WE LIVE™

VOLUME **1**

D1373085

EXTINCTION DAY

INAKI MIRANDA & ROY MIRANDA

EVA DE LA CRUZ

DAVE SHARPE

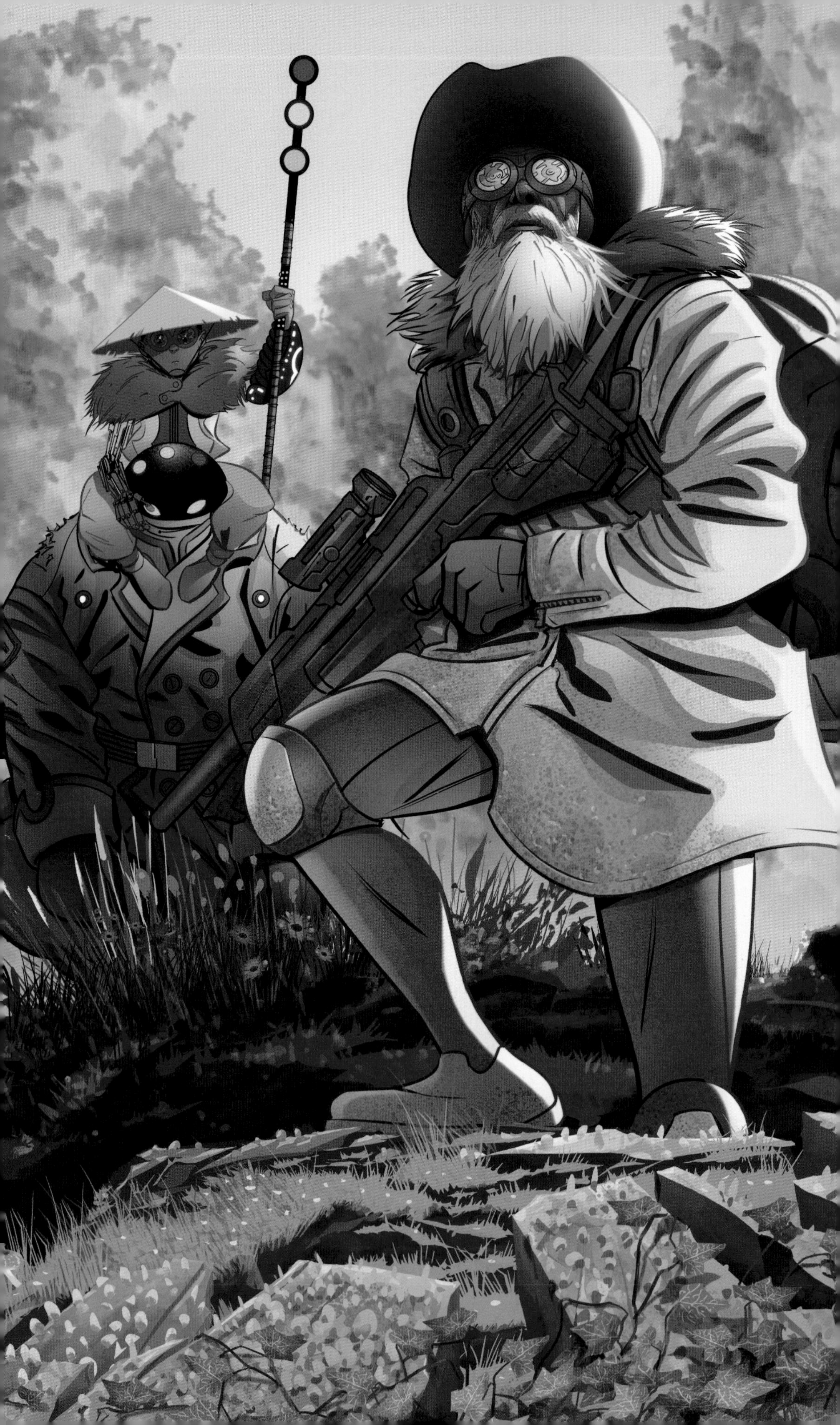

WE LIVE™

INAKI MIRANDA & ROY MIRANDA writers
INAKI MIRANDA artist

EVA DE LA CRUZ colorist

DAVE SHARPE letterer

INAKI MIRANDA front & original covers

RYAN BROWNE, IGOR LOMOV, INAKI MIRANDA, PEACH MOMOKO, DUSTIN NGUYEN, DAVID SANCHEZ & DAVID WILLIAMS variant covers

ESPINOSA.ESTUDIO logo designer

CHARLES PRITCHETT issue #1 backmatter designer

COREY BREEN book designer

MIKE MARTS editor

created by THE MIRANDA BROTHERS

AFTERSHOCK™

MIKE MARTS - Editor-in-Chief • JOE PRUETT - Publisher/CCO • LEE KRAMER - President • JON KRAMER - Chief Executive Officer
STEVE ROTTERDAM - SVP, Sales & Marketing • DAN SHIRES - VP, Film & Television UK • CHRISTINA HARRINGTON - Managing Editor
MARC HAMMOND - Sr. Retail Sales Development Manager • RUTHANN THOMPSON - Sr. Retailer Relations Manager
KATHERINE JAMISON - Marketing Manager • KELLY DIODATI - Ambassador Outreach Manager • BLAKE STOCKER - Director of Finance
AARON MARION - Publicist • LISA MOODY - Finance • RYAN CARROLL - Director, Comics/Film/TV Liaison • JAWAD QURESHI - Technology Advisor/Strategist
RACHEL PINNELAS - Social Community Manager • CHARLES PRITCHETT - Design & Production Manager • COREY BREEN - Collections Production
TEDDY LEO - Editorial Assistant • STEPHANIE CASEBIER & SARAH PRUETT - Publishing Assistants

AfterShock Logo Design by COMICRAFT
Publicity: contact AARON MARION (aaron@publichausagency.com) & RYAN CROY (ryan@publichausagency.com) at PUBLICHAUS
Special thanks to: ATOM! FREEMAN, IRA KURGAN, MARINE KSADZHIKYAN, KEITH MANZZELLA, STEPHANIE MEADOR, ANTONIA LIANOS, STEPHAN NILSON & ED ZAREMBA

PRINTED IN KOREA. Second Printing: July 2021. 10 9 8 7 6 5 4 3 2

AFTERSHOCKCOMICS.COM Follow us on social media

I N T R O D U C T I O N

Some might say that the future is the intention of the present. The world of WE LIVE might be showing us the wounded intention of our present. Yet, in this stunned present of ours, we are all able to find hope in the innocent steps of a child. Maybe WE LIVE could remind us that those same steps of ours that we once misplaced always reappear intact in a new generation that looks at us with fear and attention, with eyes full of imagination, where cruelty, despair and lies are always part of an invading army.

The book that you are holding in your hands is a story of survival, but it is not only about the survival of a human race about to become extinct, it is first and foremost about the survival of hope, imagination and innocence. It is about love, protection and sacrifice above all things. It is the story of a small vessel trying to reach its destiny through a relentless storm, that unfortunately holds an analogy that is too alive in our present.

Welcome to the odyssey of Tala and Hototo, of Humbo and Alice. Give them love and hold them close to your heart, care for them, because they carry our future.

Their path will not only be peppered with danger and tragedy. Throughout the reading you will find QR codes. Scan them with your phone's camera when you come across them. They correspond to the WE LIVE Original Soundtrack and are there to make your experience more immersive and complete.

Thanks to the sensitivity of artists Elhombreviento and Mario "Gonzo" Lorente, we have been able to work side-by-side with them, creating songs that respond to emotional, important moments of WE LIVE.

This Original Soundtrack has seven songs and a bonus track (unique for this collected edition), complemented by animated videos. You can also find the songs in any digital music platform.

1. White Whales
2. I Will Follow You
3. The Traveling
4. The Invisible Kingdom
5. Letter to Hototo
6. We Die
7. We Live: Main Theme
8. Summer Cornfields (Bonus track)

While reading, you can decide if you want to pause and extend the time of the scene (our recommendation) as you listen, or if you want to let the song run while you read the rest of the issue, as backdrop music.

We hope that the music gives you company on this trip as it did to us while creating it.

Welcome to WE LIVE. Good luck.

THE MIRANDA BROTHERS
March 2021

1

I WILL FOLLOW YOU

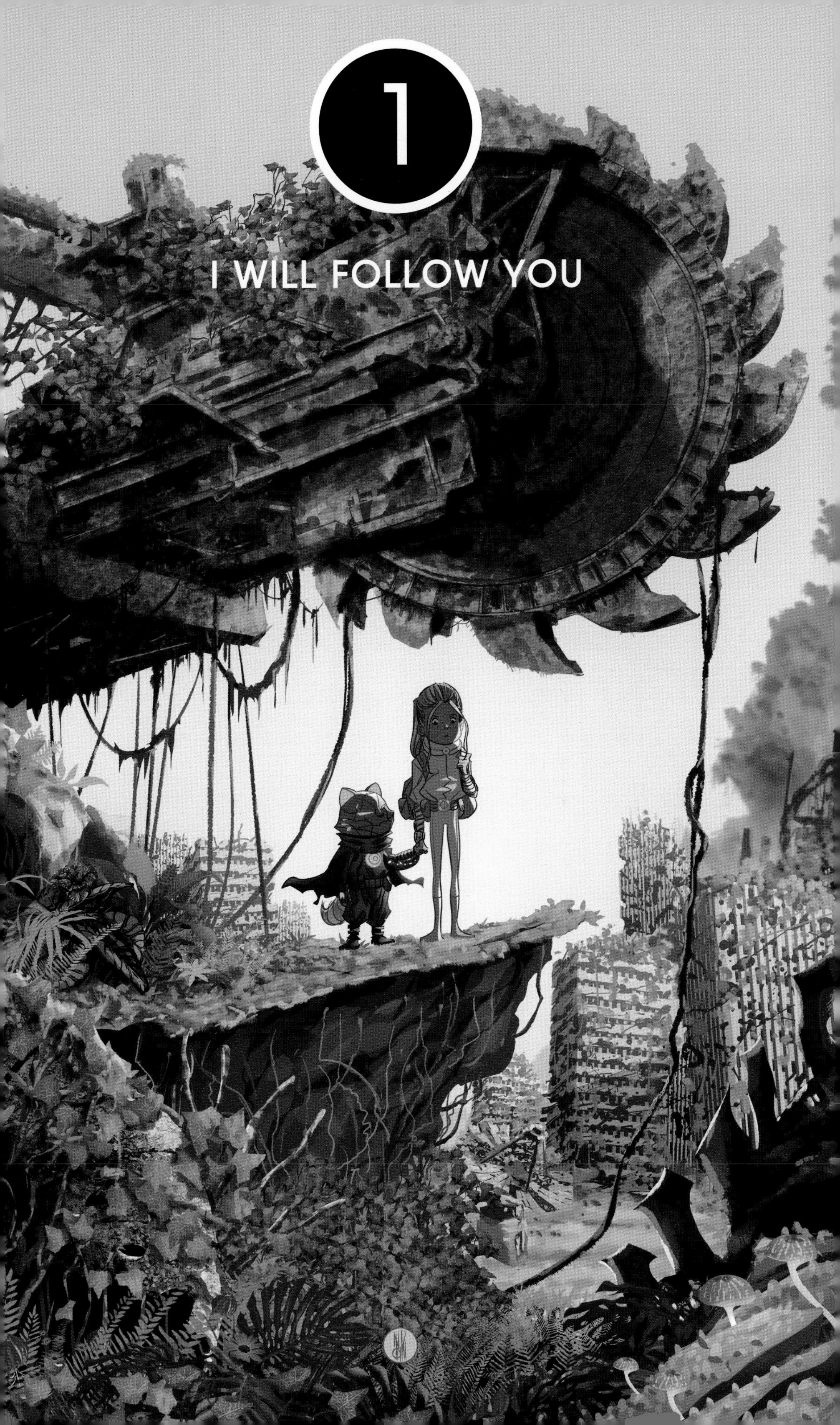

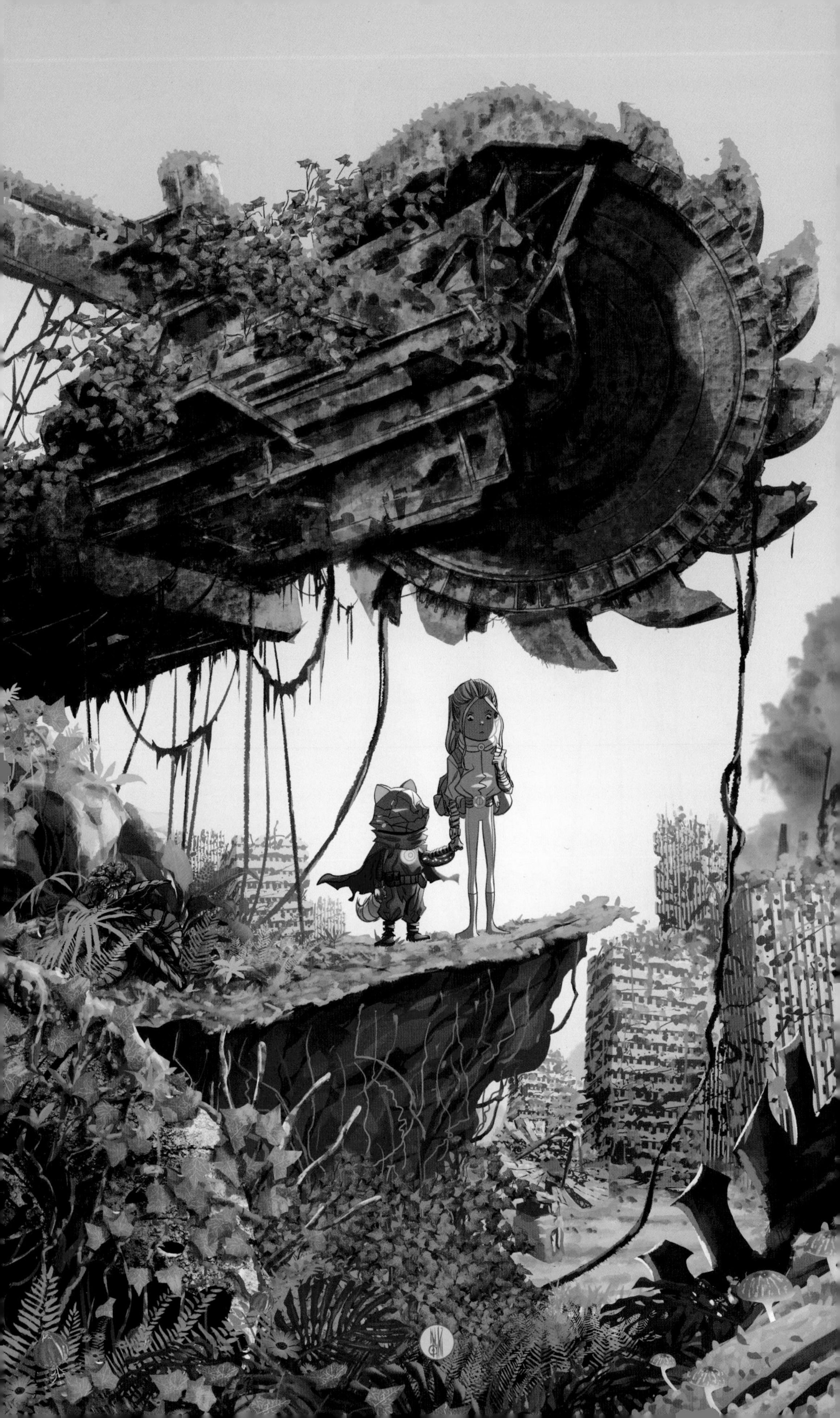

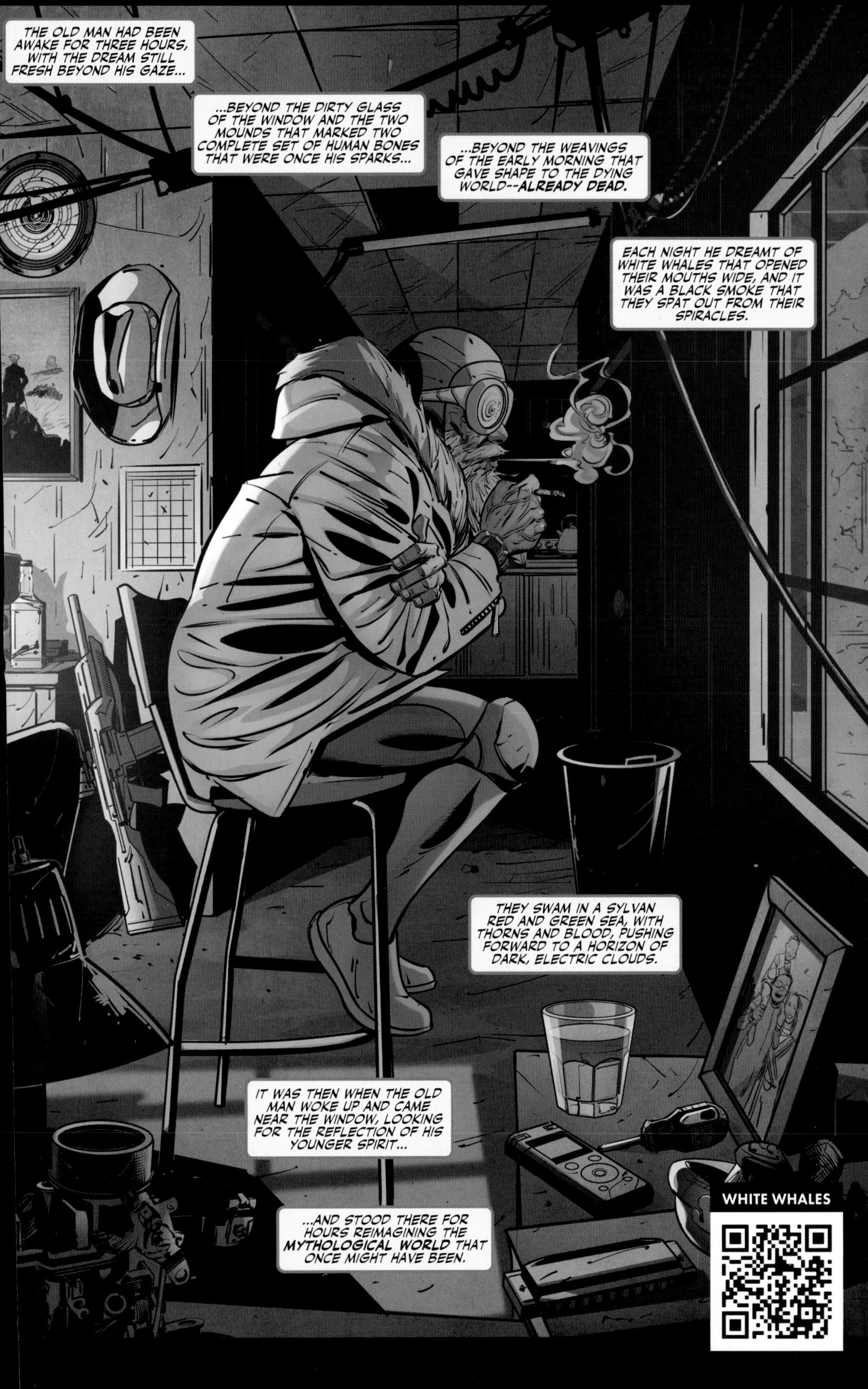
THE OLD MAN HAD BEEN AWAKE FOR THREE HOURS, WITH THE DREAM STILL FRESH BEYOND HIS GAZE...
...BEYOND THE DIRTY GLASS OF THE WINDOW AND THE TWO MOUNDS THAT MARKED TWO COMPLETE SET OF HUMAN BONES THAT WERE ONCE HIS SPARKS...
...BEYOND THE WEAVINGS OF THE EARLY MORNING THAT GAVE SHAPE TO THE DYING WORLD--**ALREADY DEAD.**
EACH NIGHT HE DREAMT OF WHITE WHALES THAT OPENED THEIR MOUTHS WIDE, AND IT WAS A BLACK SMOKE THAT THEY SPAT OUT FROM THEIR SPIRACLES.
THEY SWAM IN A SYLVAN RED AND GREEN SEA, WITH THORNS AND BLOOD, PUSHING FORWARD TO A HORIZON OF DARK, ELECTRIC CLOUDS.
IT WAS THEN WHEN THE OLD MAN WOKE UP AND CAME NEAR THE WINDOW, LOOKING FOR THE REFLECTION OF HIS YOUNGER SPIRIT...
...AND STOOD THERE FOR HOURS REIMAGINING THE **MYTHOLOGICAL WORLD** THAT ONCE MIGHT HAVE BEEN.
WHITE WHALES

THIS IS AN OFFICIAL CIVIL DEFENSE ANNOUNCEMENT

PRODUCED IN COLLABORATION BY THE NINE-MOTHER MEG...

THIS IS AN OFFICIAL CIVIL DEFENSE ANNOUNCEMENT

PRODUCED IN COLLABORATION BY THE NINE MOTHER MEGALOPOLIS

LET'S FACE TOGETHER, WITHOUT FEAR, THE REALITY OF OUR TIME. WE'VE COME A LONG WAY AS A SPECIES, WITH HITS AND MISSES.

NOW WE MUST FACE AN UNKIND DESTINY: OUR OWN *EXTINCTION.*

BUT WE ARE A SURVIVING SPECIES, OUR HISTORY WAS FORGED FIGHTING AGAINST ADVERSITIES.

WE SURVIVED **THE HOSTILE MUTATION** IN THE YEAR 2050.

WE WERE STRUCK BY COLOSSAL HURRICANES, BIBLICAL FLOODS, ELECTROMAGNETIC STORMS AND EARTHQUAKES THAT COMPLETELY CHANGED AND RESHAPED THE FACE OF THE *EARTH.*

A FURIOUS NATURE ATTACKED US FOR YEARS AND DECIMATED US. IT CREATED *NEW SPECIES,* WILD BEASTS AND GENETIC DEGENERATIONS THAT PUSHED US TOWARDS DEATH.

BUT WE FOUGHT. WE *SURVIVED.*

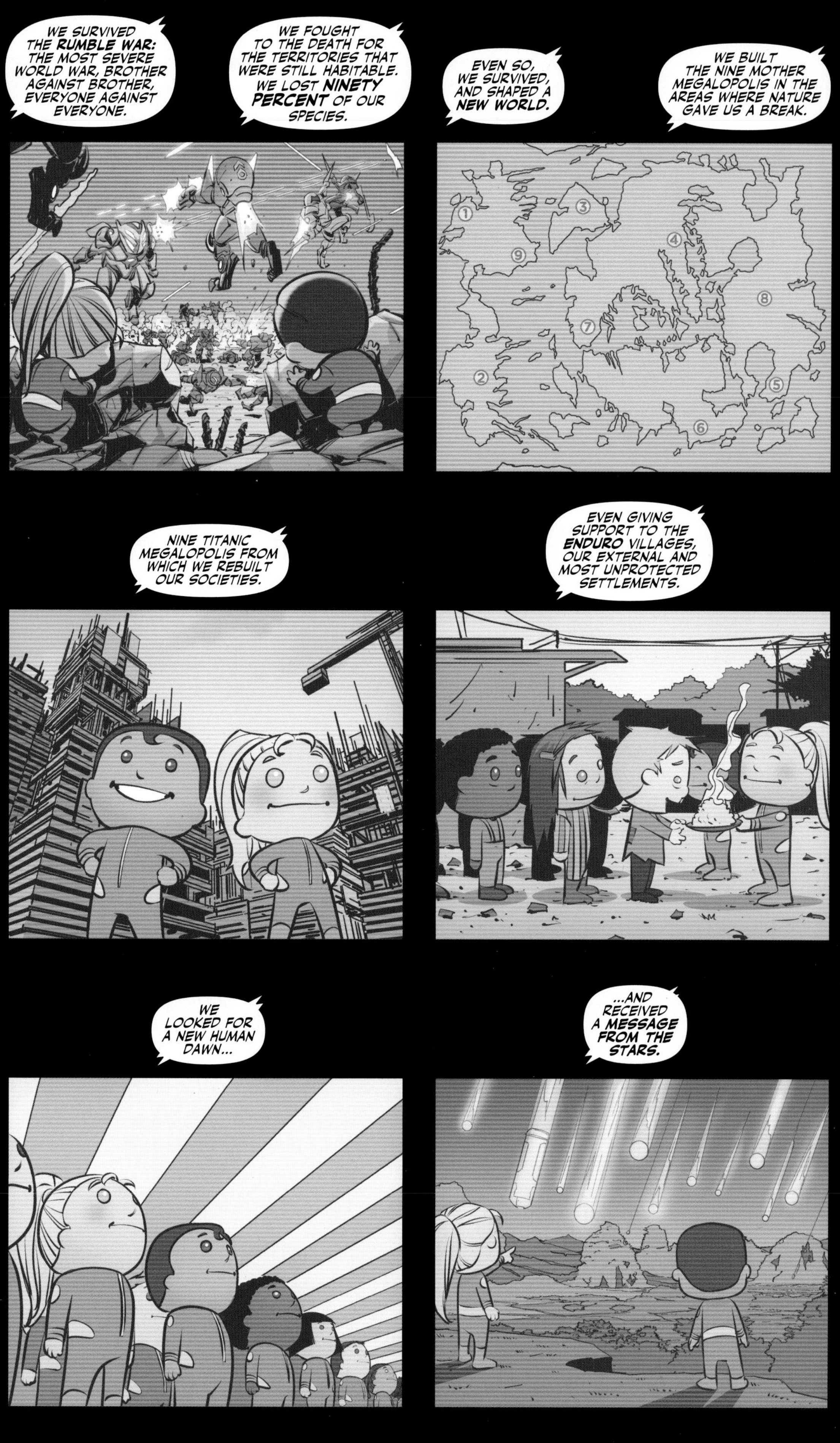
WE SURVIVED THE **RUMBLE WAR:** THE MOST SEVERE WORLD WAR, BROTHER AGAINST BROTHER, EVERYONE AGAINST EVERYONE.
WE FOUGHT TO THE DEATH FOR THE TERRITORIES THAT WERE STILL HABITABLE. WE LOST **NINETY PERCENT** OF OUR SPECIES.
EVEN SO, WE SURVIVED, AND SHAPED A **NEW WORLD.**
WE BUILT THE NINE MOTHER MEGALOPOLIS IN THE AREAS WHERE NATURE GAVE US A BREAK.
1
3
4
9
8
7
2
5
6
NINE TITANIC MEGALOPOLIS FROM WHICH WE REBUILT OUR SOCIETIES.
EVEN GIVING SUPPORT TO THE **ENDURO** VILLAGES, OUR EXTERNAL AND MOST UNPROTECTED SETTLEMENTS.
WE LOOKED FOR A NEW HUMAN DAWN...
...AND RECEIVED A **MESSAGE FROM THE STARS.**

ONE DARK MESSAGE: WE ARE GOING TO DIE. AND A HOPE OF LIFE: WE ARE BEING RESCUED.

"HUMANS: YOU FACE EXTINCTION. YOU WILL SUFFER A NEW ATTACK FROM NATURE. THIS TIME IT WILL BE DEFINITIVE. YOU WILL NOT SURVIVE. WE OFFER YOU A WAY OUT.

"5000 RESCUE BRACELETS FOR 5000 CHILDREN.

"THE RESCUE WILL TAKE PLACE AT THE NINE DESIGNATED EXTRACTION BEACONS WHEN THE COUNTDOWN REACHES ZERO. GOOD DESTINY."

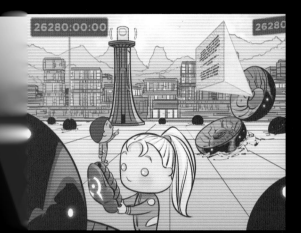

IT IS THE END OF OUR LIFE ON EARTH.

BUT WE HAVE BEEN BLESSED WITH A NEW OPPORTUNITY. EACH **RESCUE BRACELET** GUARANTEES THE RESCUE OF ONE CHILD.

5000 HUMAN CHILDREN WILL BE OUR REBIRTH IN THE STARS. A NEW PLANET. A **NEW HOME.**

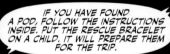

IF YOU HAVE FOUND A POD, FOLLOW THE INSTRUCTIONS INSIDE. PUT THE RESCUE BRACELET ON A CHILD. IT WILL PREPARE THEM FOR THE TRIP.

MAKE SURE TO BRING THEM TO THE NEAREST EXTRACTION BEACON **BEFORE** THE COUNTDOWN REACHES ZERO.

THERE ARE NINE BEACONS. ONE INSIDE EACH MOTHER MEGALOPOLIS.

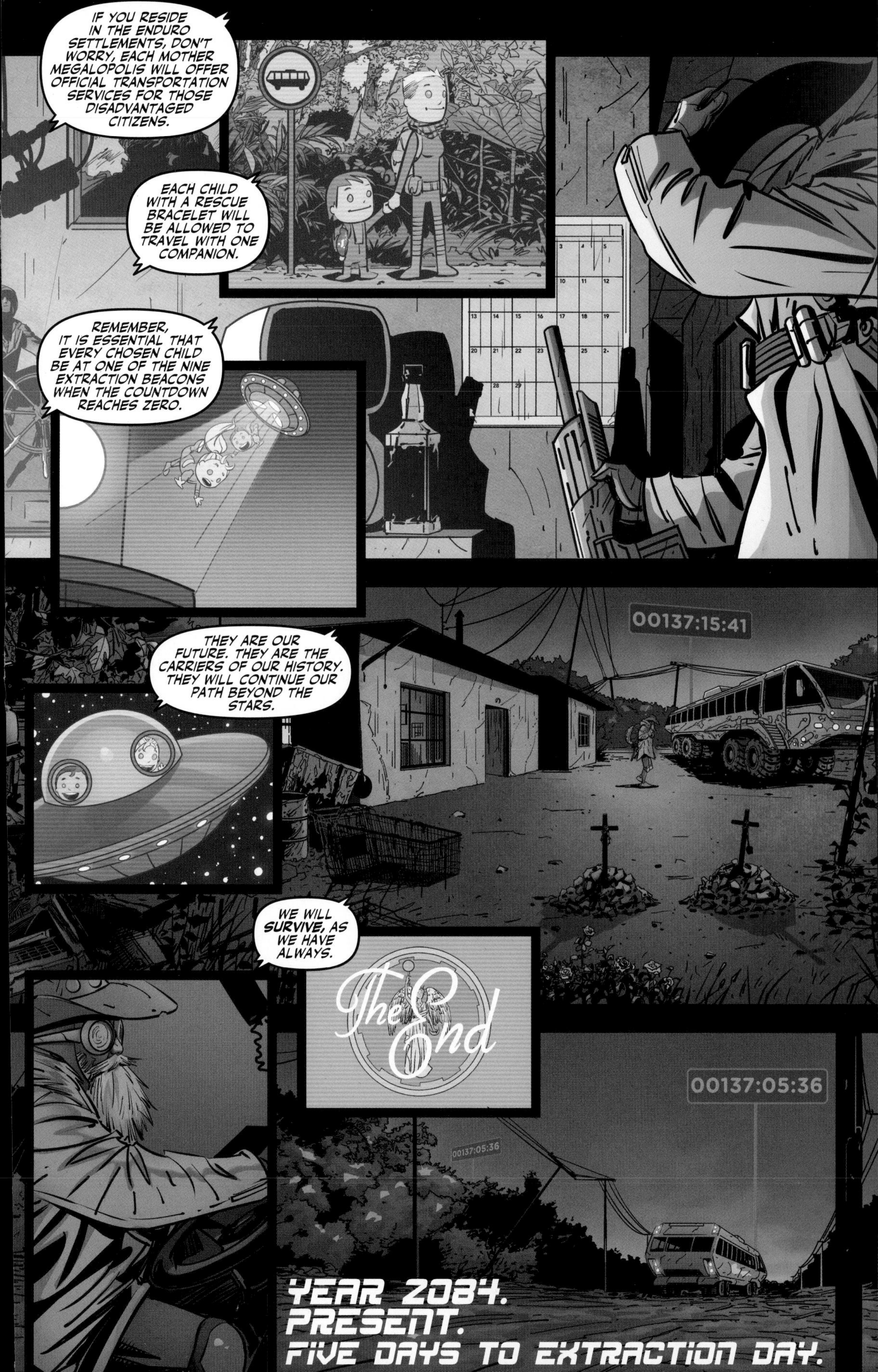
IF YOU RESIDE IN THE ENDURO SETTLEMENTS, DON'T WORRY, EACH MOTHER MEGALOPOLIS WILL OFFER OFFICIAL TRANSPORTATION SERVICES FOR THOSE DISADVANTAGED CITIZENS.
EACH CHILD WITH A RESCUE BRACELET WILL BE ALLOWED TO TRAVEL WITH ONE COMPANION.
REMEMBER, IT IS ESSENTIAL THAT EVERY CHOSEN CHILD BE AT ONE OF THE NINE EXTRACTION BEACONS WHEN THE COUNTDOWN REACHES ZERO.
THEY ARE OUR FUTURE. THEY ARE THE CARRIERS OF OUR HISTORY. THEY WILL CONTINUE OUR PATH BEYOND THE STARS.
00137:15:41
WE WILL SURVIVE, AS WE HAVE ALWAYS.
The End
00137:05:36
00137:05:36
YEAR 2084.
PRESENT.
FIVE DAYS TO EXTRACTION DAY.

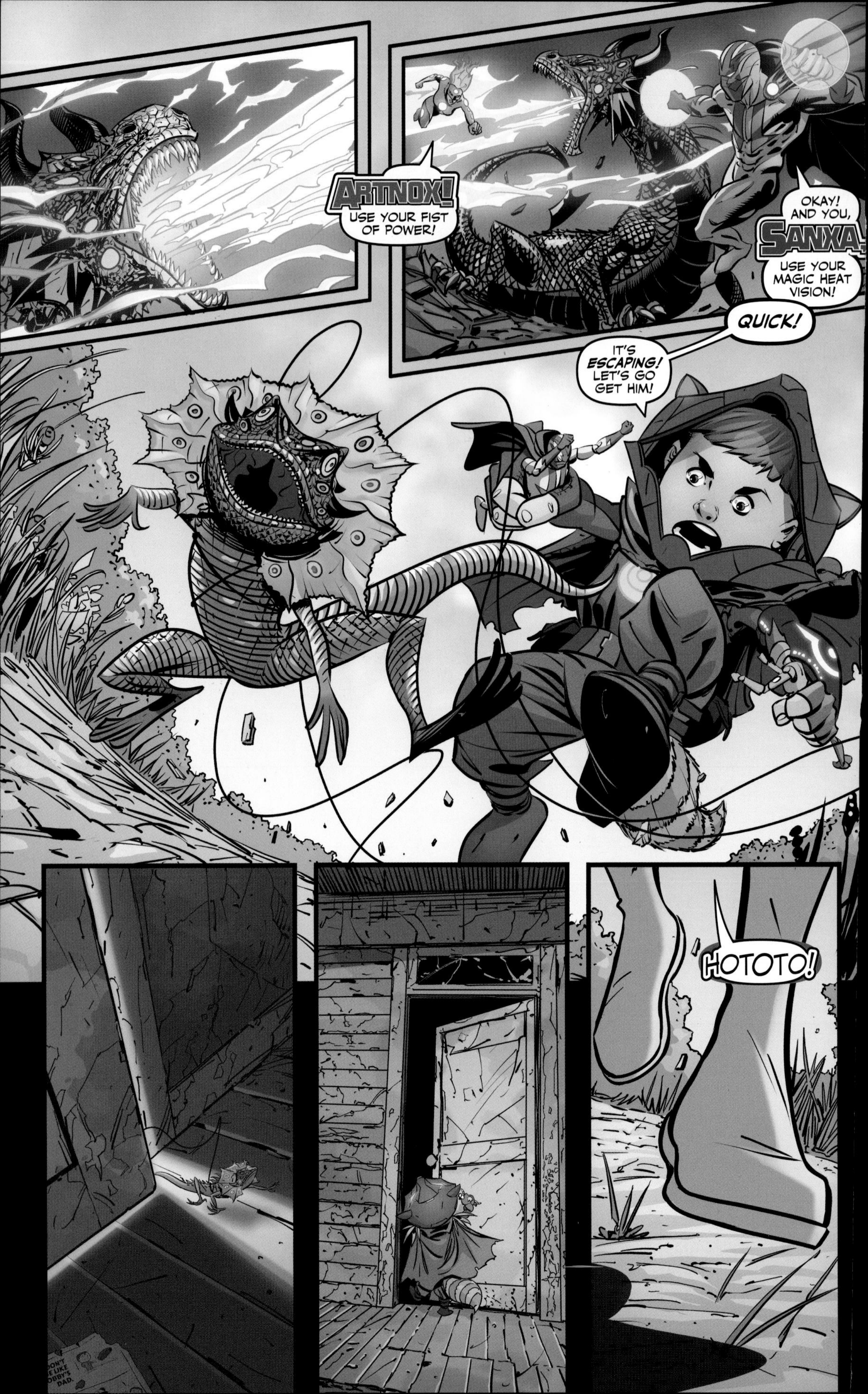
ARTNOX!
USE YOUR FIST OF POWER!
OKAY! AND YOU, SANXA,
USE YOUR MAGIC HEAT VISION!
QUICK!
IT'S ESCAPING! LET'S GO GET HIM!
HOTOTO!

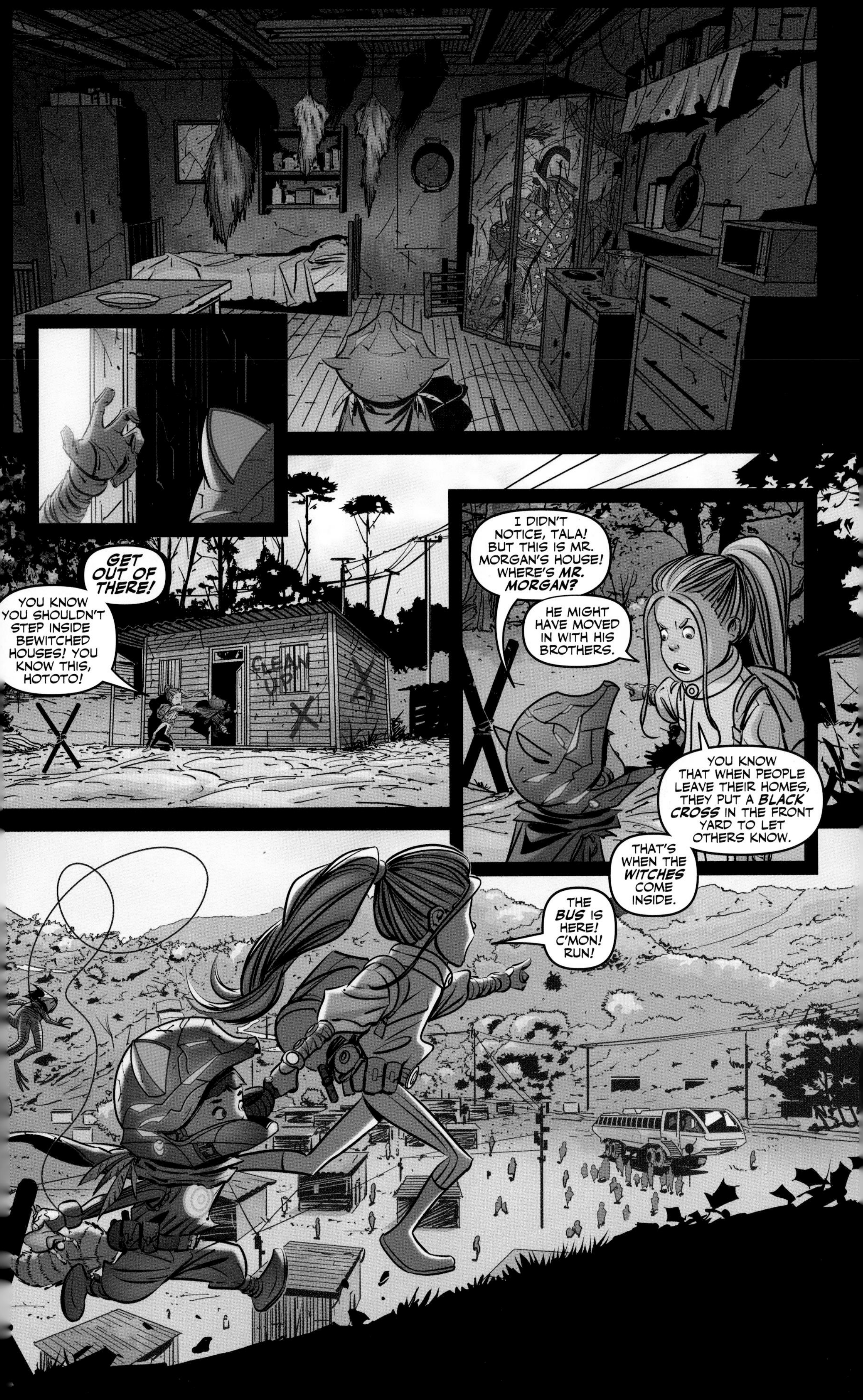
GET OUT OF THERE!
YOU KNOW YOU SHOULDN'T STEP INSIDE BEWITCHED HOUSES! YOU KNOW THIS, HOTOTO!
CLEAN UP!
I DIDN'T NOTICE, TALA! BUT THIS IS MR. MORGAN'S HOUSE! WHERE'S MR. MORGAN?
HE MIGHT HAVE MOVED IN WITH HIS BROTHERS.
YOU KNOW THAT WHEN PEOPLE LEAVE THEIR HOMES, THEY PUT A BLACK CROSS IN THE FRONT YARD TO LET OTHERS KNOW.
THAT'S WHEN THE WITCHES COME INSIDE.
THE BUS IS HERE! C'MON! RUN!

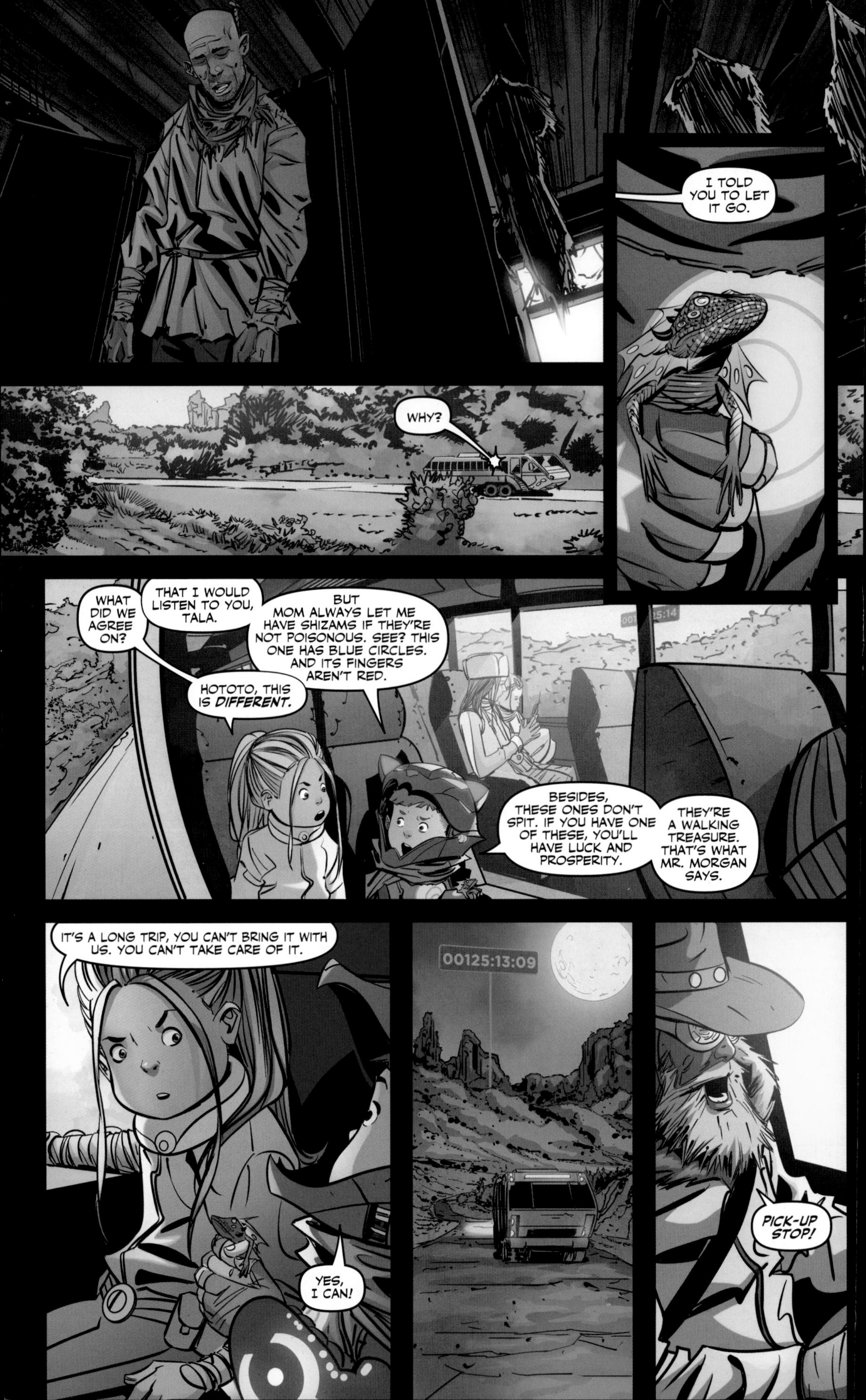
I TOLD YOU TO LET IT GO.
WHY?
WHAT DID WE AGREE ON?
THAT I WOULD LISTEN TO YOU, TALA.
BUT MOM ALWAYS LET ME HAVE SHIZAMS IF THEY'RE NOT POISONOUS. SEE? THIS ONE HAS BLUE CIRCLES. AND ITS FINGERS AREN'T RED.
HOTOTO, THIS IS *DIFFERENT.*
BESIDES, THESE ONES DON'T SPIT. IF YOU HAVE ONE OF THESE, YOU'LL HAVE LUCK AND PROSPERITY.
THEY'RE A WALKING TREASURE. THAT'S WHAT MR. MORGAN SAYS.
IT'S A LONG TRIP, YOU CAN'T BRING IT WITH US. YOU CAN'T TAKE CARE OF IT.
YES, I CAN!
00125:13:09
PICK-UP STOP!

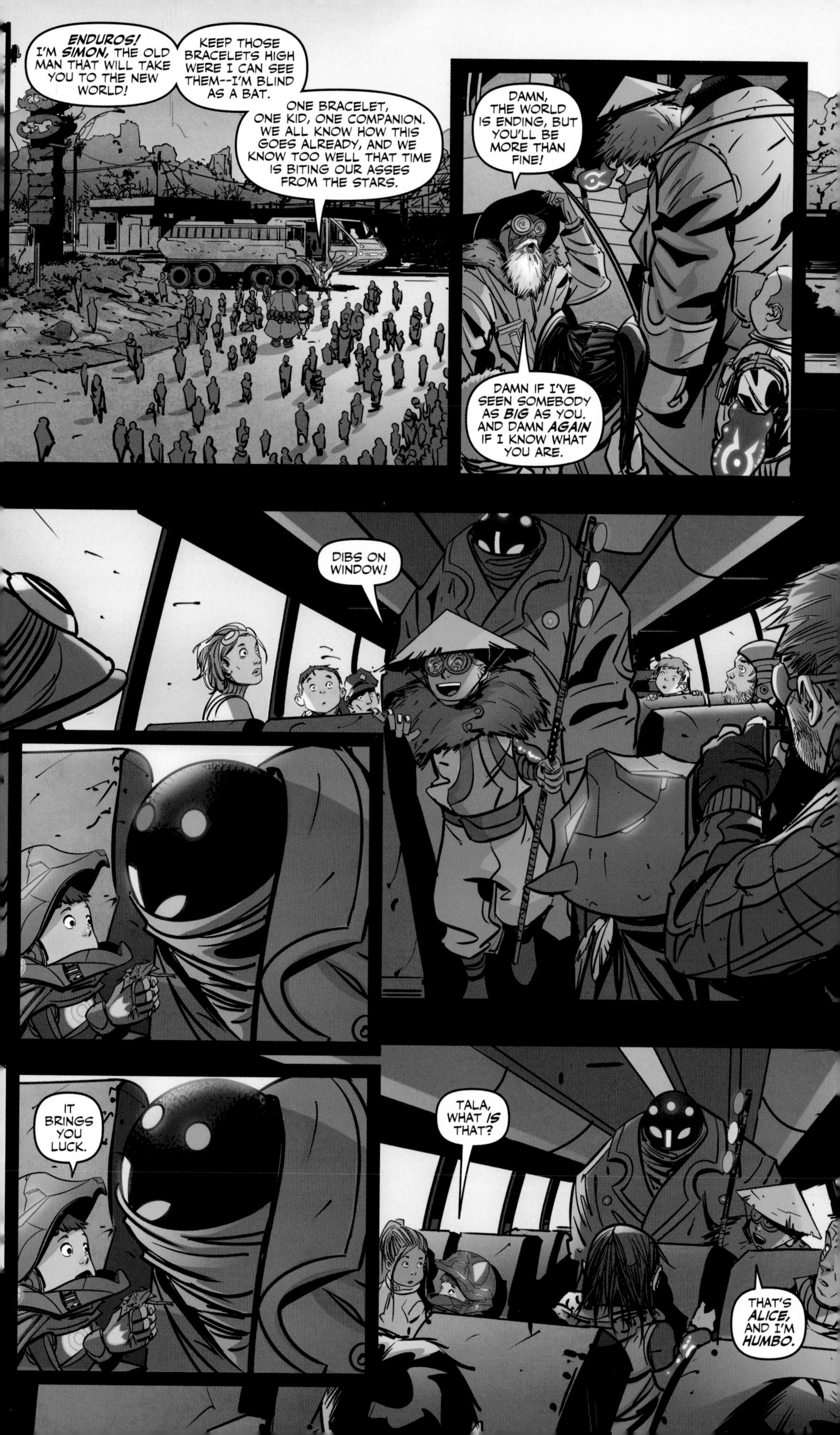
ENDUROS! I'M SIMON, THE OLD MAN THAT WILL TAKE YOU TO THE NEW WORLD!
KEEP THOSE BRACELETS HIGH WERE I CAN SEE THEM--I'M BLIND AS A BAT.
ONE BRACELET, ONE KID, ONE COMPANION. WE ALL KNOW HOW THIS GOES ALREADY, AND WE KNOW TOO WELL THAT TIME IS BITING OUR ASSES FROM THE STARS.
DAMN, THE WORLD IS ENDING, BUT YOU'LL BE MORE THAN FINE!
DAMN IF I'VE SEEN SOMEBODY AS BIG AS YOU. AND DAMN AGAIN IF I KNOW WHAT YOU ARE.
DIBS ON WINDOW!
IT BRINGS YOU LUCK.
TALA, WHAT IS THAT?
THAT'S ALICE, AND I'M HUMBO.

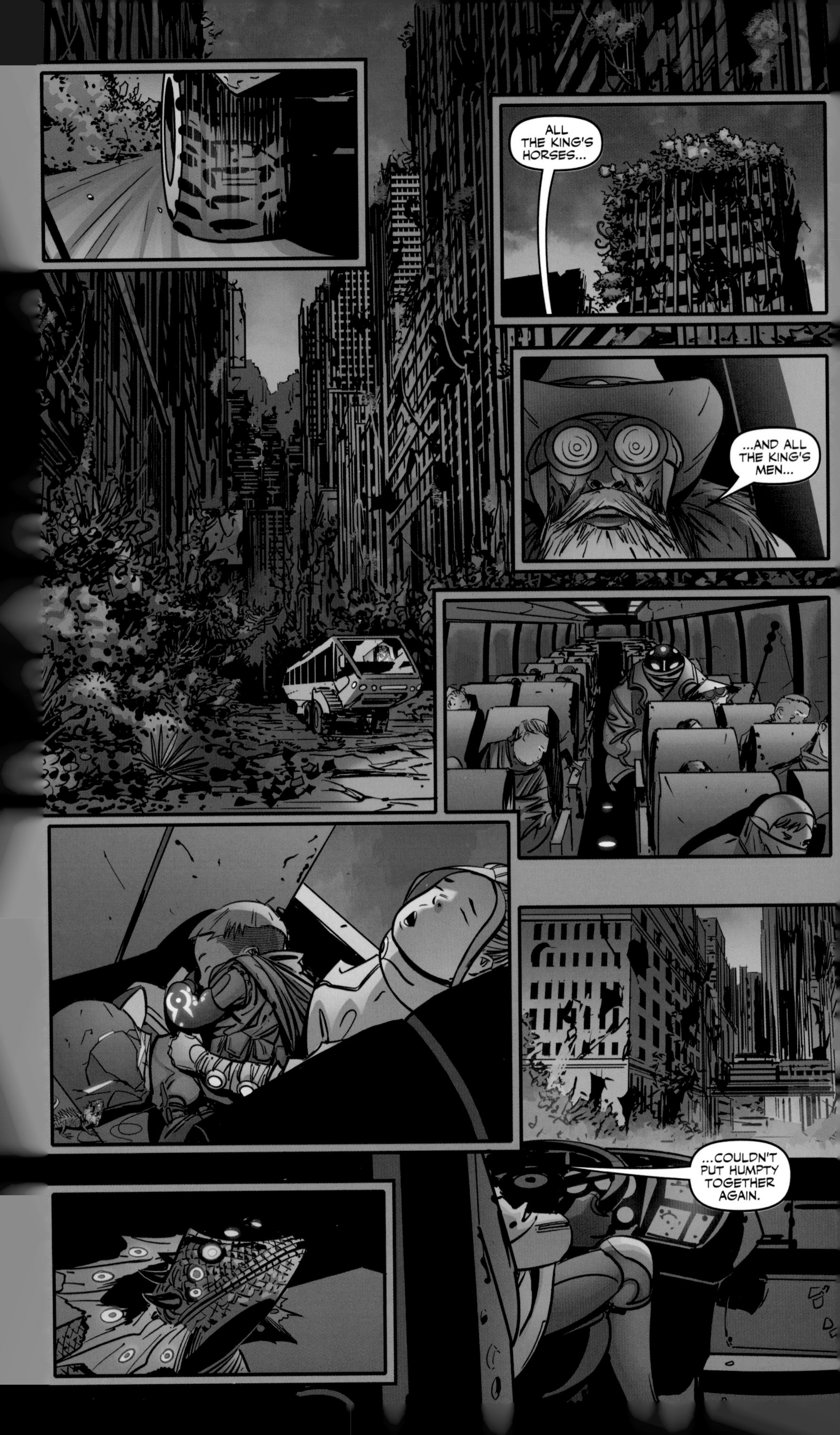
ALL THE KING'S HORSES...
...AND ALL THE KING'S MEN...
...COULDN'T PUT HUMPTY TOGETHER AGAIN.

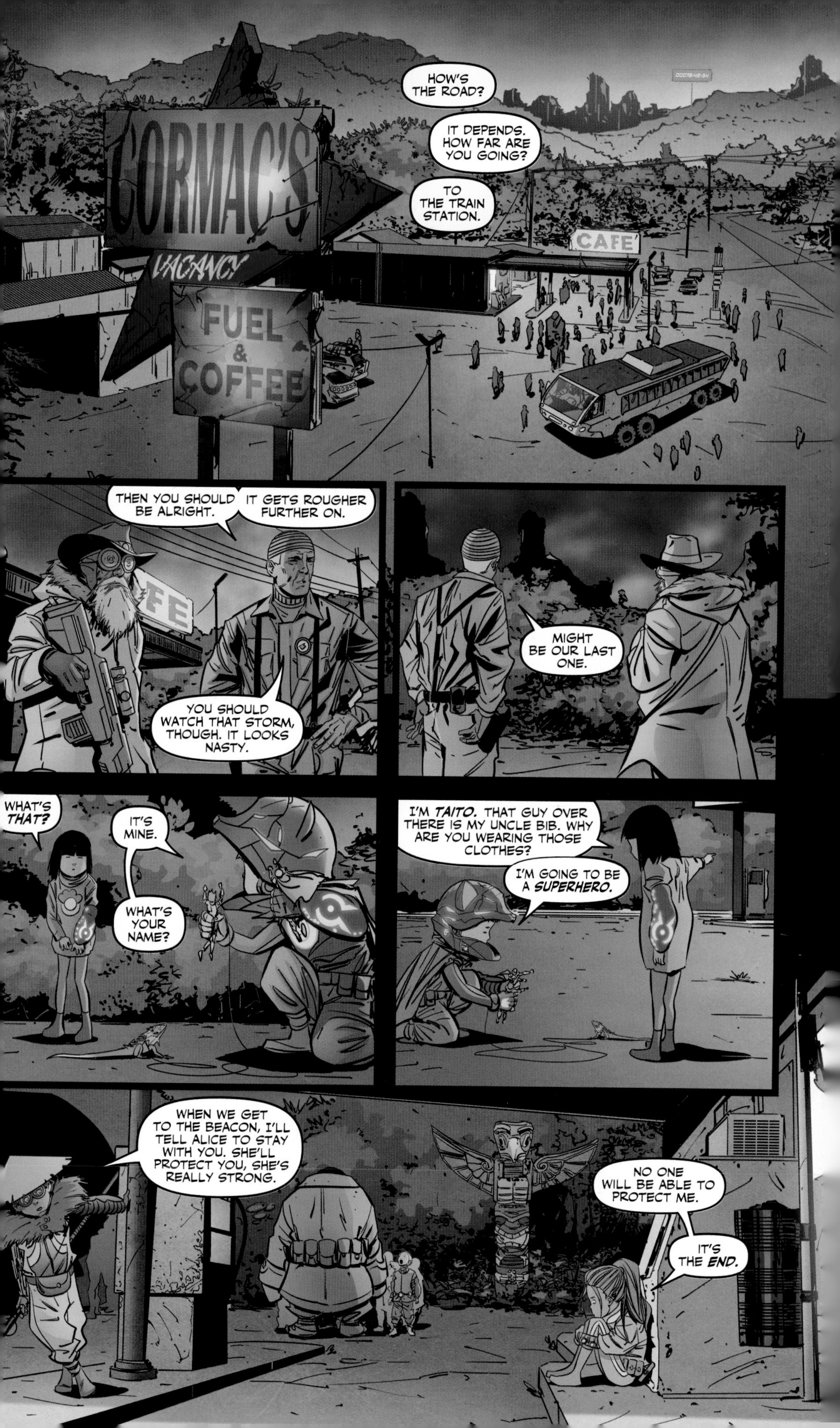
CORMAC'S
VACANCY
FUEL & COFFEE
CAFE
HOW'S THE ROAD?
IT DEPENDS. HOW FAR ARE YOU GOING?
TO THE TRAIN STATION.
THEN YOU SHOULD BE ALRIGHT.
IT GETS ROUGHER FURTHER ON.
YOU SHOULD WATCH THAT STORM, THOUGH. IT LOOKS NASTY.
MIGHT BE OUR LAST ONE.
WHAT'S *THAT?*
IT'S MINE.
WHAT'S YOUR NAME?
I'M *TAITO.* THAT GUY OVER THERE IS MY UNCLE BIB. WHY ARE YOU WEARING THOSE CLOTHES?
I'M GOING TO BE A *SUPERHERO.*
WHEN WE GET TO THE BEACON, I'LL TELL ALICE TO STAY WITH YOU. SHE'LL PROTECT YOU, SHE'S REALLY STRONG.
NO ONE WILL BE ABLE TO PROTECT ME.
IT'S THE *END.*

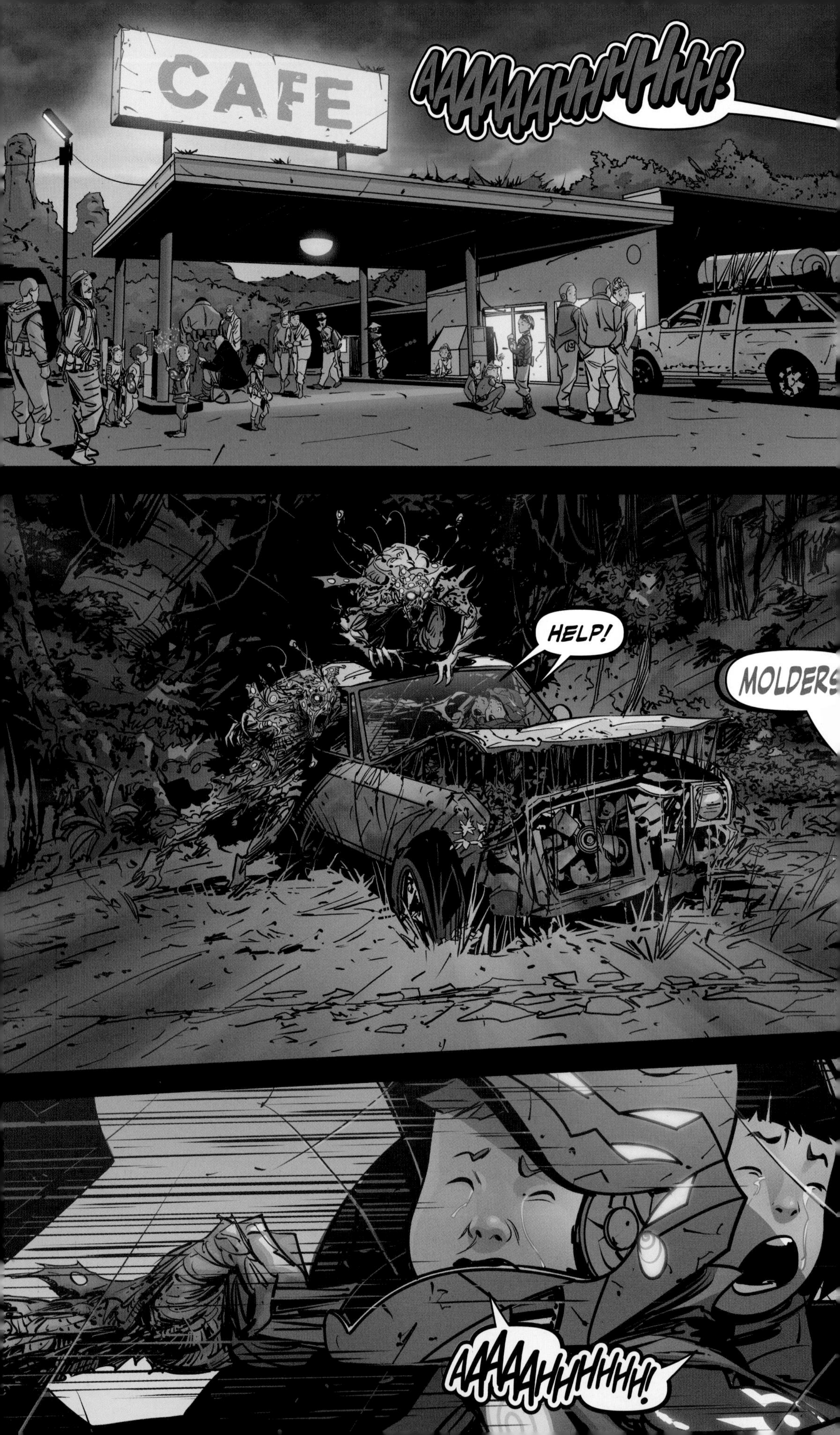
CAFE
AAAAAAHHHHHHH!
HELP!
MOLDERS
AAAAAHHHHHH!

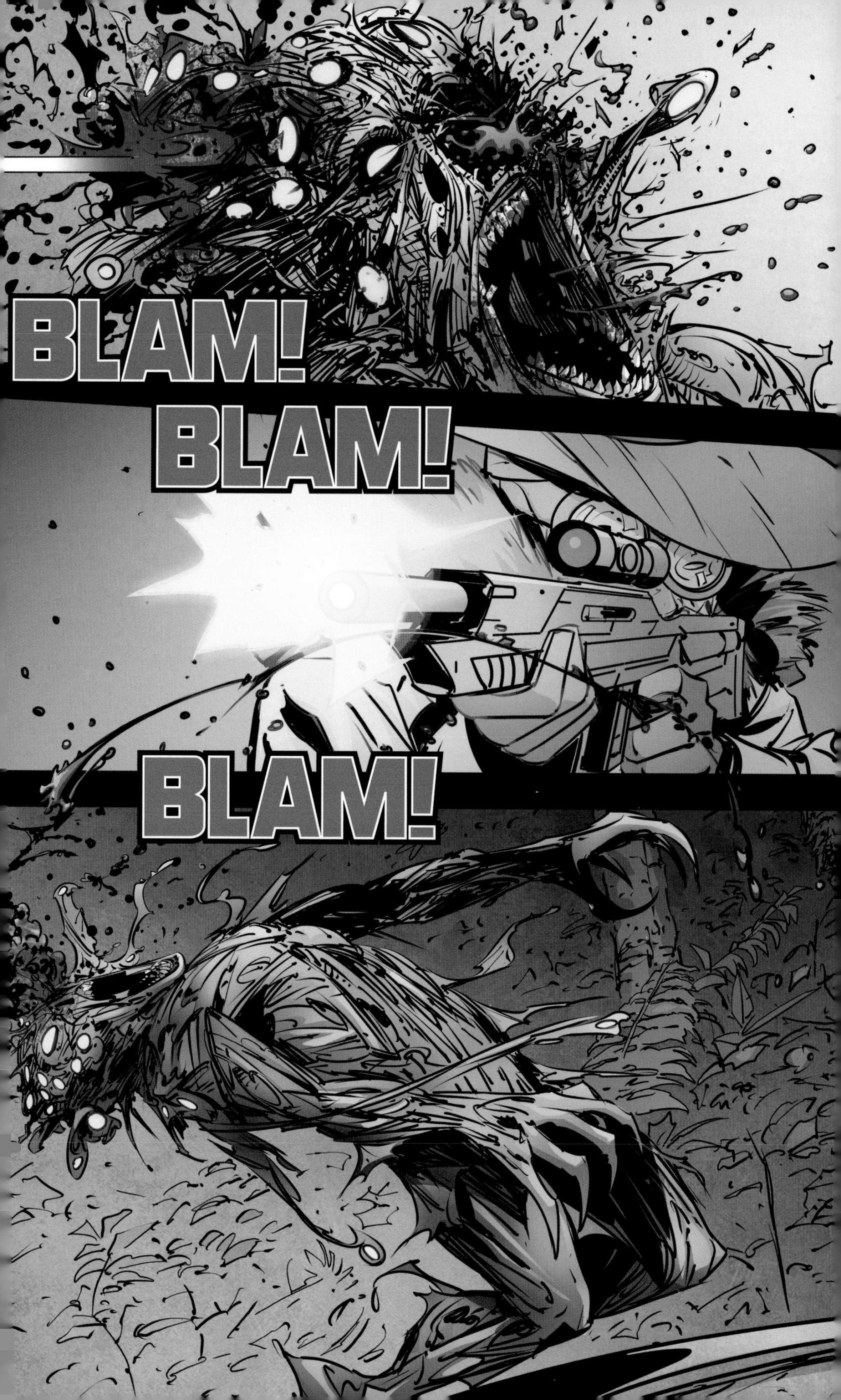
BLAM!
BLAM!
BLAM!

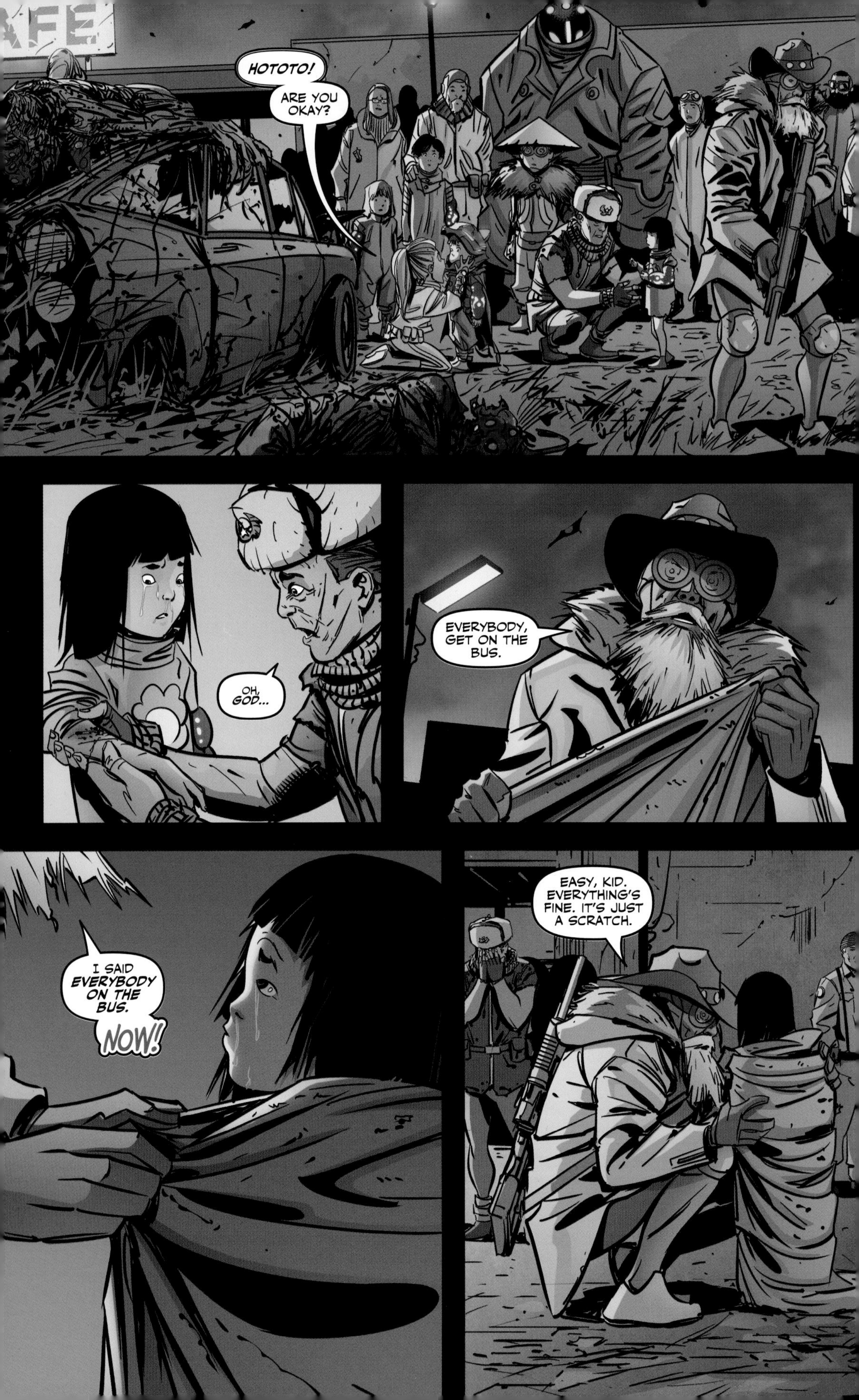
AFE
HOTOTO!
ARE YOU OKAY?
OH, GOD...
EVERYBODY, GET ON THE BUS.
I SAID EVERYBODY ON THE BUS.
NOW!
EASY, KID. EVERYTHING'S FINE. IT'S JUST A SCRATCH.

THIS WILL BE THE FIRST TIME I SHOOT A CHILD.
HAND ME THE REVOLVER.
GRRHARG
THIS IS NO LONGER A CHILD.
CLICK
BLAM!

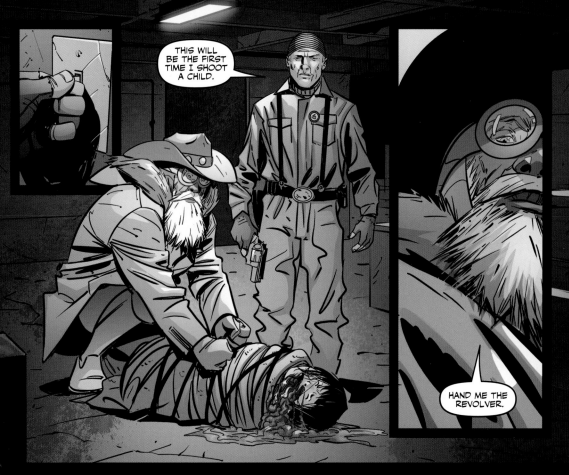

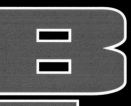

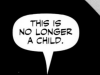

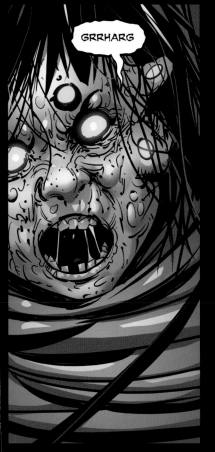

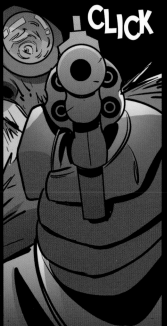

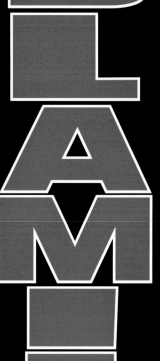

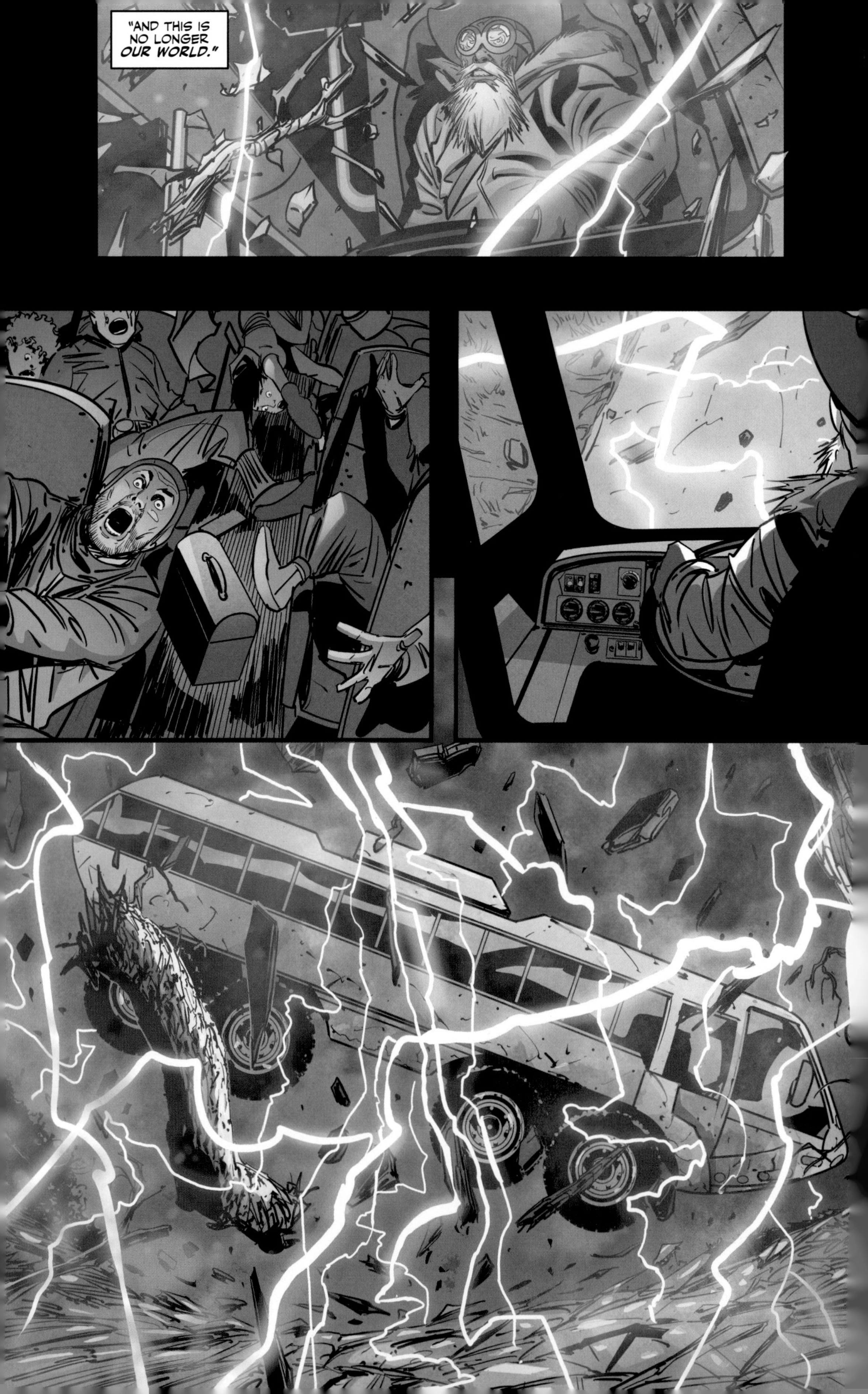
"AND THIS IS NO LONGER OUR WORLD."

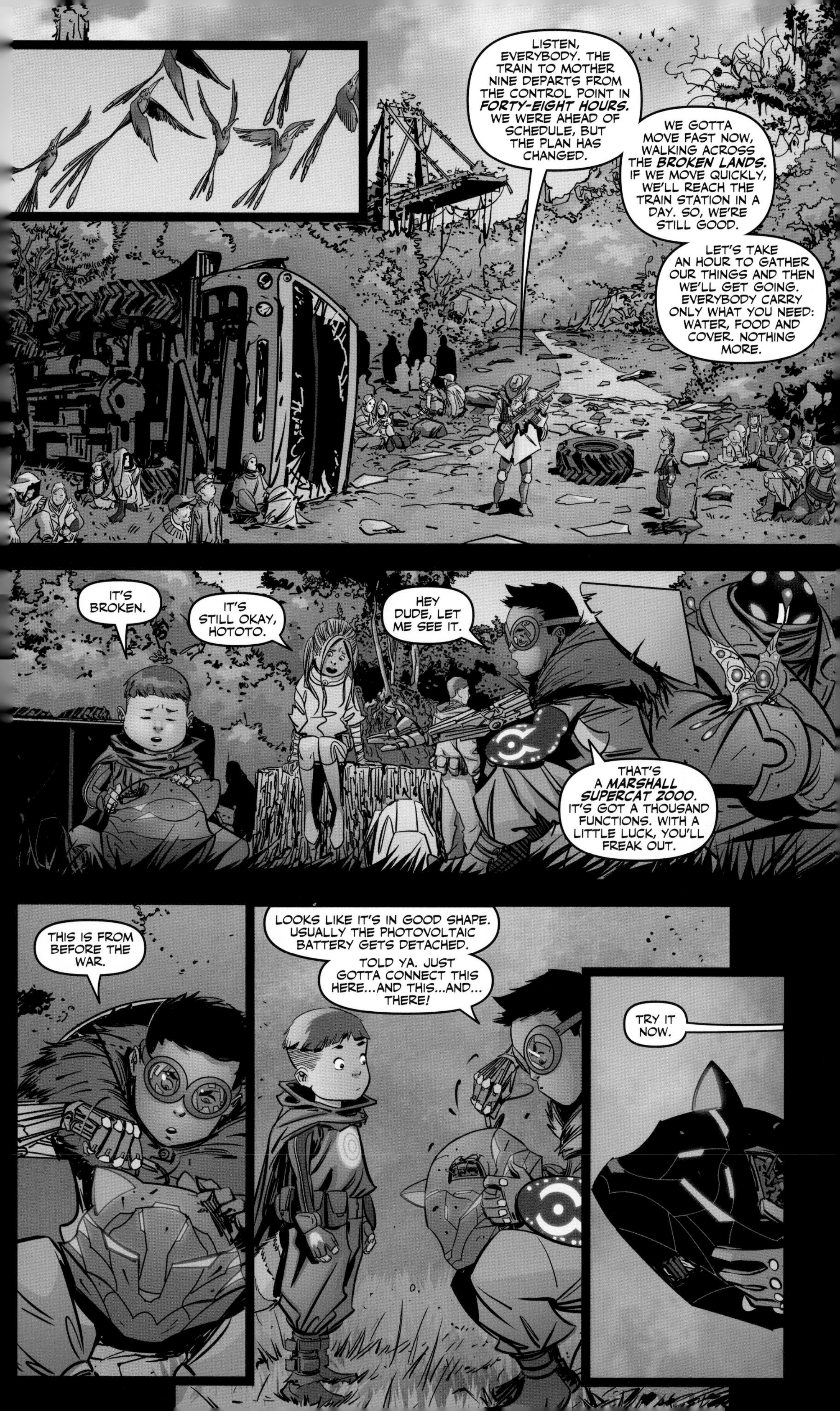

LISTEN, EVERYBODY. THE TRAIN TO MOTHER NINE DEPARTS FROM THE CONTROL POINT IN *FORTY-EIGHT HOURS.* WE WERE AHEAD OF SCHEDULE, BUT THE PLAN HAS CHANGED.
WE GOTTA MOVE FAST NOW, WALKING ACROSS THE *BROKEN LANDS.* IF WE MOVE QUICKLY, WE'LL REACH THE TRAIN STATION IN A DAY. SO, WE'RE STILL GOOD.
LET'S TAKE AN HOUR TO GATHER OUR THINGS AND THEN WE'LL GET GOING. EVERYBODY CARRY ONLY WHAT YOU NEED: WATER, FOOD AND COVER. NOTHING MORE.
IT'S BROKEN.
IT'S STILL OKAY, HOTOTO.
HEY DUDE, LET ME SEE IT.
THAT'S A *MARSHALL SUPERCAT 2000.* IT'S GOT A THOUSAND FUNCTIONS. WITH A LITTLE LUCK, YOU'LL FREAK OUT.
THIS IS FROM BEFORE THE WAR.
LOOKS LIKE IT'S IN GOOD SHAPE. USUALLY THE PHOTOVOLTAIC BATTERY GETS DETACHED.
TOLD YA. JUST GOTTA CONNECT THIS HERE...AND THIS...AND... THERE!
TRY IT NOW.

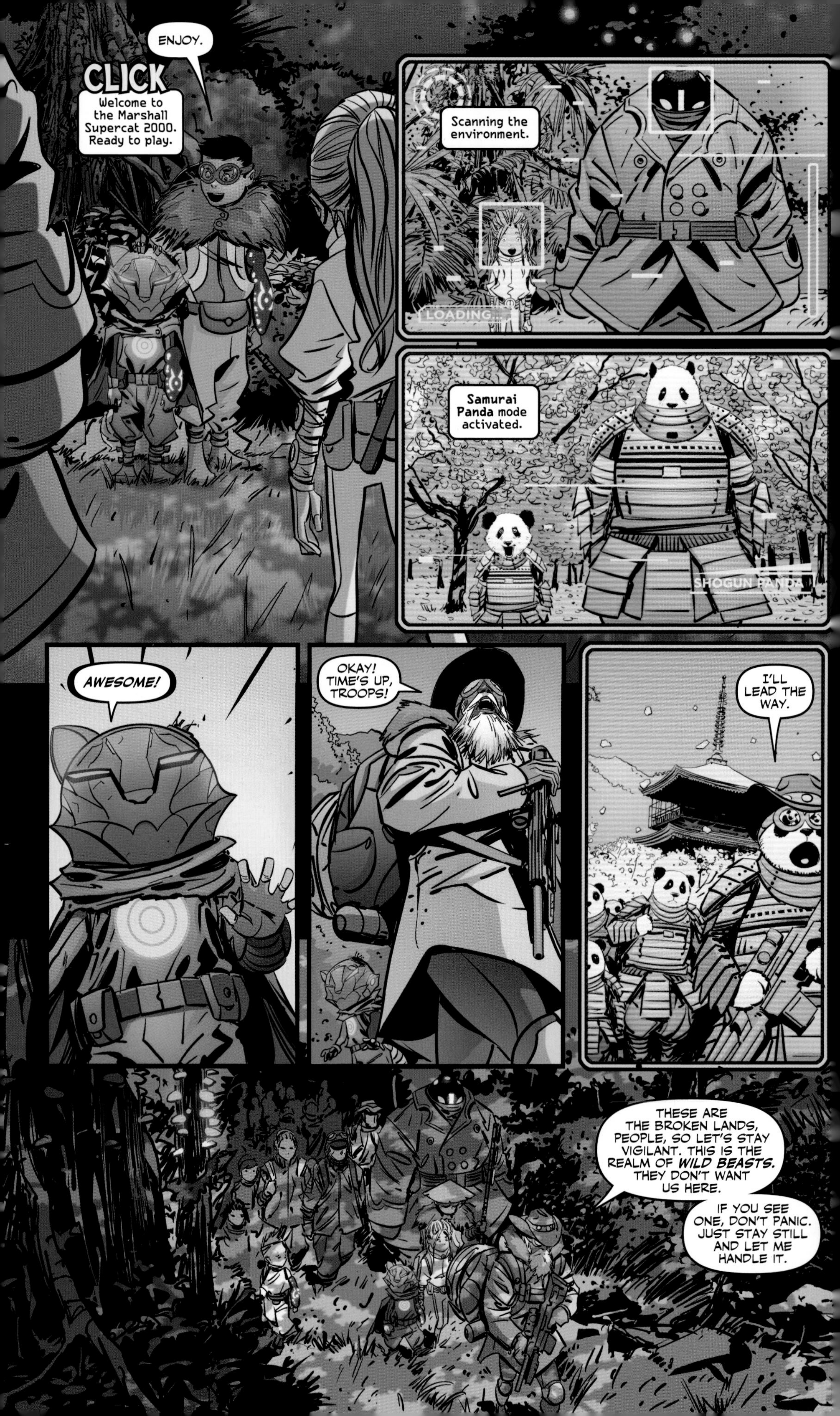
ENJOY.
CLICK
Welcome to the Marshall Supercat 2000. Ready to play.
Scanning the environment.
LOADING...
Samurai Panda mode activated.
SHOGUN PANDA
AWESOME!
OKAY! TIME'S UP, TROOPS!
I'LL LEAD THE WAY.
THESE ARE THE BROKEN LANDS, PEOPLE, SO LET'S STAY VIGILANT. THIS IS THE REALM OF WILD BEASTS. THEY DON'T WANT US HERE.
IF YOU SEE ONE, DON'T PANIC. JUST STAY STILL AND LET ME HANDLE IT.

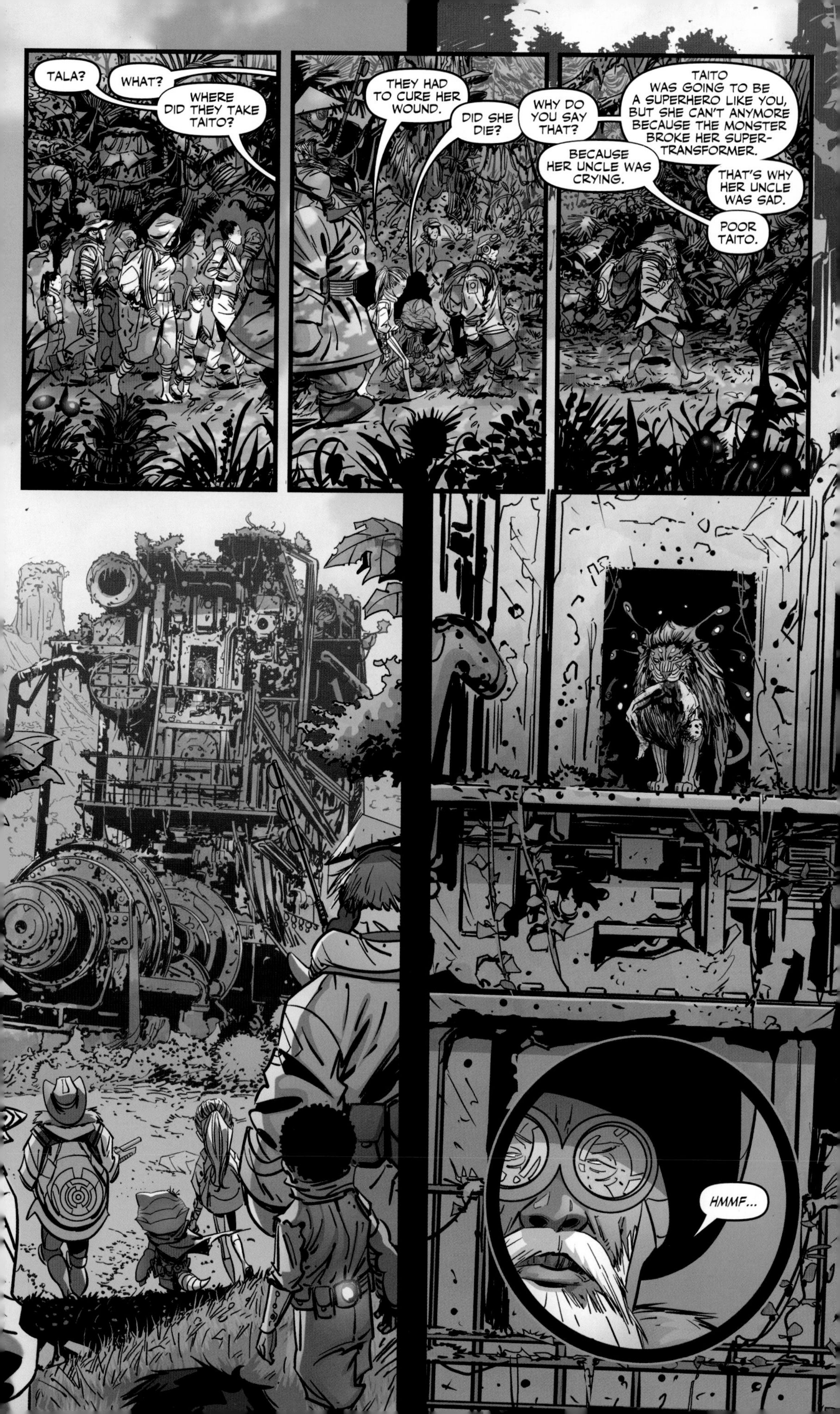
TALA?
WHAT?
WHERE DID THEY TAKE TAITO?
THEY HAD TO CURE HER WOUND.
DID SHE DIE?
WHY DO YOU SAY THAT?
BECAUSE HER UNCLE WAS CRYING.
TAITO WAS GOING TO BE A SUPERHERO LIKE YOU, BUT SHE CAN'T ANYMORE BECAUSE THE MONSTER BROKE HER SUPER-TRANSFORMER.
THAT'S WHY HER UNCLE WAS SAD.
POOR TAITO.
HMMF...

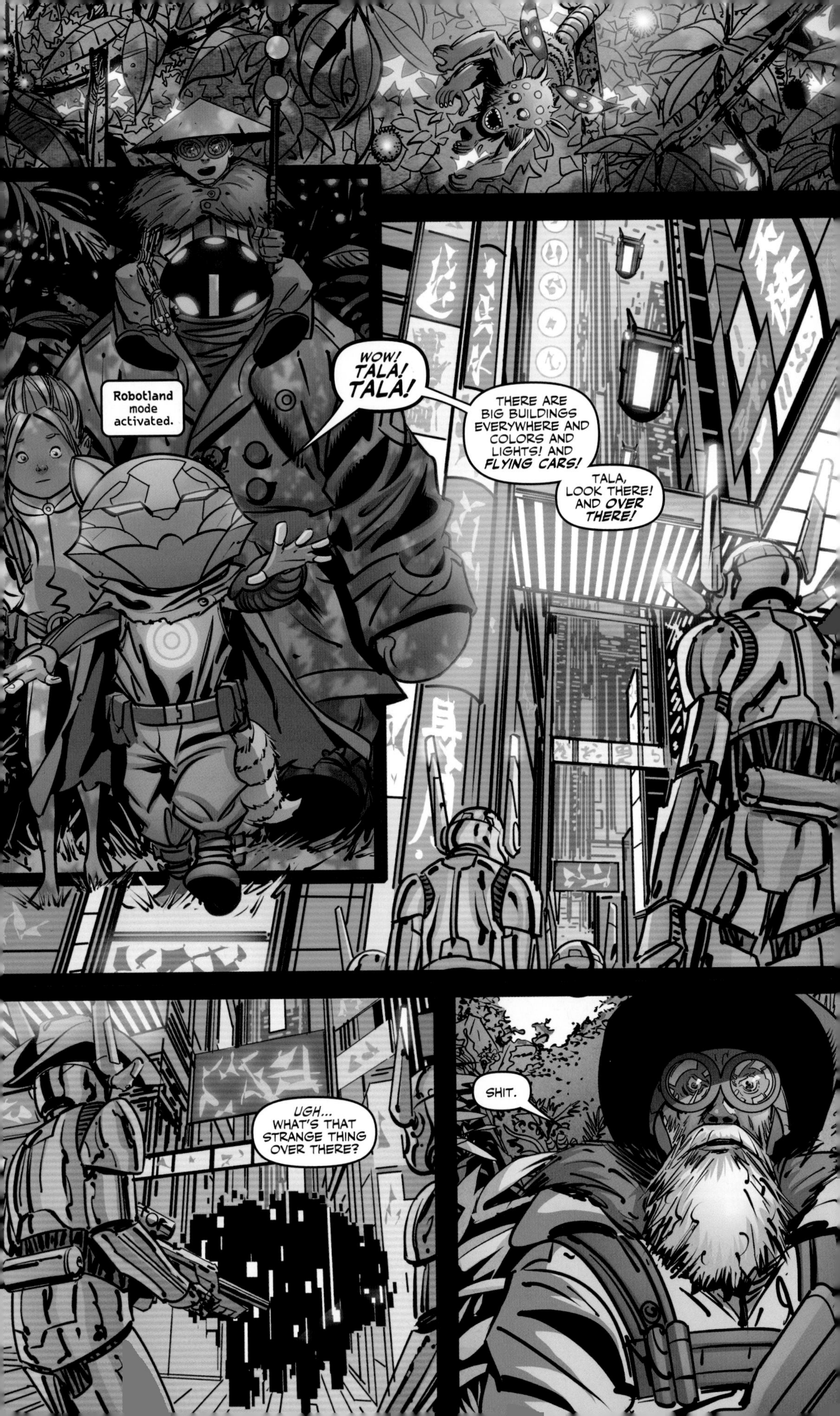
Robotland mode activated.
WOW! TALA! TALA!
THERE ARE BIG BUILDINGS EVERYWHERE AND COLORS AND LIGHTS! AND FLYING CARS!
TALA, LOOK THERE! AND OVER THERE!
UGH... WHAT'S THAT STRANGE THING OVER THERE?
SHIT.

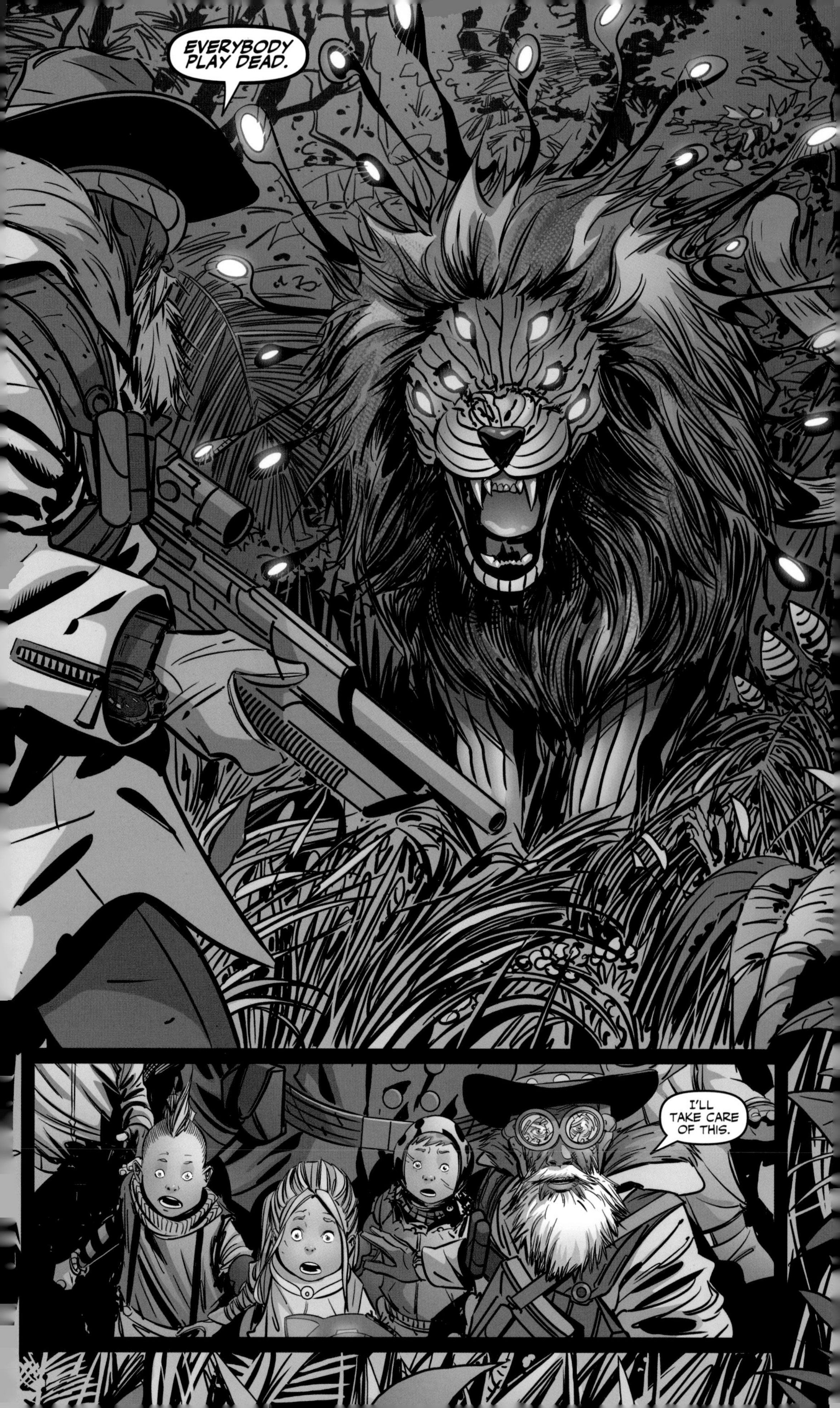
EVERYBODY PLAY DEAD.
I'LL TAKE CARE OF THIS.

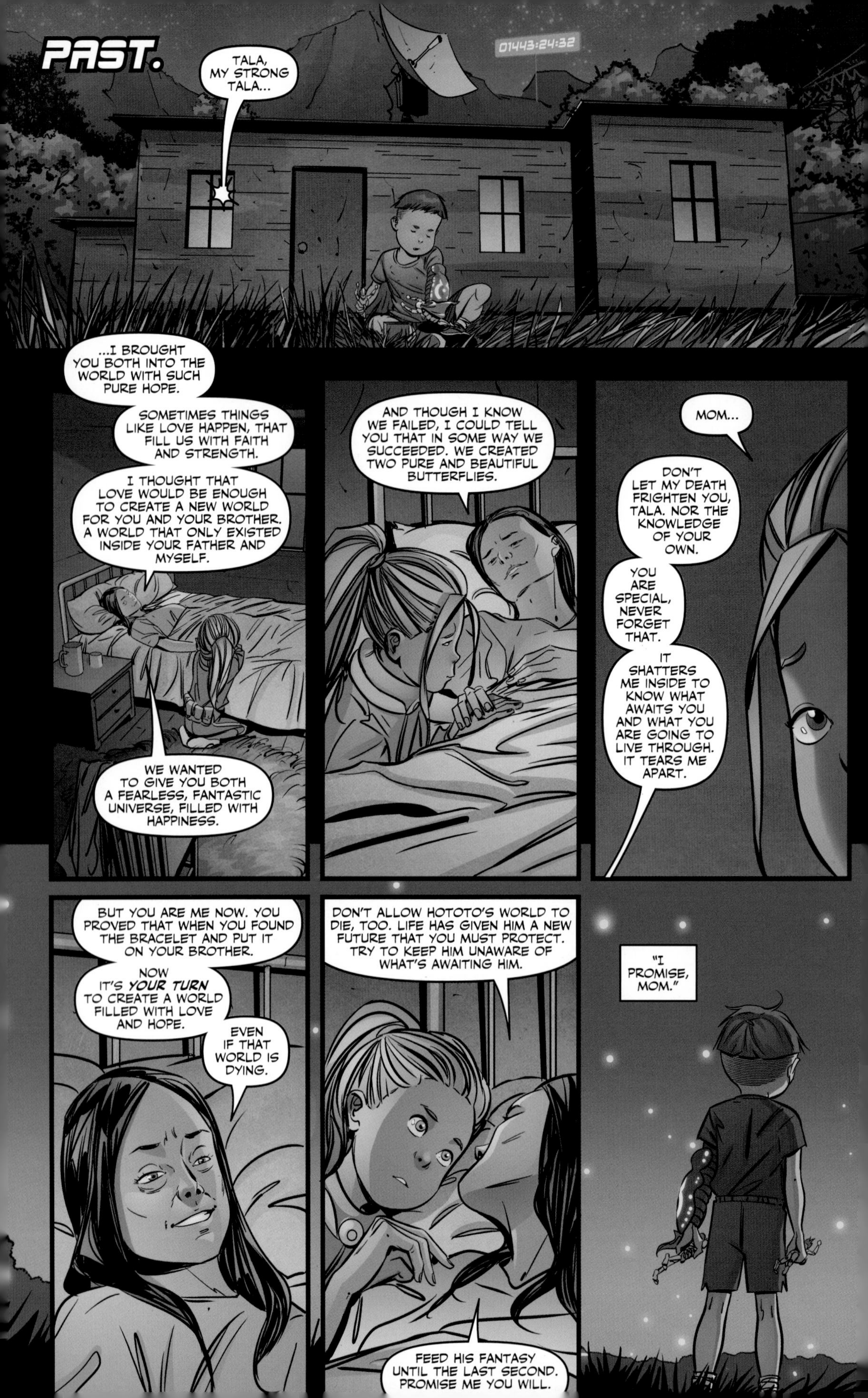
PAST.
01443:24:32
TALA, MY STRONG TALA...
...I BROUGHT YOU BOTH INTO THE WORLD WITH SUCH PURE HOPE.
SOMETIMES THINGS LIKE LOVE HAPPEN, THAT FILL US WITH FAITH AND STRENGTH.
I THOUGHT THAT LOVE WOULD BE ENOUGH TO CREATE A NEW WORLD FOR YOU AND YOUR BROTHER. A WORLD THAT ONLY EXISTED INSIDE YOUR FATHER AND MYSELF.
WE WANTED TO GIVE YOU BOTH A FEARLESS, FANTASTIC UNIVERSE, FILLED WITH HAPPINESS.
AND THOUGH I KNOW WE FAILED, I COULD TELL YOU THAT IN SOME WAY WE SUCCEEDED. WE CREATED TWO PURE AND BEAUTIFUL BUTTERFLIES.
MOM...
DON'T LET MY DEATH FRIGHTEN YOU, TALA. NOR THE KNOWLEDGE OF YOUR OWN.
YOU ARE SPECIAL, NEVER FORGET THAT.
IT SHATTERS ME INSIDE TO KNOW WHAT AWAITS YOU AND WHAT YOU ARE GOING TO LIVE THROUGH. IT TEARS ME APART.
BUT YOU ARE ME NOW. YOU PROVED THAT WHEN YOU FOUND THE BRACELET AND PUT IT ON YOUR BROTHER.
NOW IT'S *YOUR TURN* TO CREATE A WORLD FILLED WITH LOVE AND HOPE.
EVEN IF THAT WORLD IS DYING.
DON'T ALLOW HOTOTO'S WORLD TO DIE, TOO. LIFE HAS GIVEN HIM A NEW FUTURE THAT YOU MUST PROTECT. TRY TO KEEP HIM UNAWARE OF WHAT'S AWAITING HIM.
FEED HIS FANTASY UNTIL THE LAST SECOND. PROMISE ME YOU WILL.
"I PROMISE, MOM."

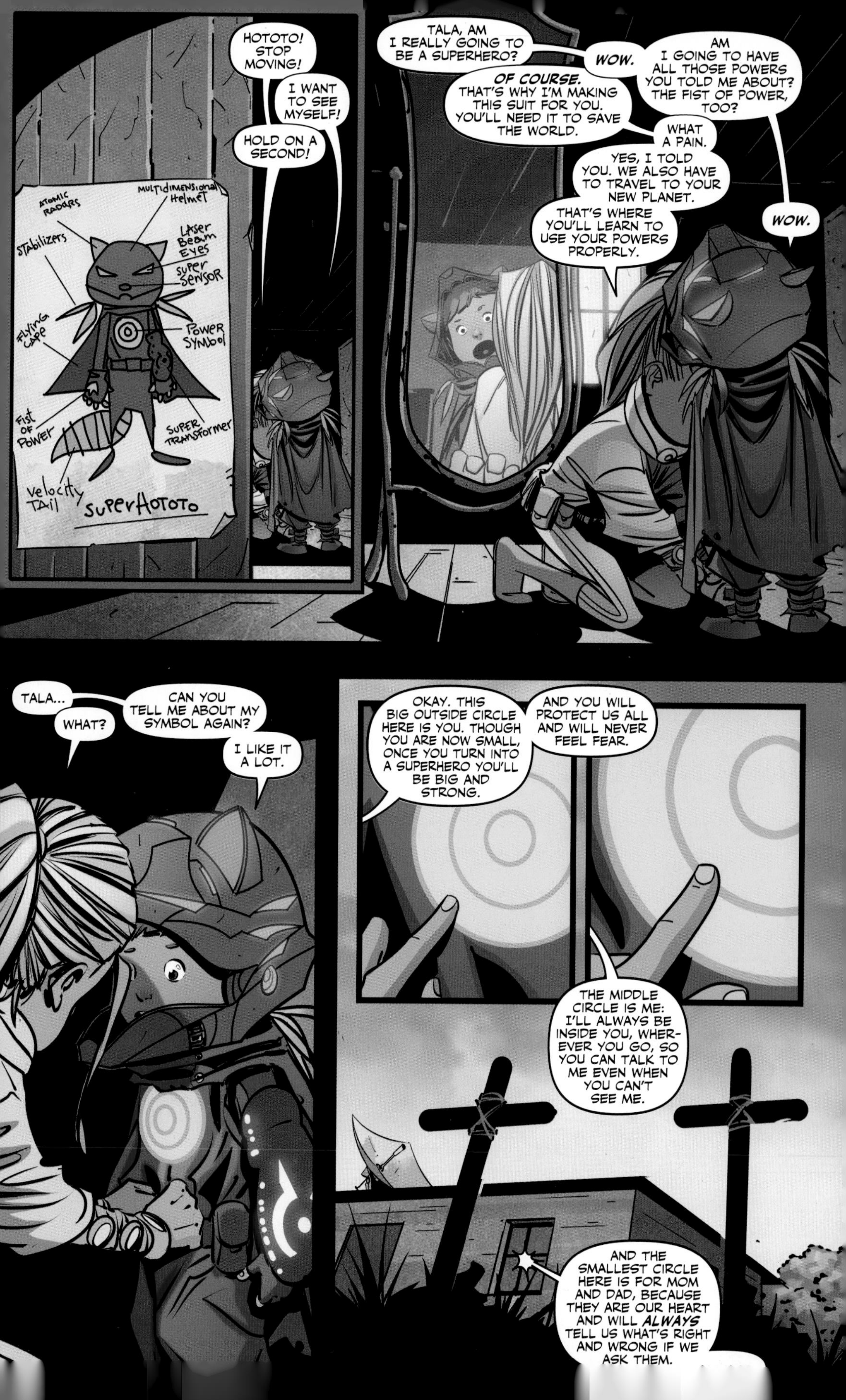
HOTOTO! STOP MOVING!
I WANT TO SEE MYSELF!
HOLD ON A SECOND!
ATOMIC RADARS
MULTIDIMENSIONAL HELMET
STABILIZERS
LASER BEAM EYES
SUPER SENSOR
FLYING CAPE
POWER SYMBOL
FIST OF POWER
SUPER TRANSFORMER
VELOCITY TAIL
SUPERHOTOTO
TALA, AM I REALLY GOING TO BE A SUPERHERO?
OF COURSE. THAT'S WHY I'M MAKING THIS SUIT FOR YOU. YOU'LL NEED IT TO SAVE THE WORLD.
WOW.
AM I GOING TO HAVE ALL THOSE POWERS YOU TOLD ME ABOUT? THE FIST OF POWER, TOO?
WHAT A PAIN.
YES, I TOLD YOU. WE ALSO HAVE TO TRAVEL TO YOUR NEW PLANET.
THAT'S WHERE YOU'LL LEARN TO USE YOUR POWERS PROPERLY.
WOW.
TALA...
WHAT?
CAN YOU TELL ME ABOUT MY SYMBOL AGAIN?
I LIKE IT A LOT.
OKAY. THIS BIG OUTSIDE CIRCLE HERE IS YOU. THOUGH YOU ARE NOW SMALL, ONCE YOU TURN INTO A SUPERHERO YOU'LL BE BIG AND STRONG.
AND YOU WILL PROTECT US ALL AND WILL NEVER FEEL FEAR.
THE MIDDLE CIRCLE IS ME: I'LL ALWAYS BE INSIDE YOU, WHEREVER YOU GO, SO YOU CAN TALK TO ME EVEN WHEN YOU CAN'T SEE ME.
AND THE SMALLEST CIRCLE HERE IS FOR MOM AND DAD, BECAUSE THEY ARE OUR HEART AND WILL ALWAYS TELL US WHAT'S RIGHT AND WRONG IF WE ASK THEM.

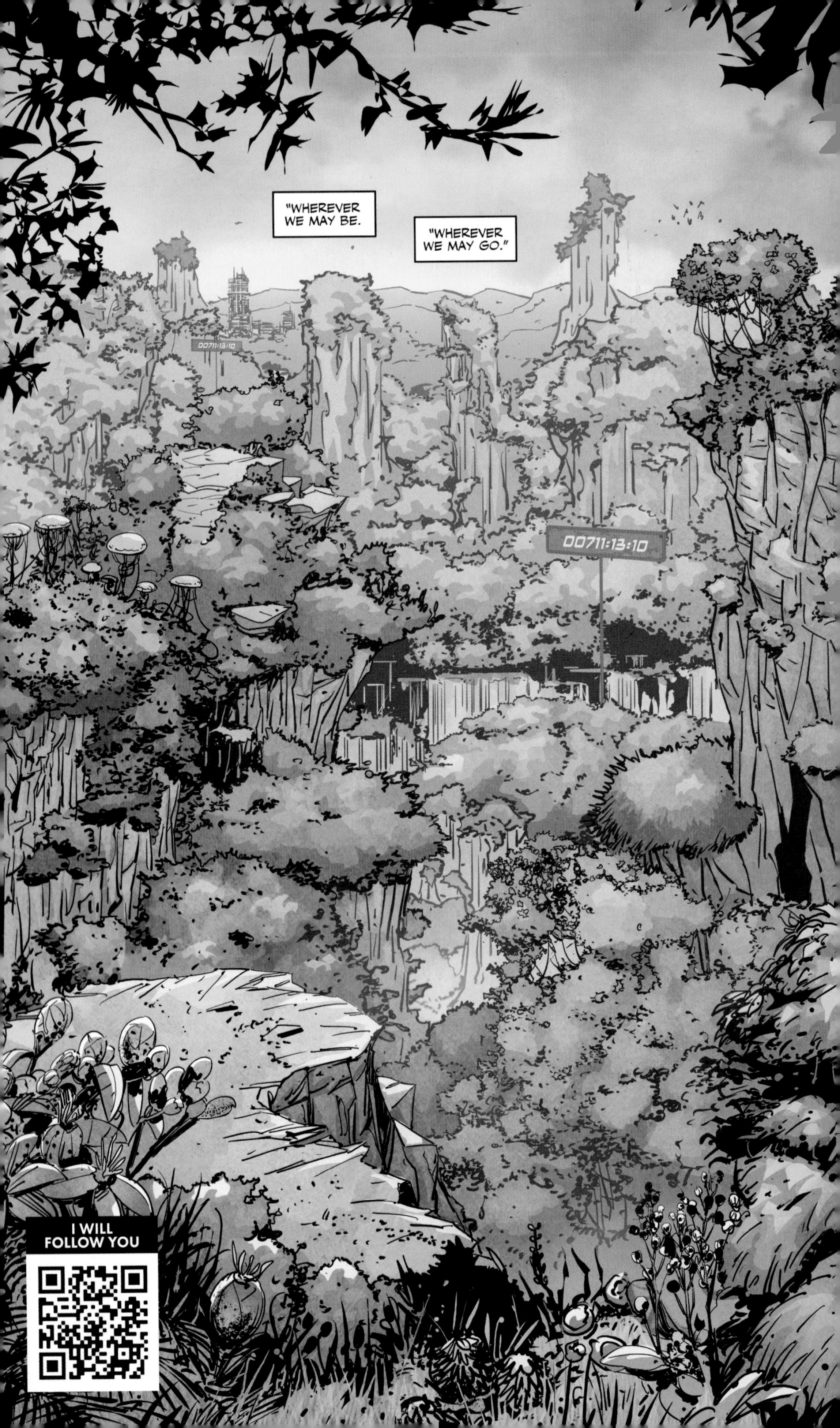
"WHEREVER WE MAY BE.
"WHEREVER WE MAY GO."
00711:13:10
00711:13:10
I WILL FOLLOW YOU

2

JADE ALGAE

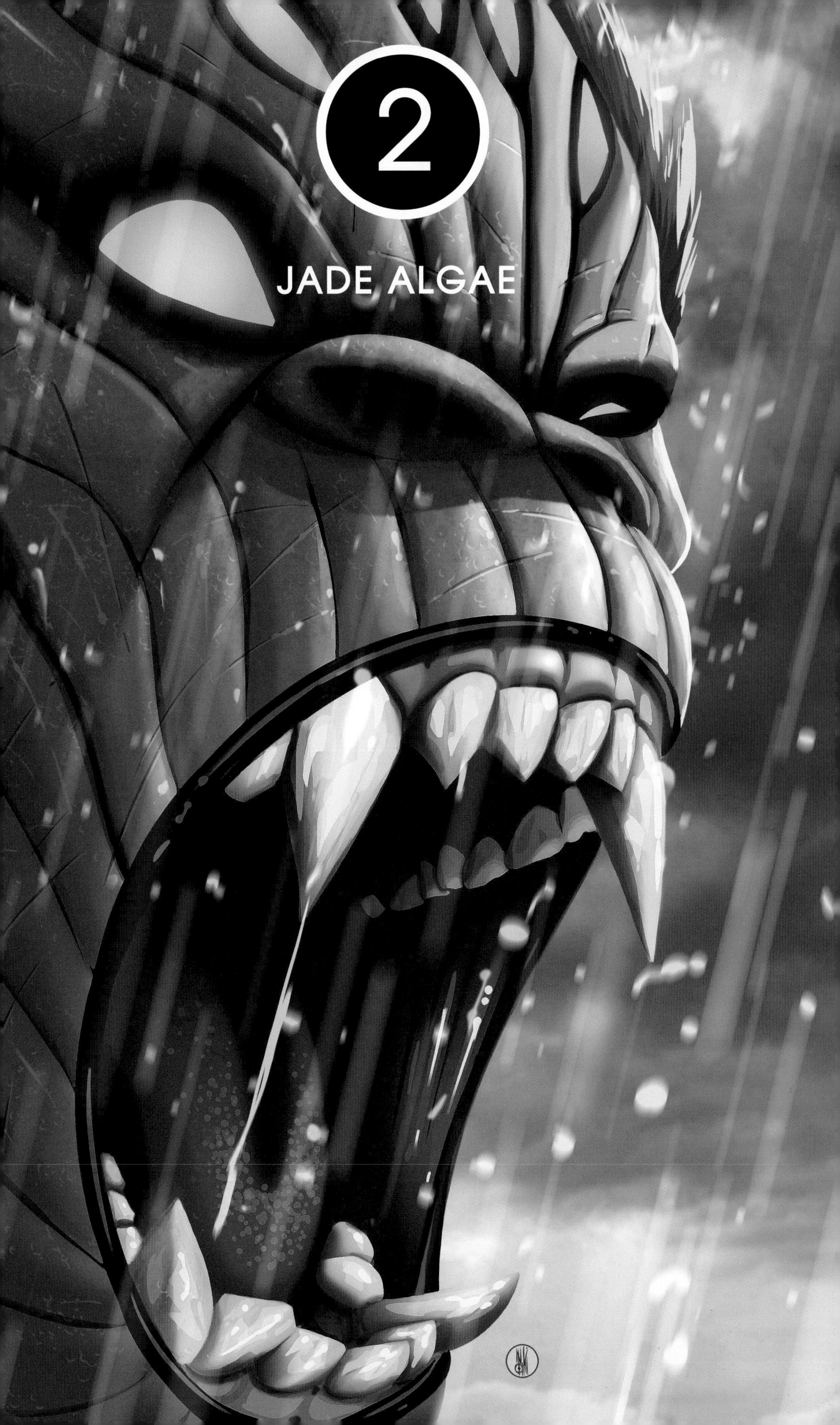

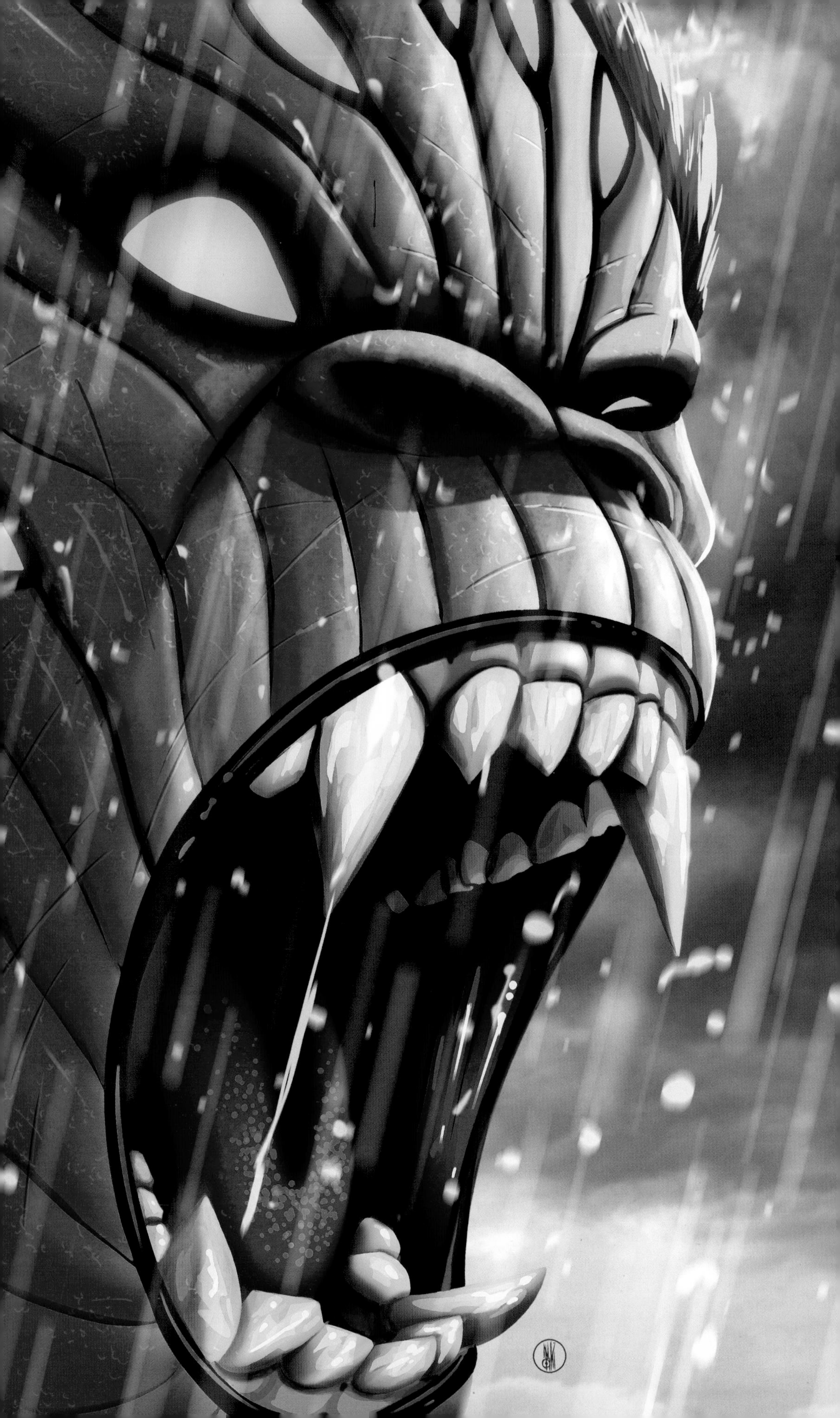

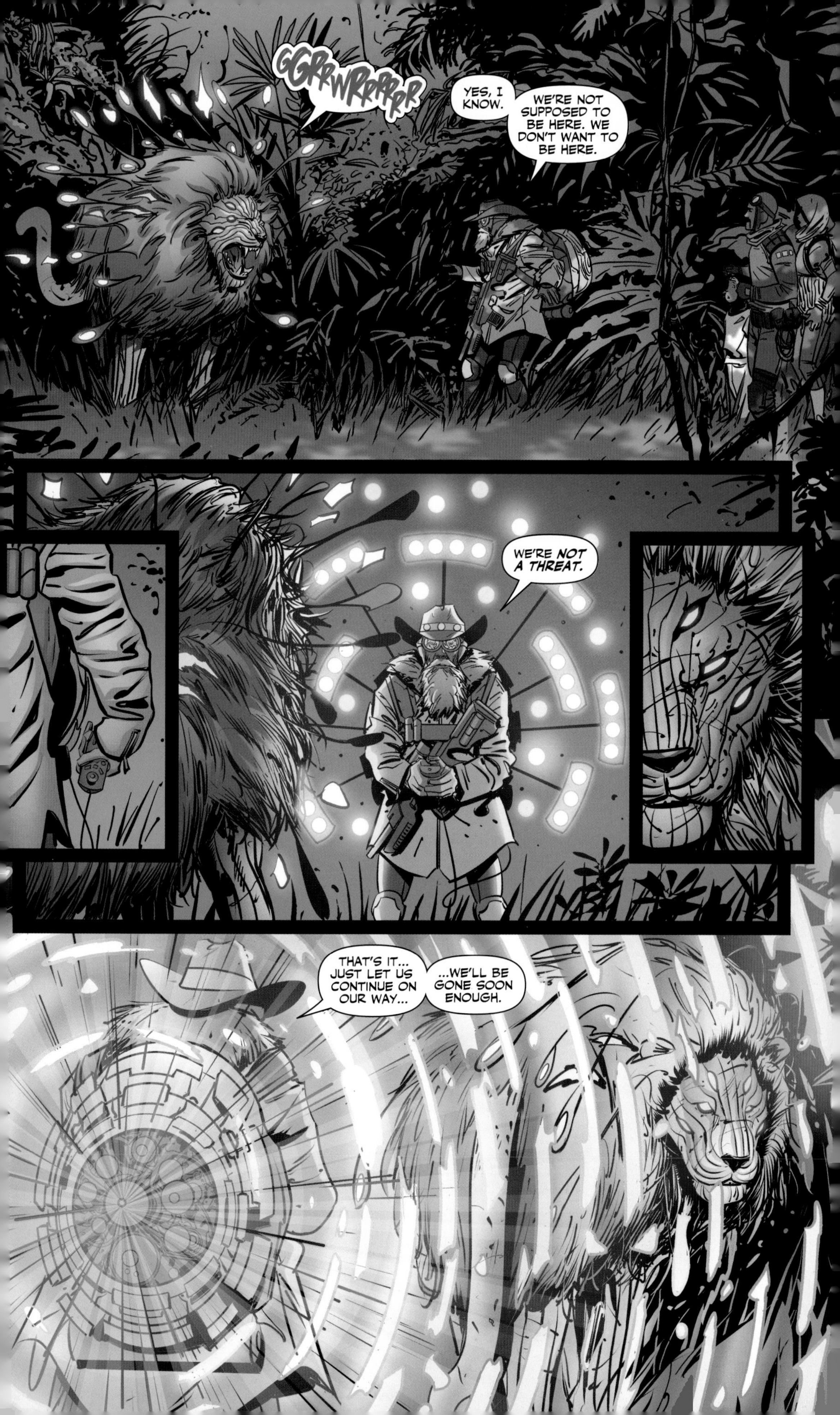
GGRRRWRRRRRR
YES, I KNOW.
WE'RE NOT SUPPOSED TO BE HERE. WE DON'T WANT TO BE HERE.
WE'RE NOT A THREAT.
THAT'S IT... JUST LET US CONTINUE ON OUR WAY...
...WE'LL BE GONE SOON ENOUGH.

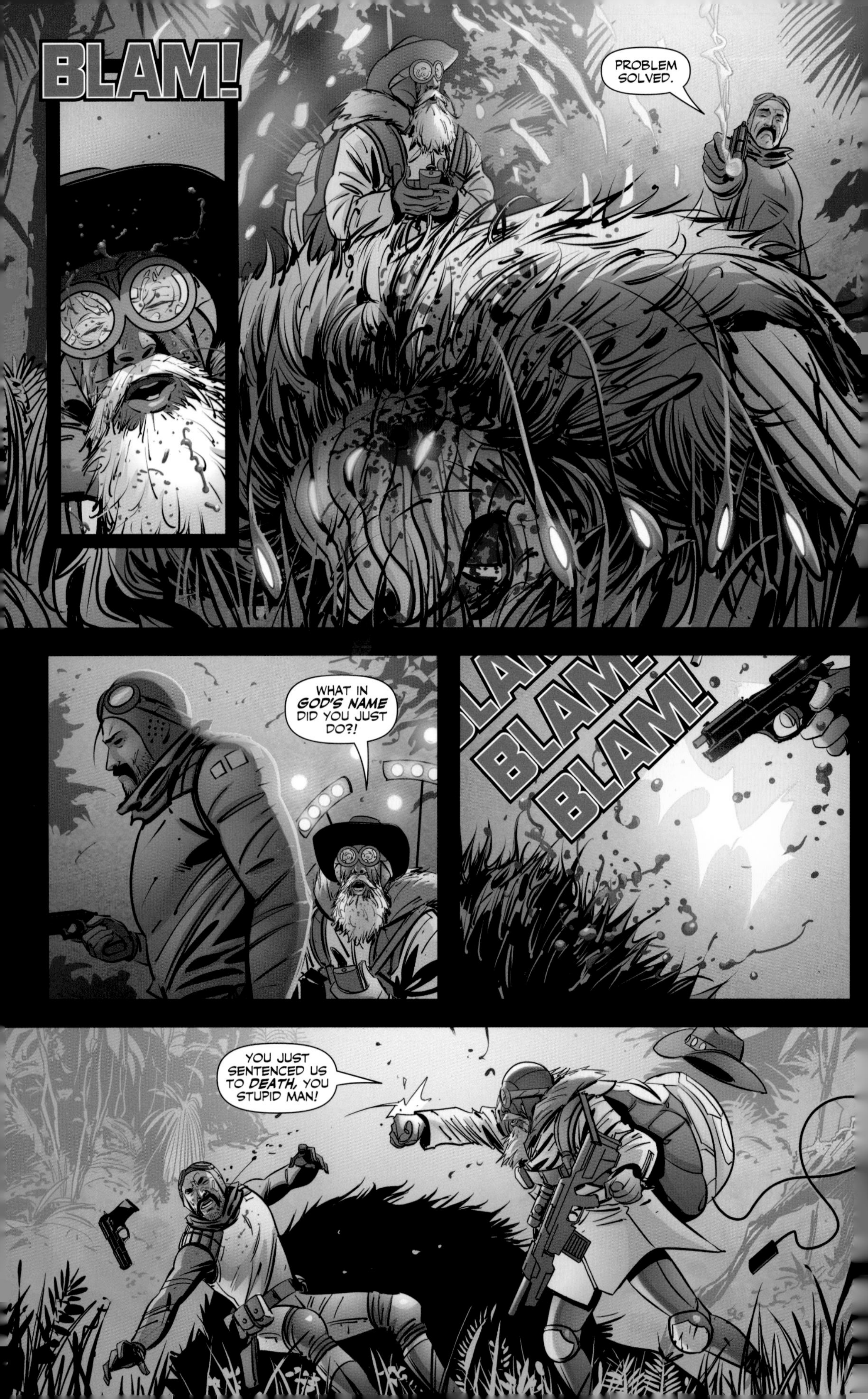
BLAM!
PROBLEM SOLVED.
WHAT IN GOD'S NAME DID YOU JUST DO?!
BLAM! BLAM! BLAM!
YOU JUST SENTENCED US TO DEATH, YOU STUPID MAN!

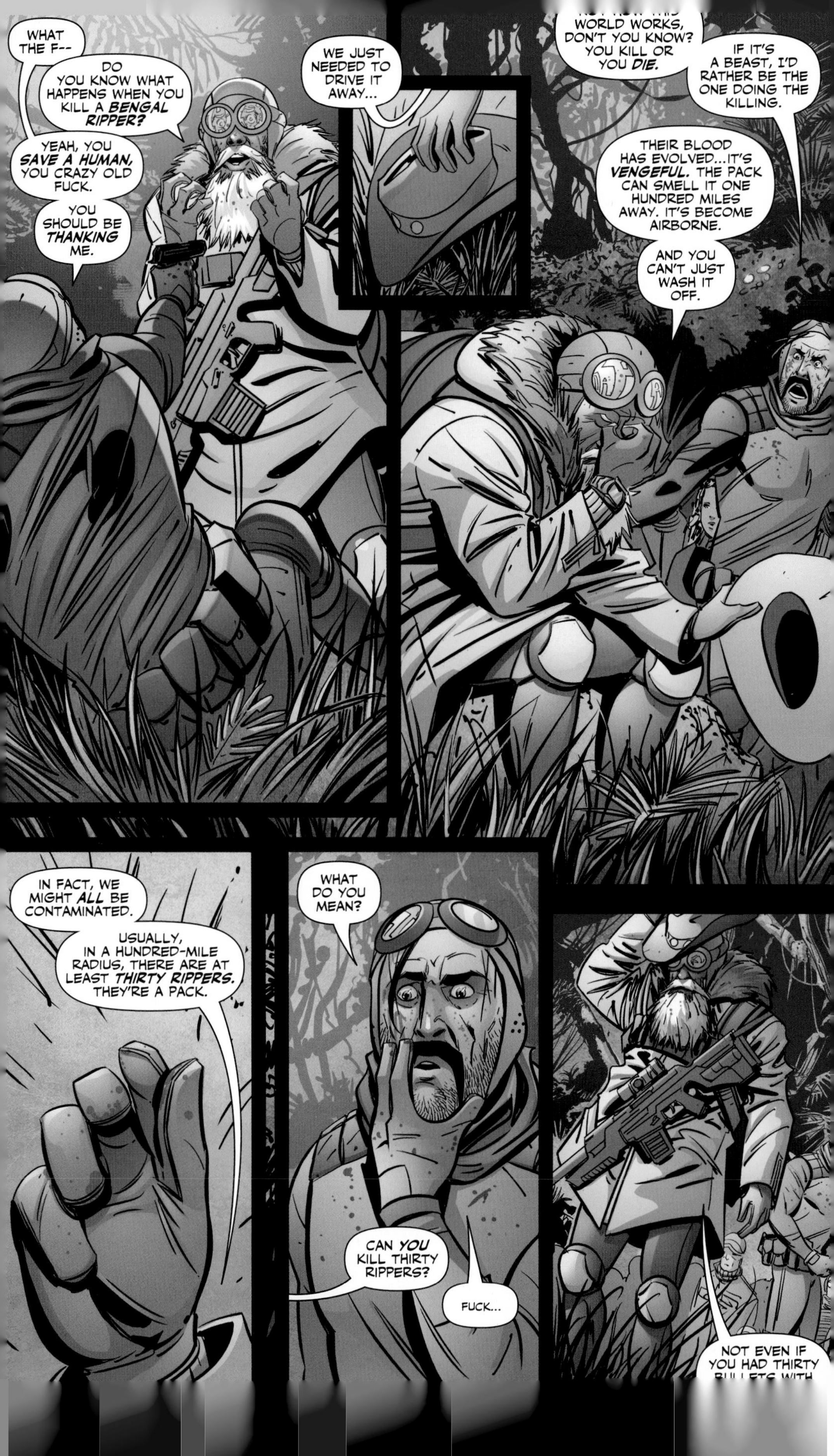
WHAT THE F--
DO YOU KNOW WHAT HAPPENS WHEN YOU KILL A BENGAL RIPPER?
YEAH, YOU SAVE A HUMAN, YOU CRAZY OLD FUCK.
YOU SHOULD BE THANKING ME.
WE JUST NEEDED TO DRIVE IT AWAY...
WORLD WORKS, DON'T YOU KNOW? YOU KILL OR YOU DIE.
IF IT'S A BEAST, I'D RATHER BE THE ONE DOING THE KILLING.
THEIR BLOOD HAS EVOLVED...IT'S VENGEFUL. THE PACK CAN SMELL IT ONE HUNDRED MILES AWAY. IT'S BECOME AIRBORNE.
AND YOU CAN'T JUST WASH IT OFF.
IN FACT, WE MIGHT ALL BE CONTAMINATED.
USUALLY, IN A HUNDRED-MILE RADIUS, THERE ARE AT LEAST THIRTY RIPPERS. THEY'RE A PACK.
WHAT DO YOU MEAN?
CAN YOU KILL THIRTY RIPPERS?
FUCK...
NOT EVEN IF YOU HAD THIRTY

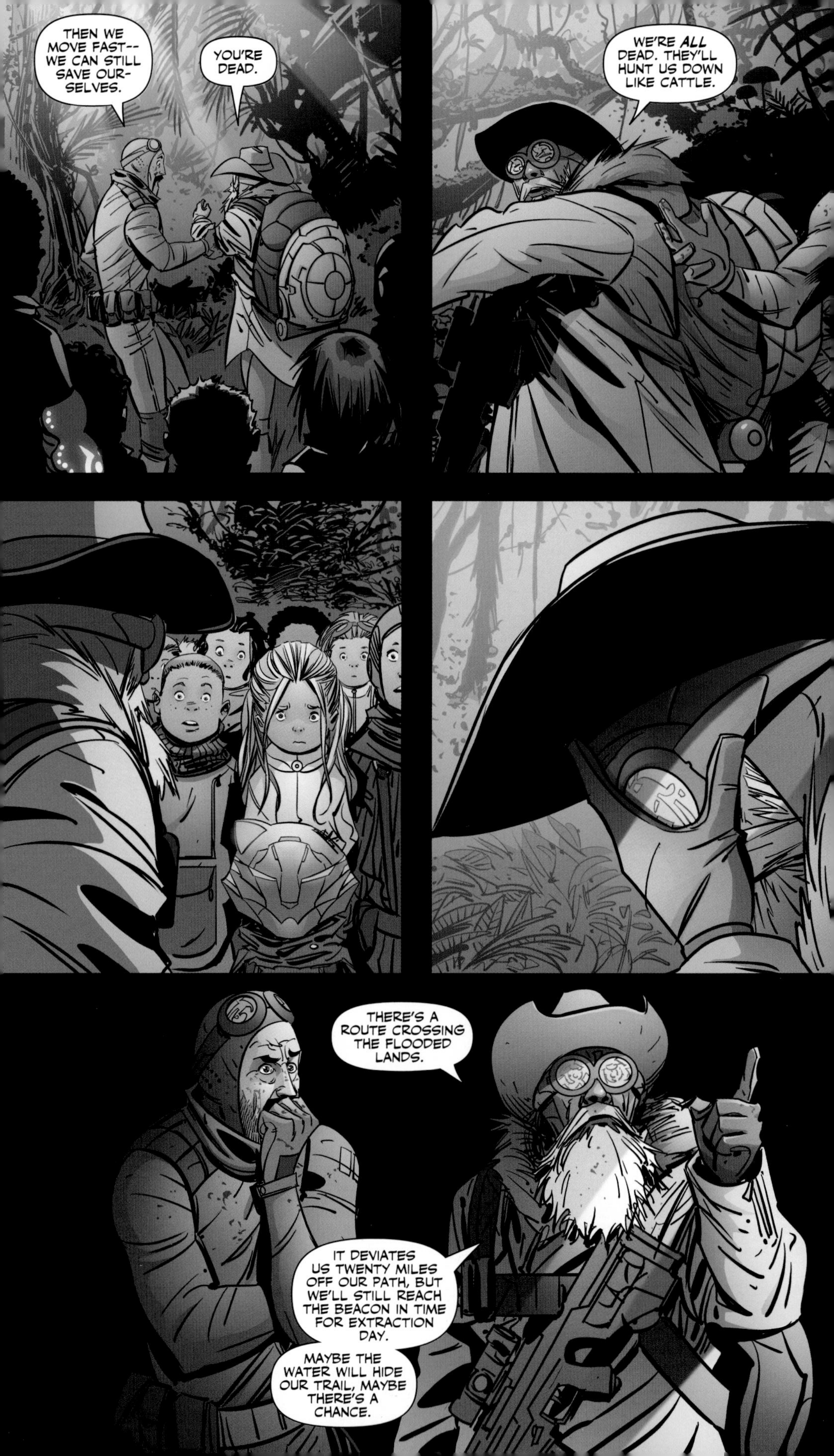
THEN WE MOVE FAST-- WE CAN STILL SAVE OUR-SELVES.
YOU'RE DEAD.
WE'RE *ALL* DEAD. THEY'LL HUNT US DOWN LIKE CATTLE.
THERE'S A ROUTE CROSSING THE FLOODED LANDS.
IT DEVIATES US TWENTY MILES OFF OUR PATH, BUT WE'LL STILL REACH THE BEACON IN TIME FOR EXTRACTION DAY.
MAYBE THE WATER WILL HIDE OUR TRAIL, MAYBE THERE'S A CHANCE.

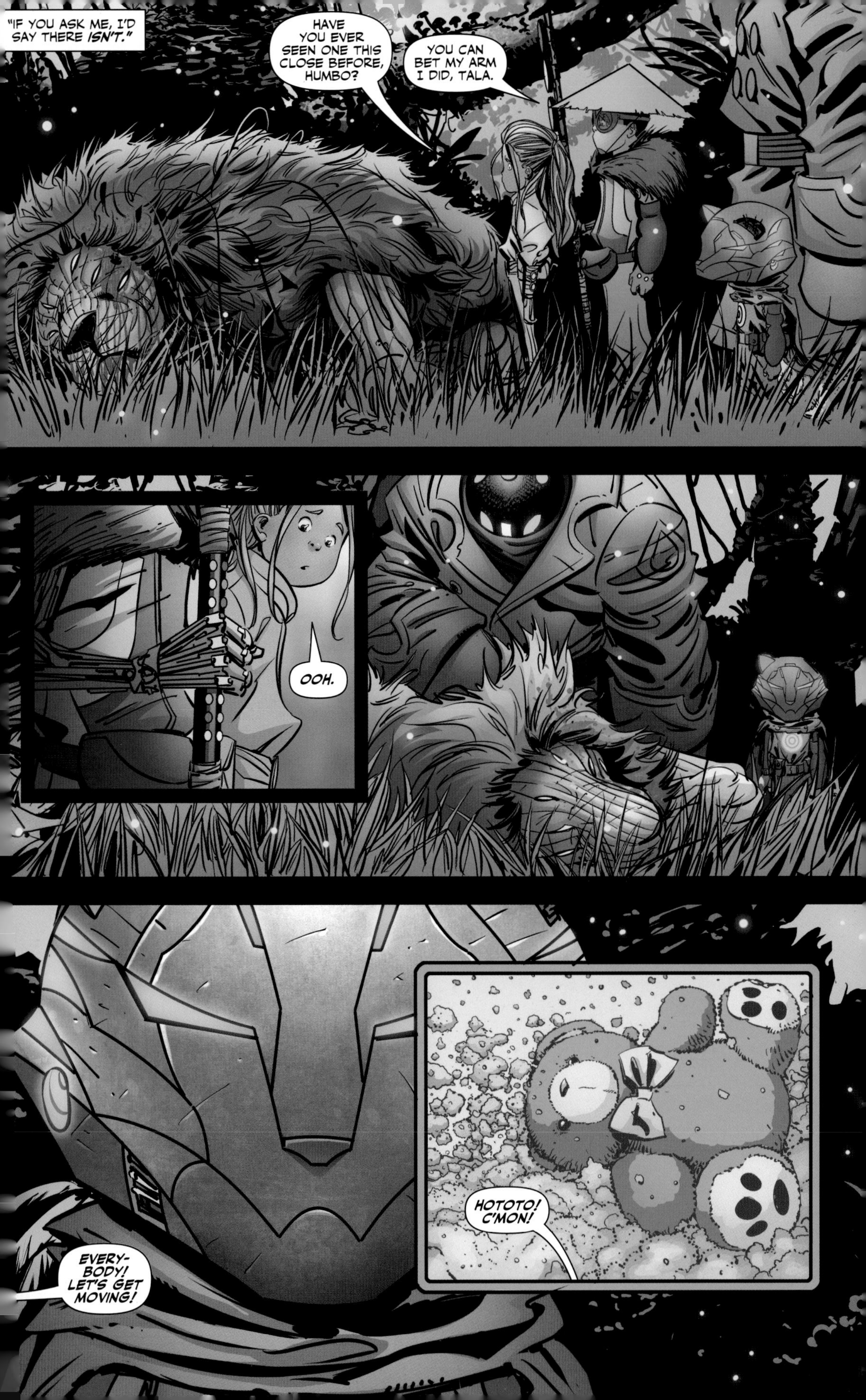
"IF YOU ASK ME, I'D SAY THERE ISN'T."
HAVE YOU EVER SEEN ONE THIS CLOSE BEFORE, HUMBO?
YOU CAN BET MY ARM I DID, TALA.
OOH.
HOTOTO! C'MON!
EVERY-BODY! LET'S GET MOVING!

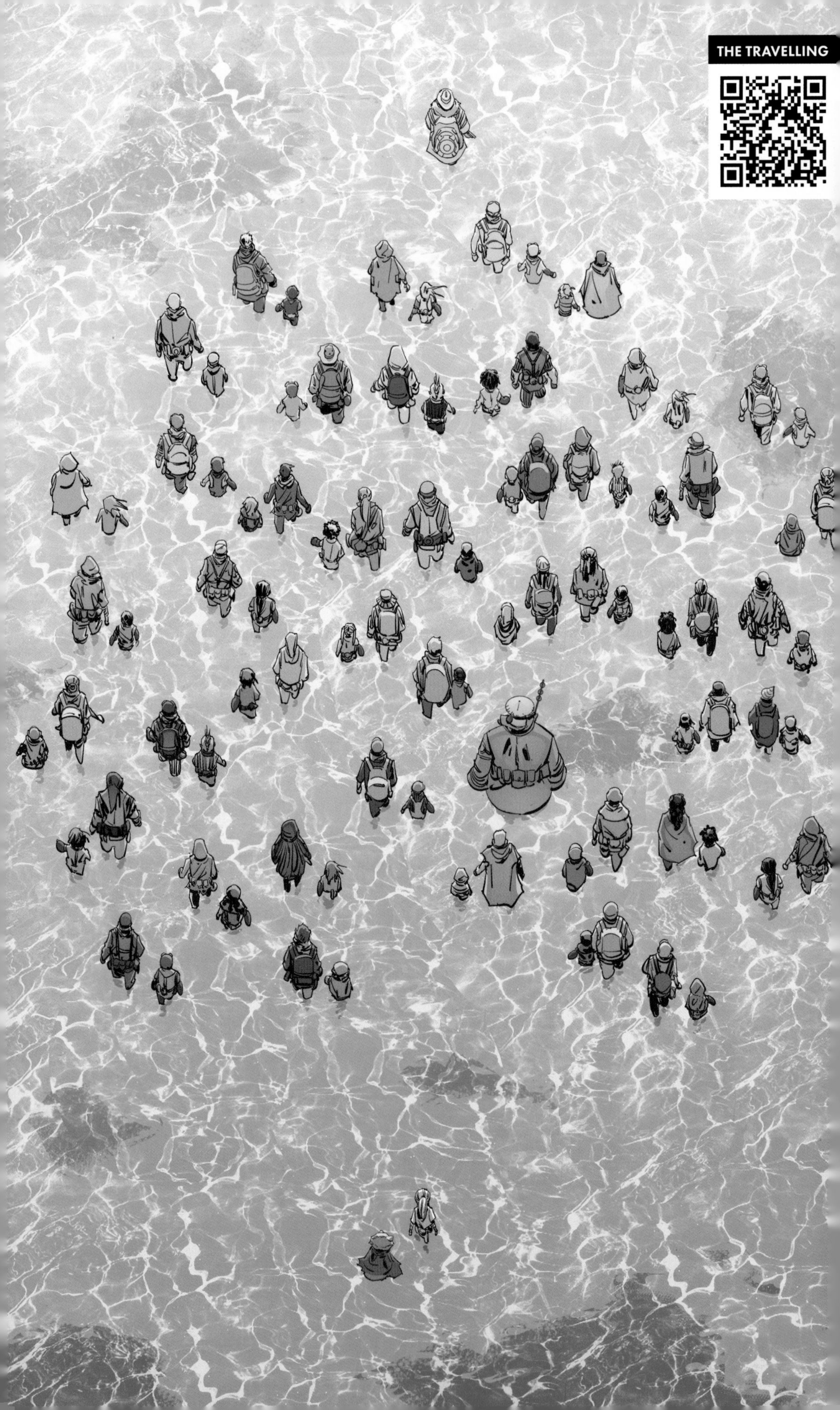
THE TRAVELLING

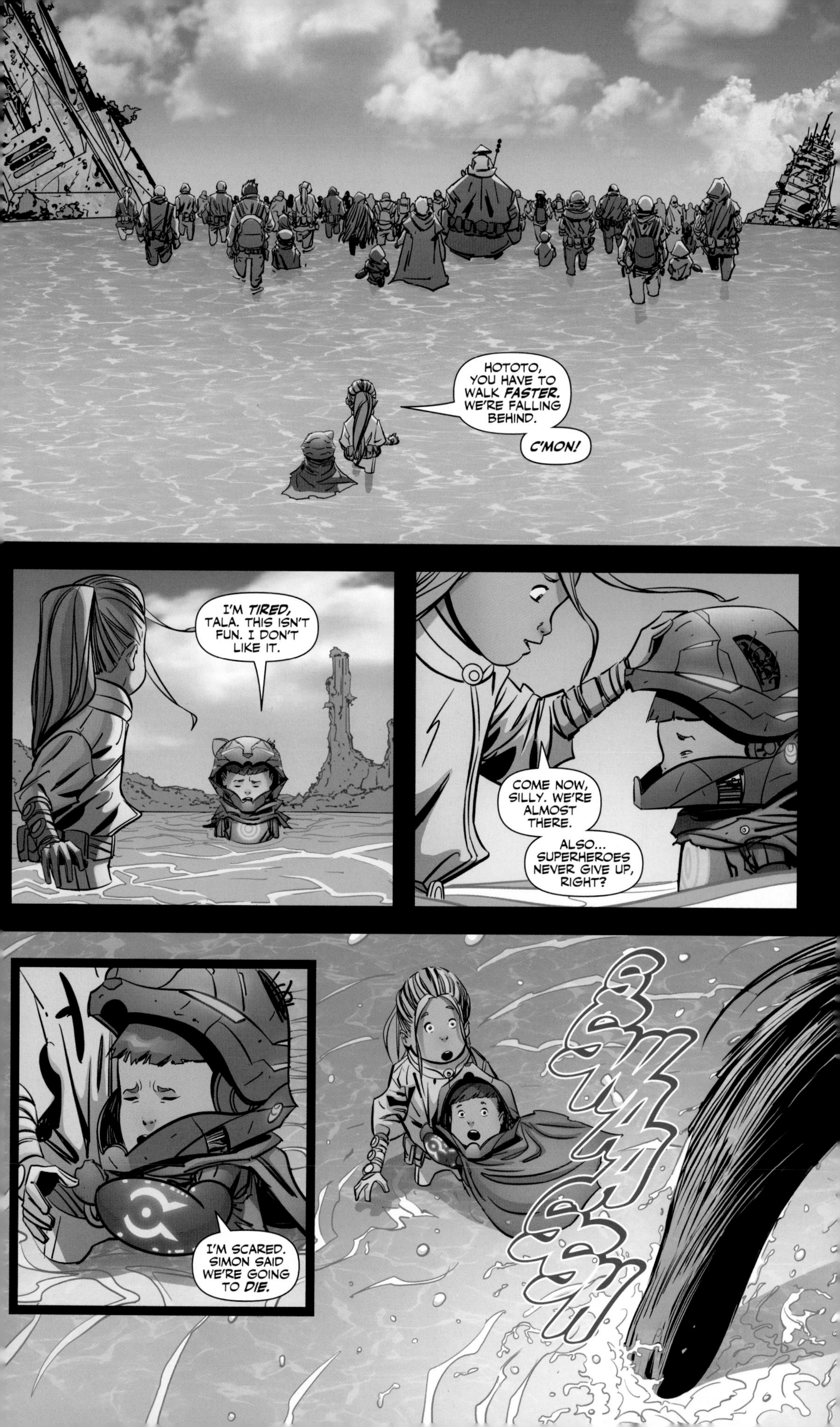
HOTOTO, YOU HAVE TO WALK FASTER. WE'RE FALLING BEHIND.
C'MON!
I'M TIRED, TALA. THIS ISN'T FUN. I DON'T LIKE IT.
COME NOW, SILLY. WE'RE ALMOST THERE.
ALSO... SUPERHEROES NEVER GIVE UP, RIGHT?
I'M SCARED. SIMON SAID WE'RE GOING TO DIE.

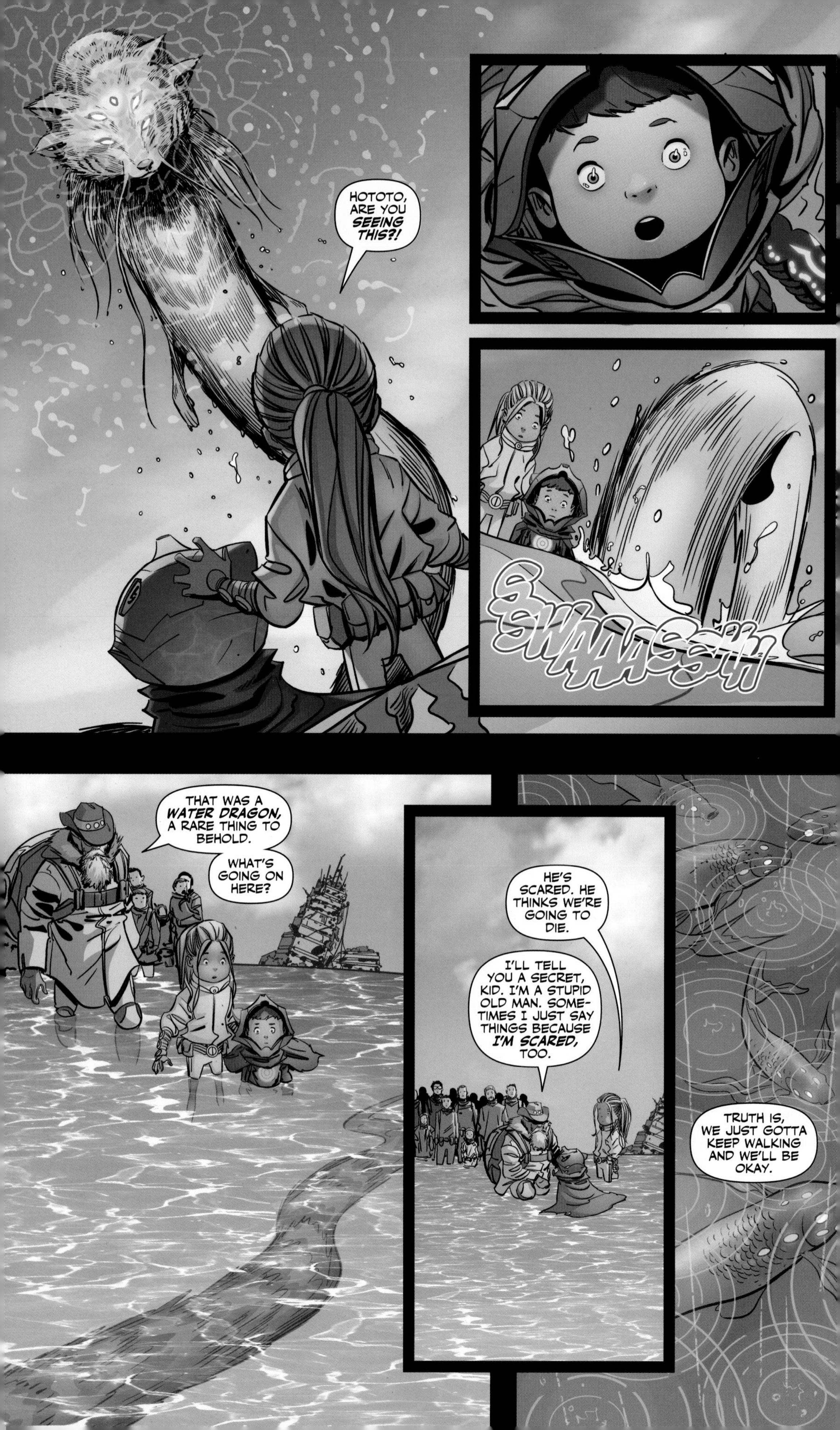
HOTOTO, ARE YOU *SEEING THIS?!*
SWAAASSSH
THAT WAS A *WATER DRAGON,* A RARE THING TO BEHOLD.
WHAT'S GOING ON HERE?
HE'S SCARED. HE THINKS WE'RE GOING TO DIE.
I'LL TELL YOU A SECRET, KID. I'M A STUPID OLD MAN. SOMETIMES I JUST SAY THINGS BECAUSE *I'M SCARED,* TOO.
TRUTH IS, WE JUST GOTTA KEEP WALKING AND WE'LL BE OKAY.

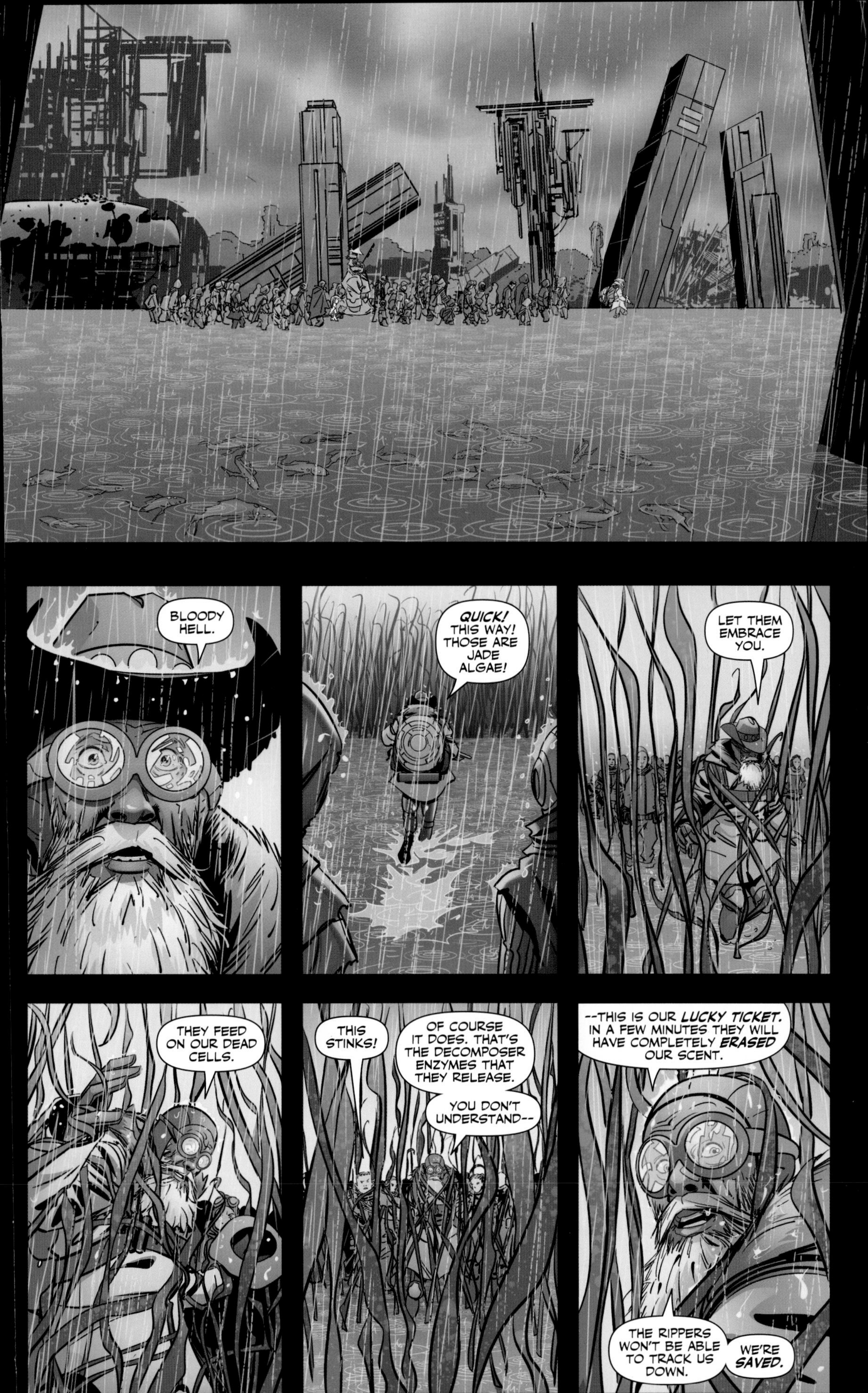
BLOODY HELL.
QUICK! THIS WAY! THOSE ARE JADE ALGAE!
LET THEM EMBRACE YOU.
THEY FEED ON OUR DEAD CELLS.
THIS STINKS!
OF COURSE IT DOES. THAT'S THE DECOMPOSER ENZYMES THAT THEY RELEASE.
YOU DON'T UNDERSTAND--
--THIS IS OUR *LUCKY TICKET.* IN A FEW MINUTES THEY WILL HAVE COMPLETELY *ERASED* OUR SCENT.
THE RIPPERS WON'T BE ABLE TO TRACK US DOWN.
WE'RE *SAVED.*

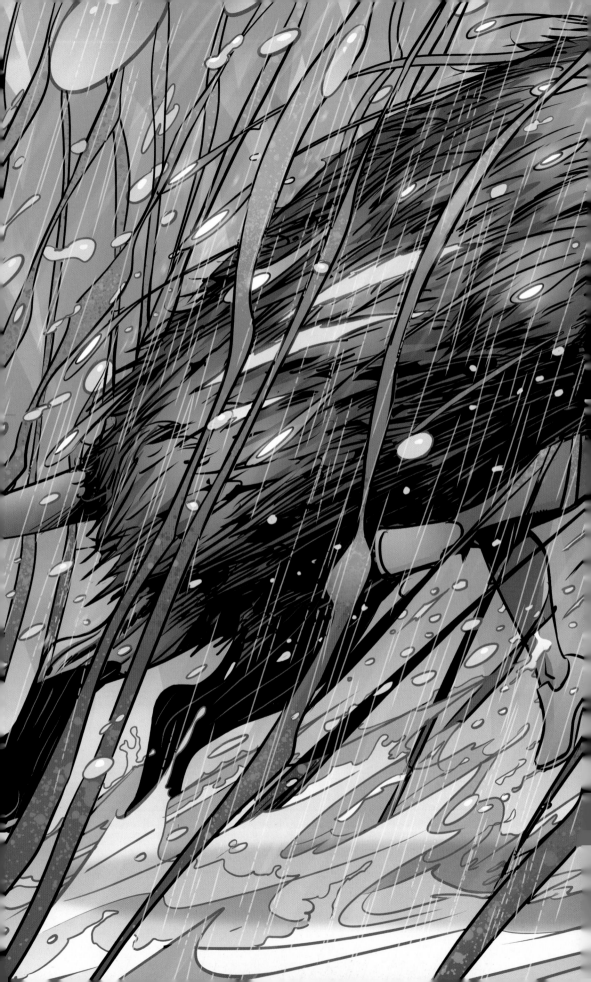

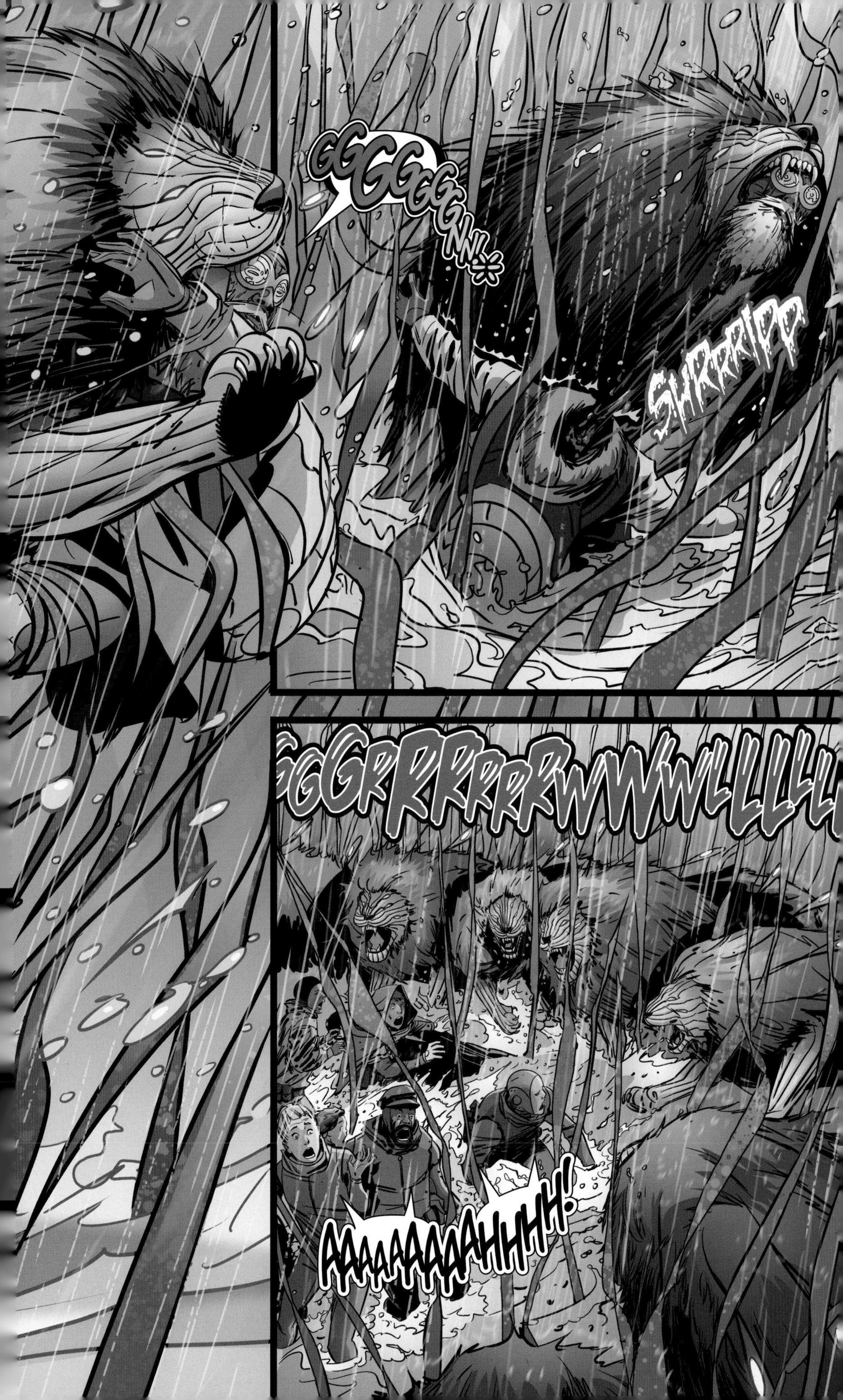
GGGGGGNN!*
SHRRIPP
GGGRRRRRRWWWLLLLL
AAAAAAAAAHHHH!

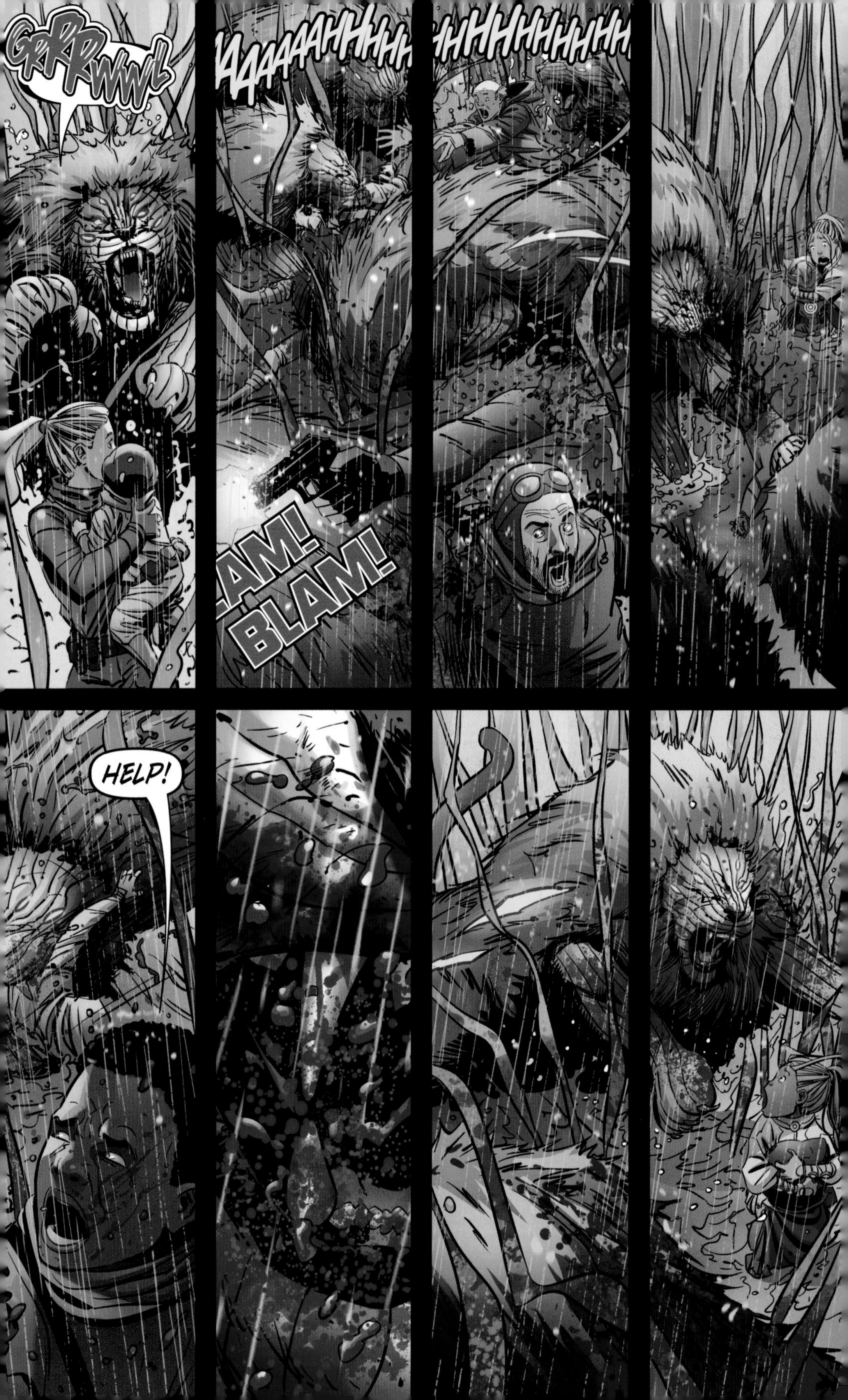
GRRRWWWL
AAAAAAAHHHHH
HHHHHHHHHHH
BLAM! BLAM!
HELP!

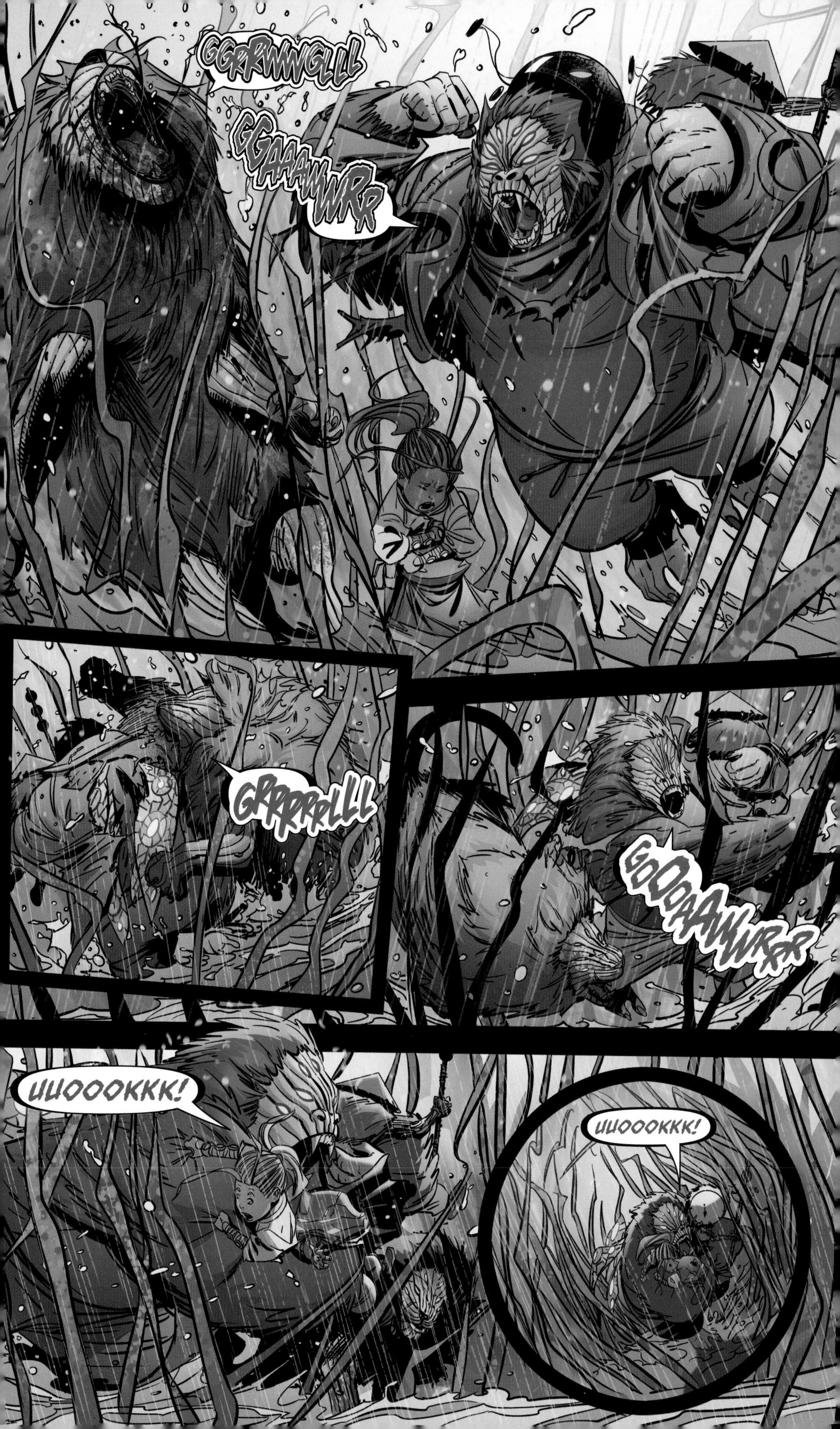
GGRRWWGLLL
GGAAAAWRR
GRRRRRLLLL
GOOOAAWRRR
UUOOOKKK!
UUOOOKKK!

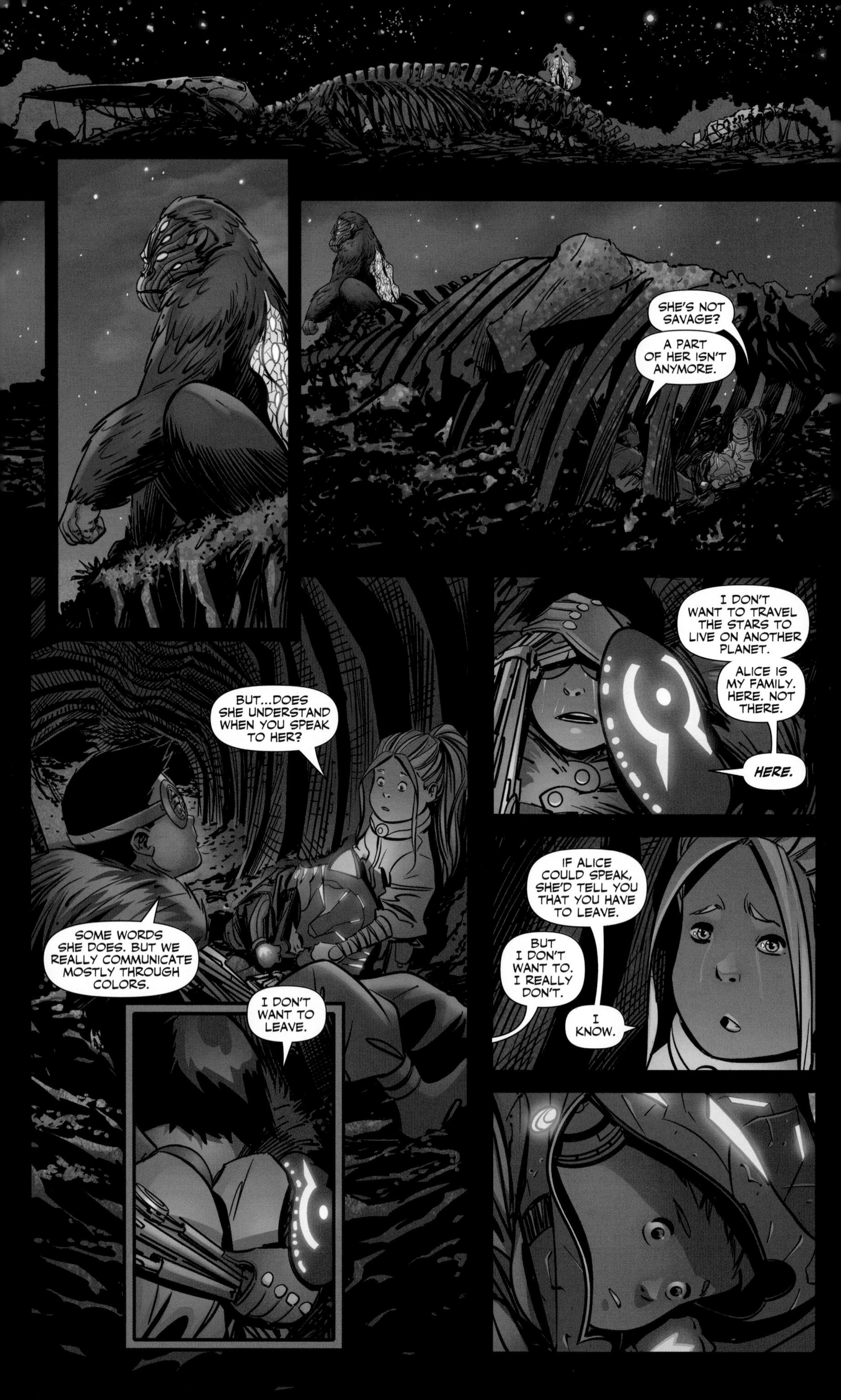
SHE'S NOT SAVAGE?
A PART OF HER ISN'T ANYMORE.
BUT...DOES SHE UNDERSTAND WHEN YOU SPEAK TO HER?
SOME WORDS SHE DOES. BUT WE REALLY COMMUNICATE MOSTLY THROUGH COLORS.
I DON'T WANT TO LEAVE.
I DON'T WANT TO TRAVEL THE STARS TO LIVE ON ANOTHER PLANET.
ALICE IS MY FAMILY. HERE. NOT THERE.
HERE.
IF ALICE COULD SPEAK, SHE'D TELL YOU THAT YOU HAVE TO LEAVE.
BUT I DON'T WANT TO. I REALLY DON'T.
I KNOW.

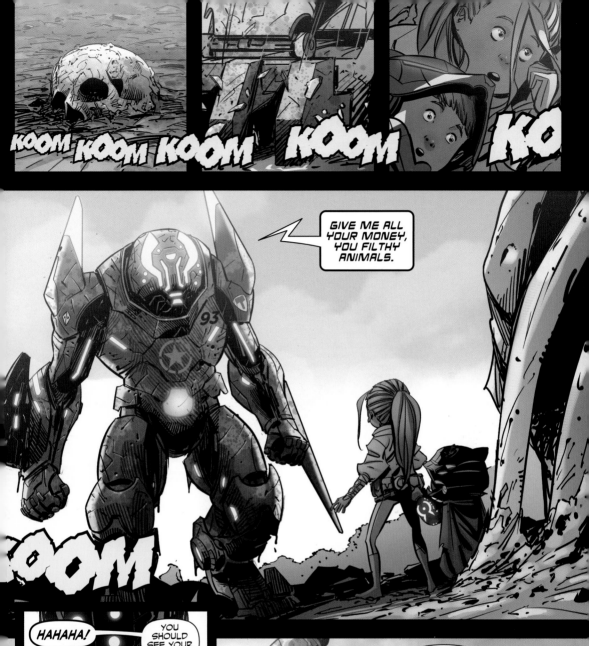

KOOM KOOM KOOM KOOM KO

GIVE ME ALL YOUR MONEY, YOU FILTHY ANIMALS.

OOM

HAHAHA!

YOU SHOULD SEE YOUR FACES!

I FOUND THIS HOPPER AND I MANAGED TO TURN IT ON.

IT HAS A GPS THAT CAN SHOW US THE ROUTE TO THE STATION!

HUMBO, WHAT'S A HOPPER?

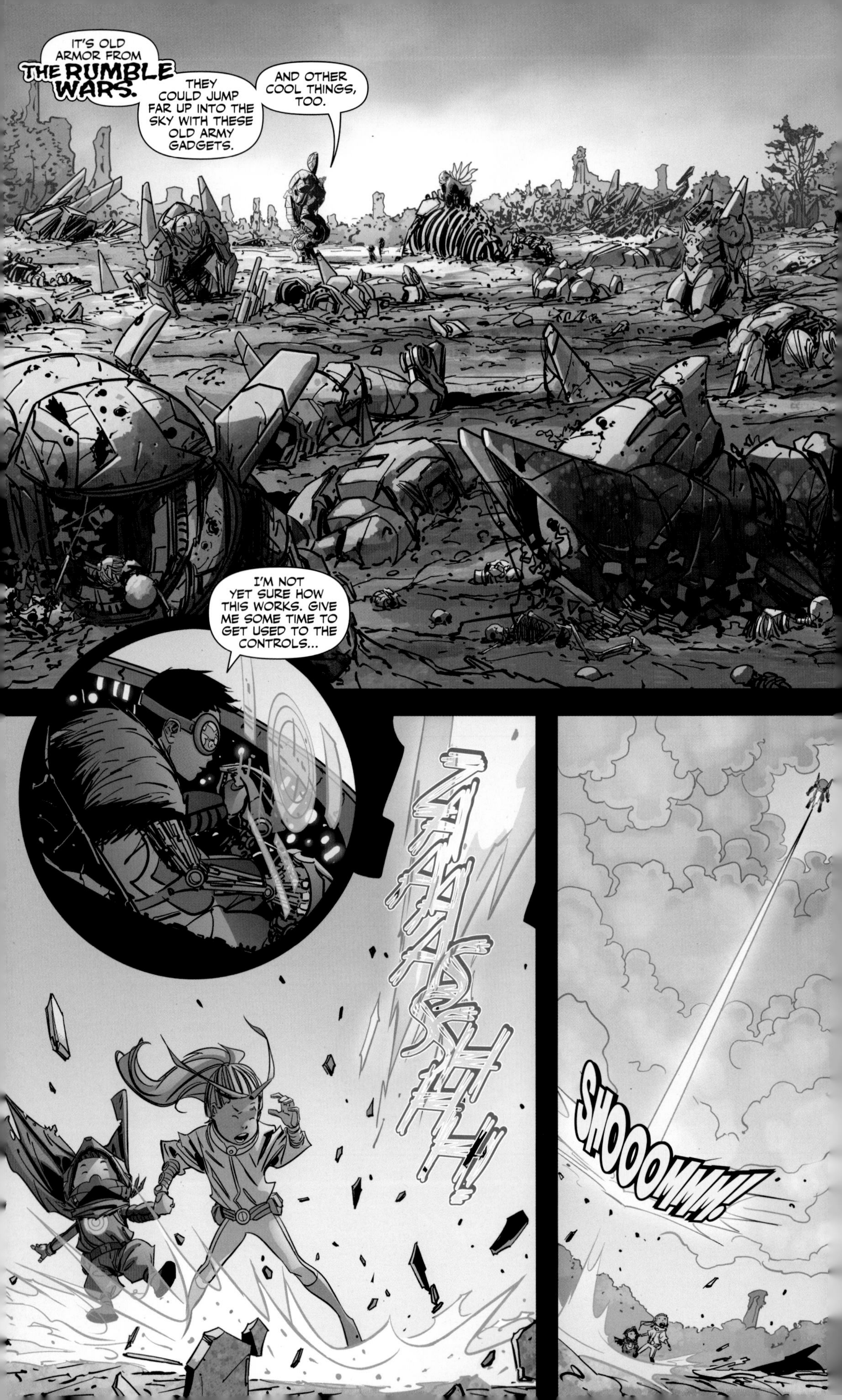
IT'S OLD ARMOR FROM THE RUMBLE WARS.
THEY COULD JUMP FAR UP INTO THE SKY WITH THESE OLD ARMY GADGETS.
AND OTHER COOL THINGS, TOO.
I'M NOT YET SURE HOW THIS WORKS. GIVE ME SOME TIME TO GET USED TO THE CONTROLS...
SHOOOMMM!

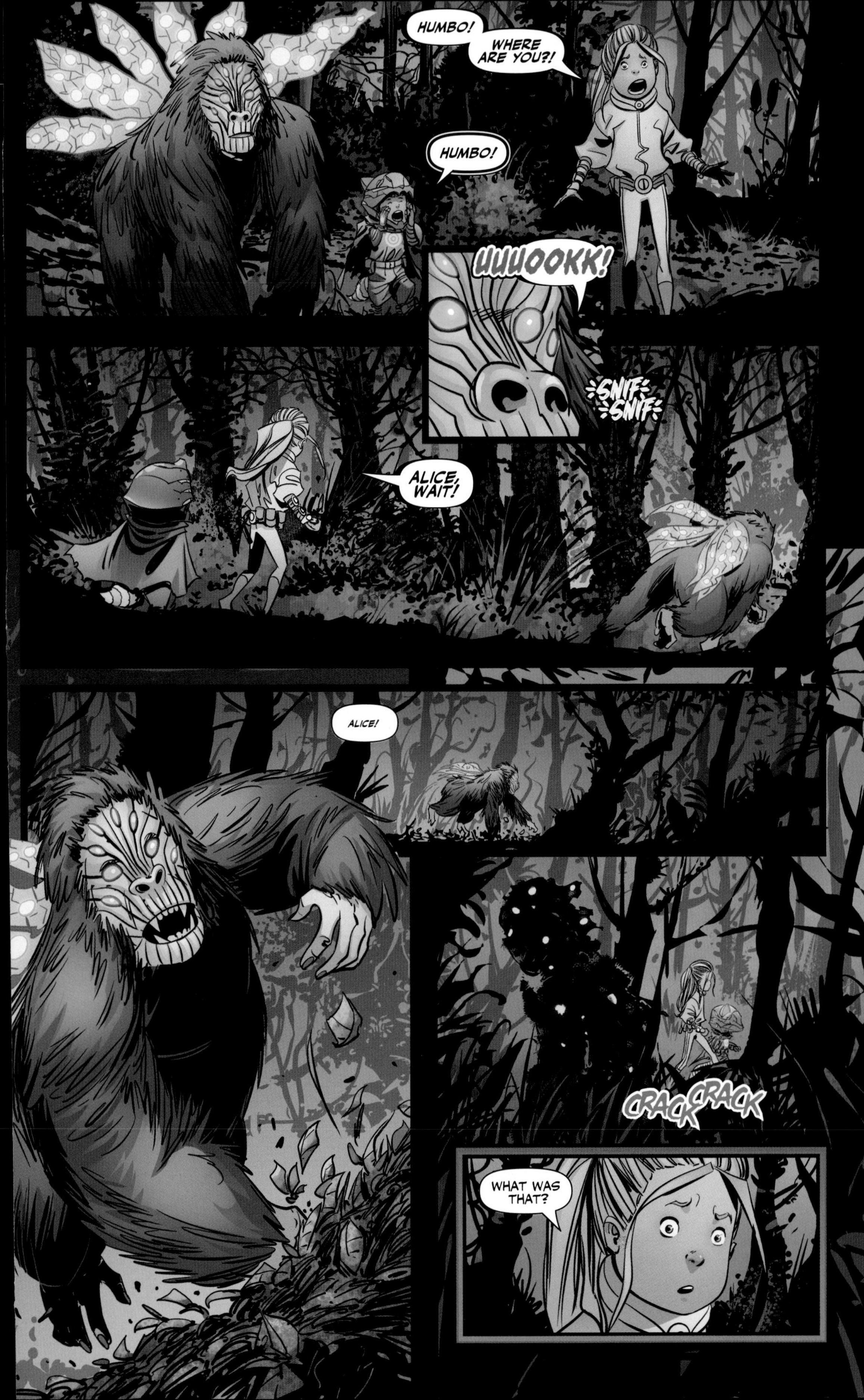
HUMBO!
WHERE ARE YOU?!
HUMBO!
UUUOOKK!
SNIF SNIF
ALICE, WAIT!
ALICE!
CRACK CRACK
WHAT WAS THAT?

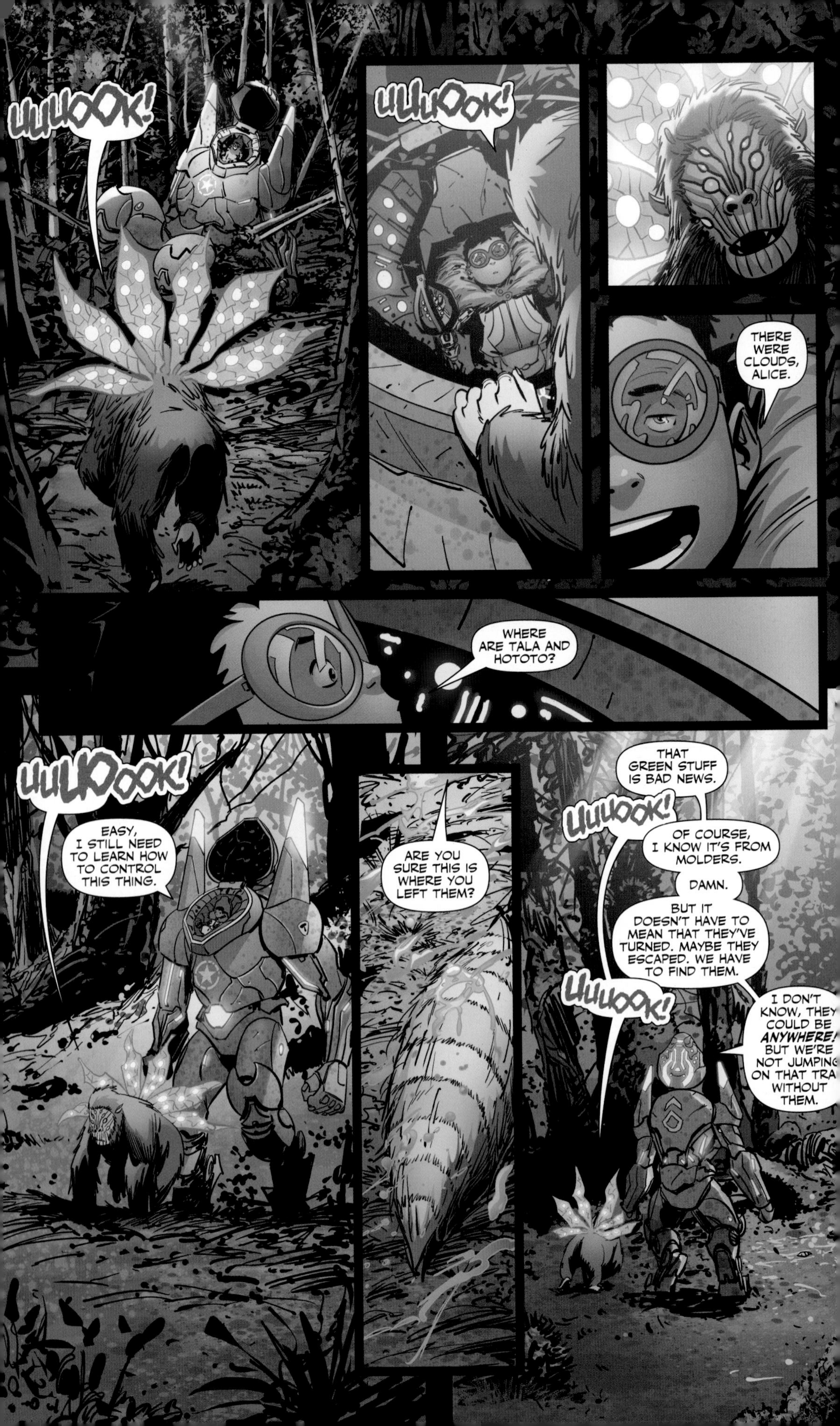
UULLOOK!
UULLOOK!
THERE WERE CLOUDS, ALICE.
WHERE ARE TALA AND HOTOTO?
UULLOOOK!
EASY, I STILL NEED TO LEARN HOW TO CONTROL THIS THING.
ARE YOU SURE THIS IS WHERE YOU LEFT THEM?
THAT GREEN STUFF IS BAD NEWS.
UULLOOK!
OF COURSE, I KNOW IT'S FROM MOLDERS.
DAMN.
BUT IT DOESN'T HAVE TO MEAN THAT THEY'VE TURNED. MAYBE THEY ESCAPED. WE HAVE TO FIND THEM.
UULLOOK!
I DON'T KNOW, THEY COULD BE *ANYWHERE!* BUT WE'RE NOT JUMPING ON THAT TRA WITHOUT THEM.

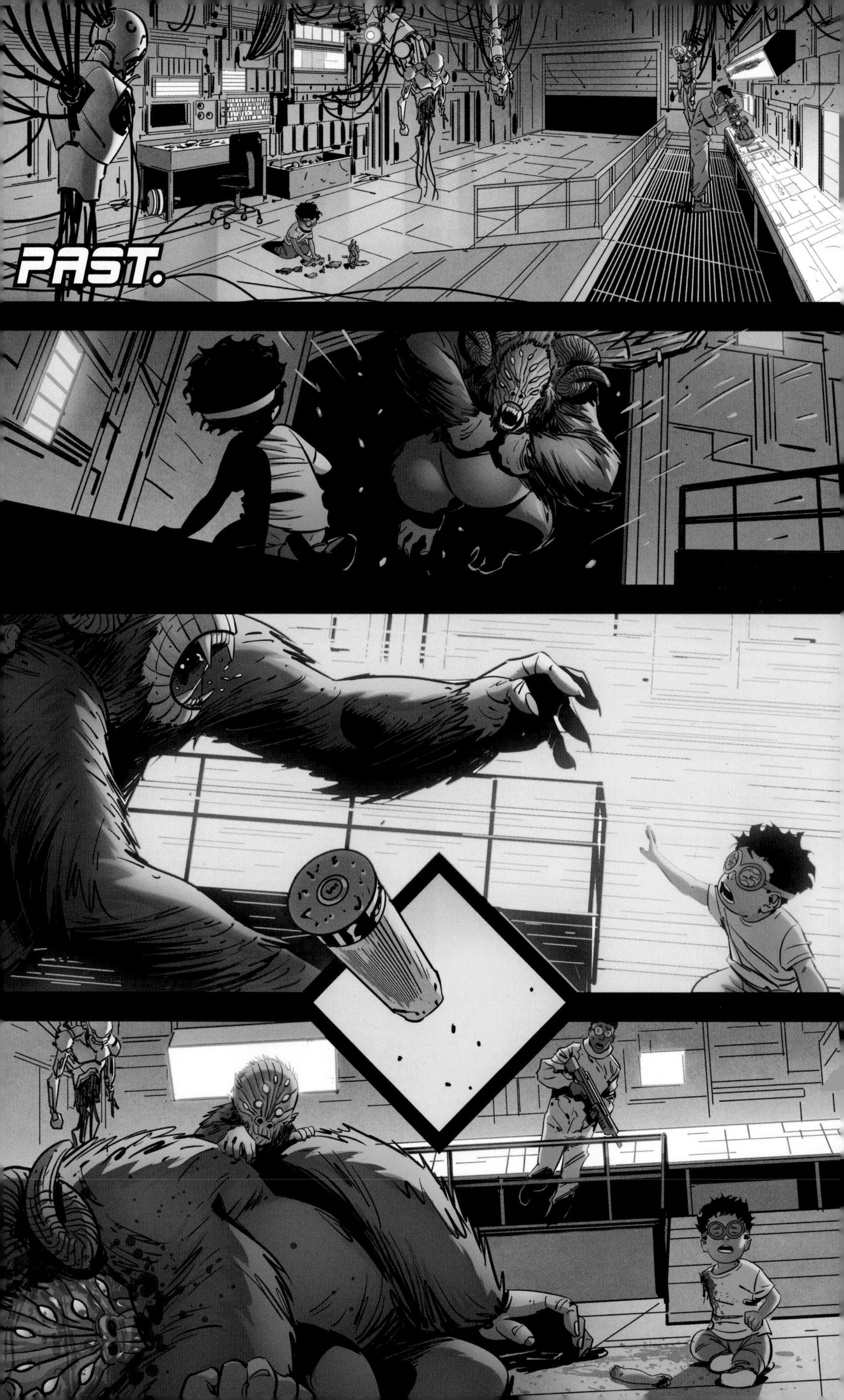
PAST.

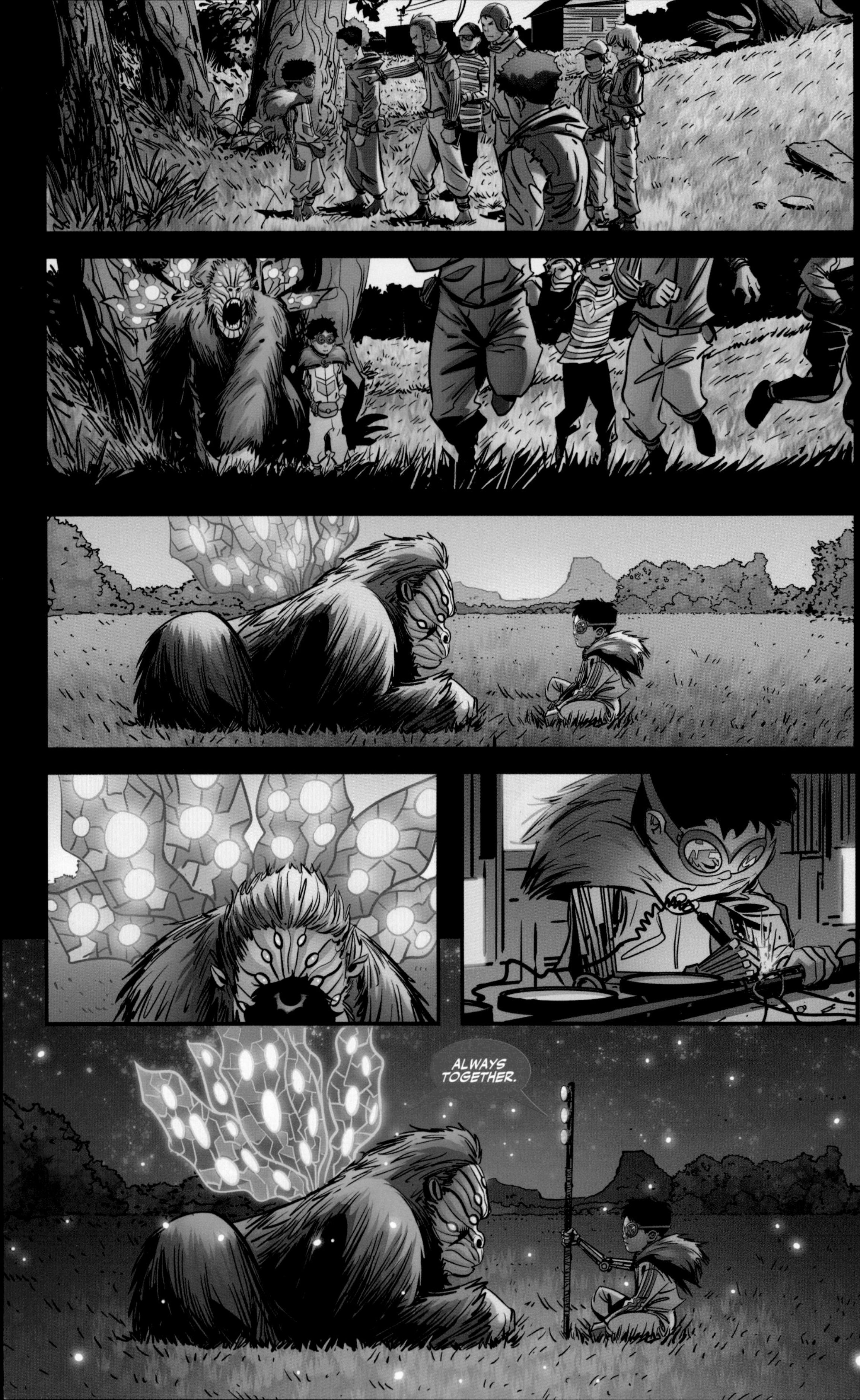
ALWAYS TOGETHER.

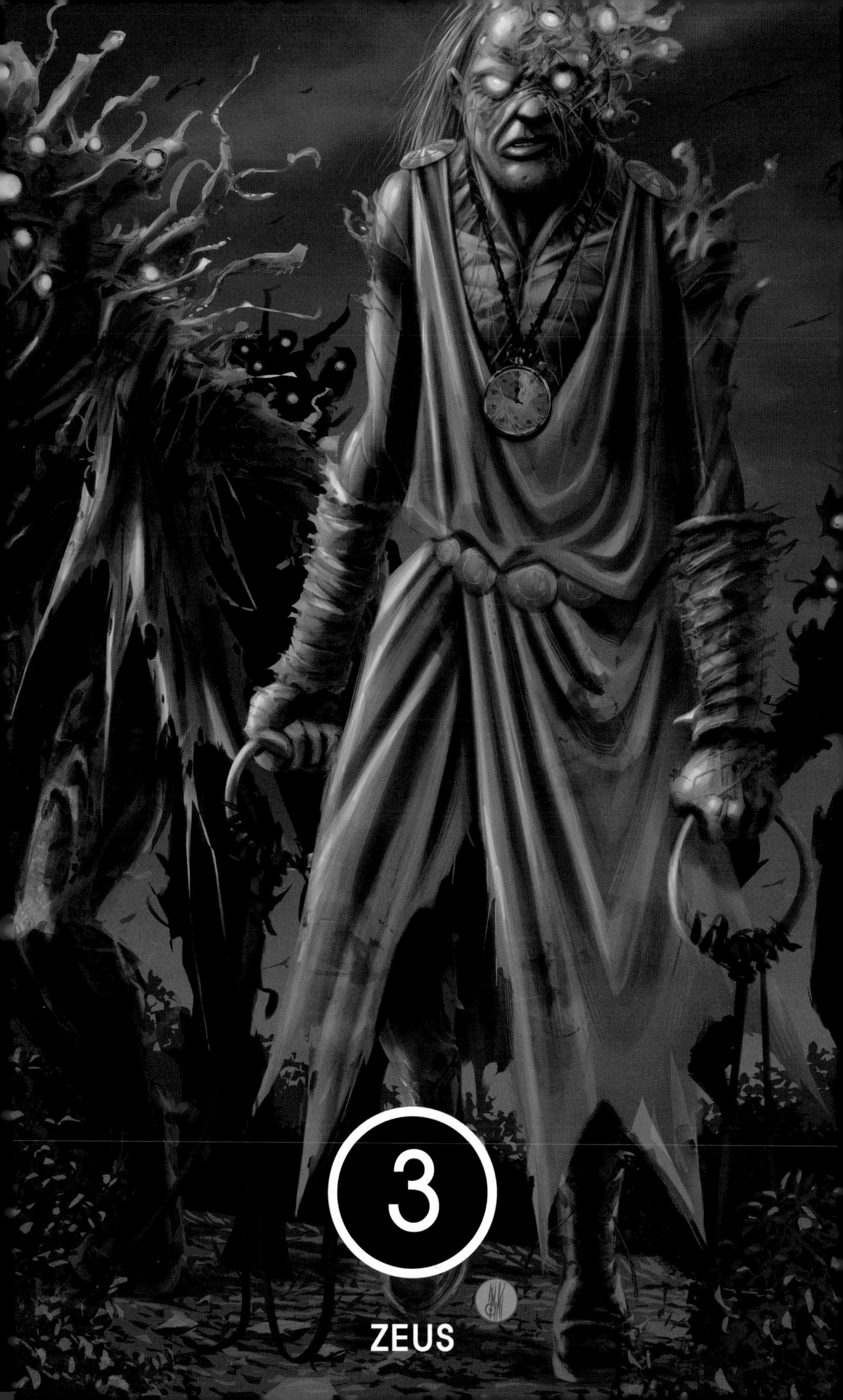
3
ZEUS

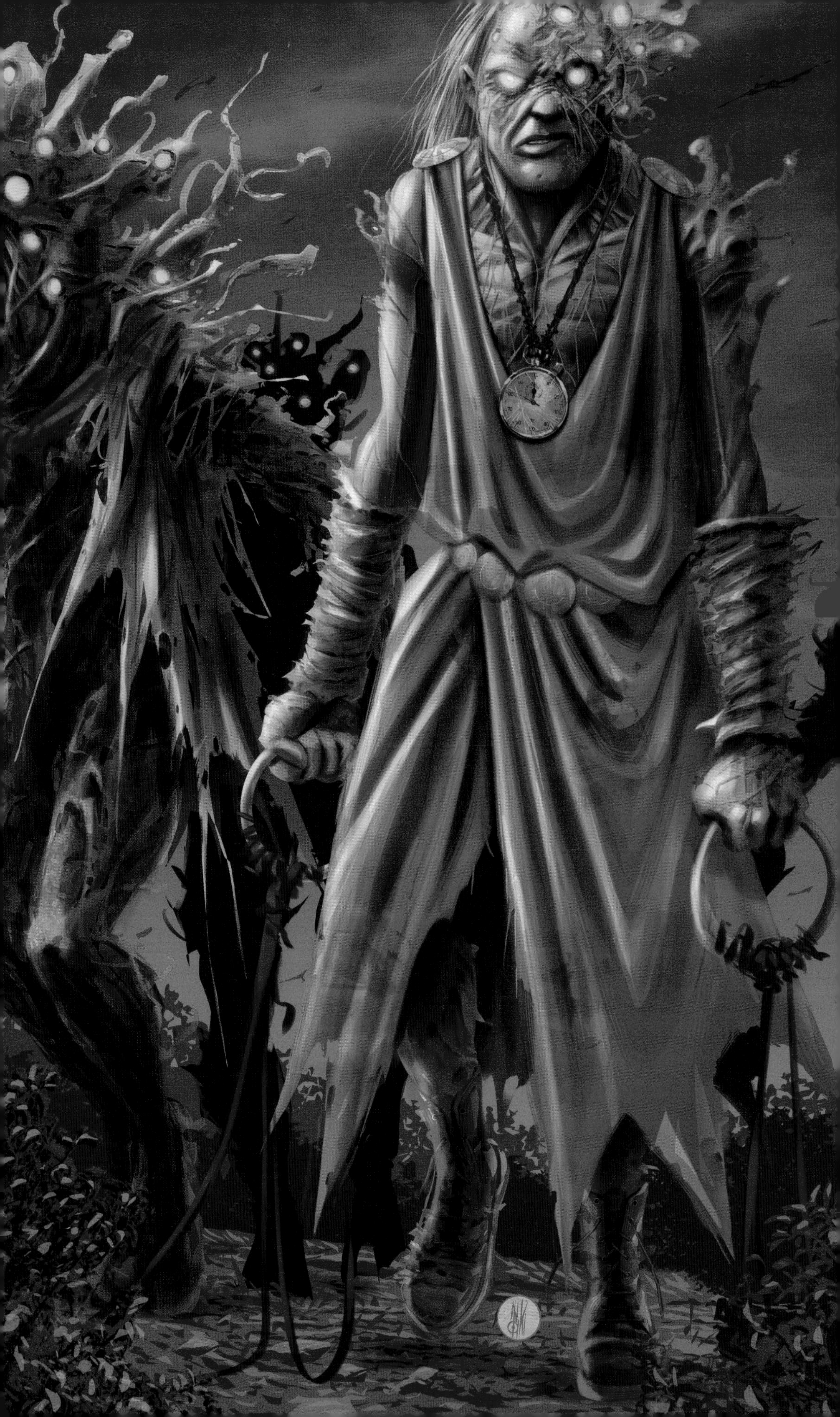

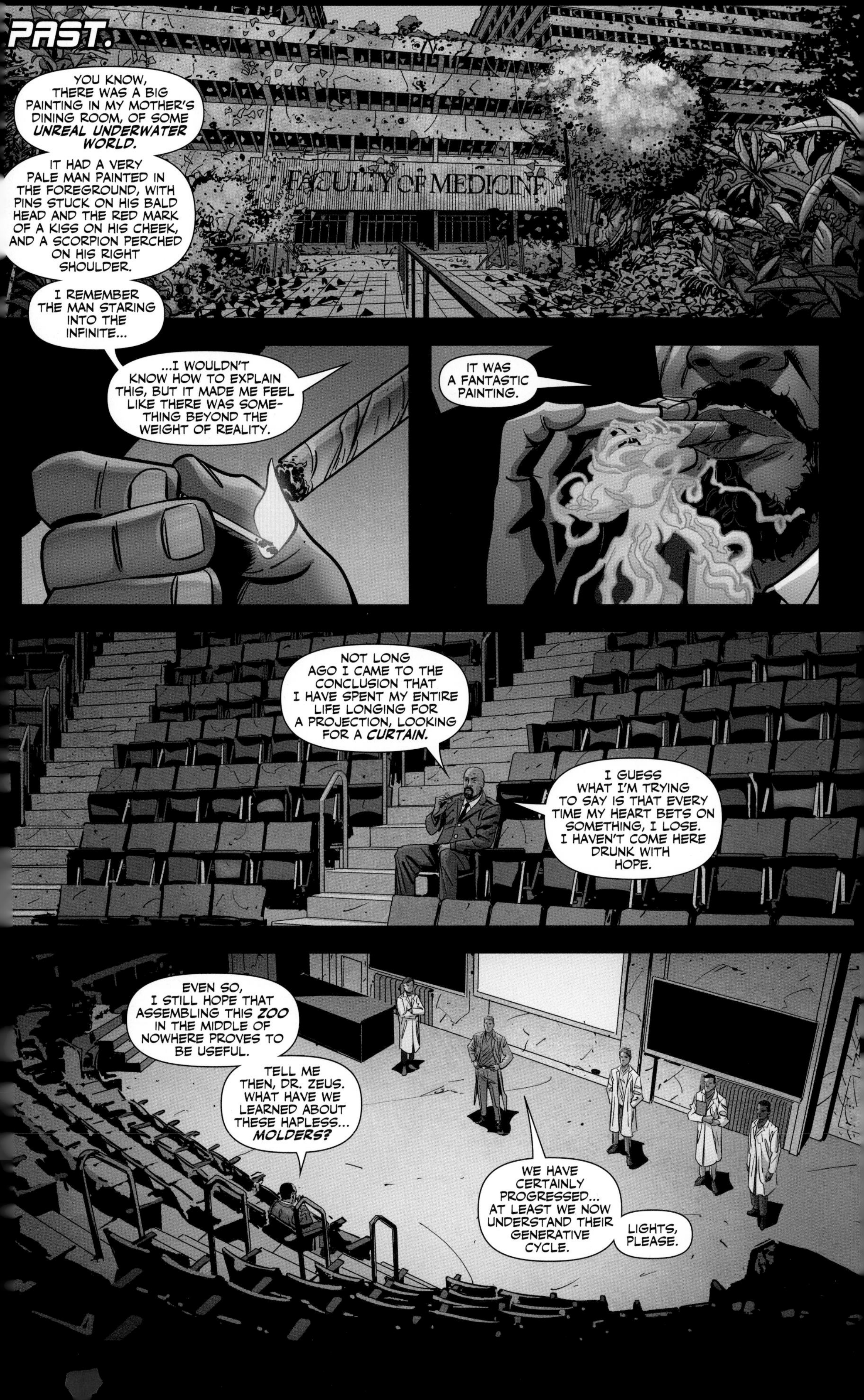
PAST.
YOU KNOW, THERE WAS A BIG PAINTING IN MY MOTHER'S DINING ROOM, OF SOME UNREAL UNDERWATER WORLD.
IT HAD A VERY PALE MAN PAINTED IN THE FOREGROUND, WITH PINS STUCK ON HIS BALD HEAD AND THE RED MARK OF A KISS ON HIS CHEEK, AND A SCORPION PERCHED ON HIS RIGHT SHOULDER.
I REMEMBER THE MAN STARING INTO THE INFINITE...
FACULTY OF MEDICINE
...I WOULDN'T KNOW HOW TO EXPLAIN THIS, BUT IT MADE ME FEEL LIKE THERE WAS SOME-THING BEYOND THE WEIGHT OF REALITY.
IT WAS A FANTASTIC PAINTING.
NOT LONG AGO I CAME TO THE CONCLUSION THAT I HAVE SPENT MY ENTIRE LIFE LONGING FOR A PROJECTION, LOOKING FOR A CURTAIN.
I GUESS WHAT I'M TRYING TO SAY IS THAT EVERY TIME MY HEART BETS ON SOMETHING, I LOSE. I HAVEN'T COME HERE DRUNK WITH HOPE.
EVEN SO, I STILL HOPE THAT ASSEMBLING THIS ZOO IN THE MIDDLE OF NOWHERE PROVES TO BE USEFUL.
TELL ME THEN, DR. ZEUS. WHAT HAVE WE LEARNED ABOUT THESE HAPLESS... MOLDERS?
WE HAVE CERTAINLY PROGRESSED... AT LEAST WE NOW UNDERSTAND THEIR GENERATIVE CYCLE.
LIGHTS, PLEASE.

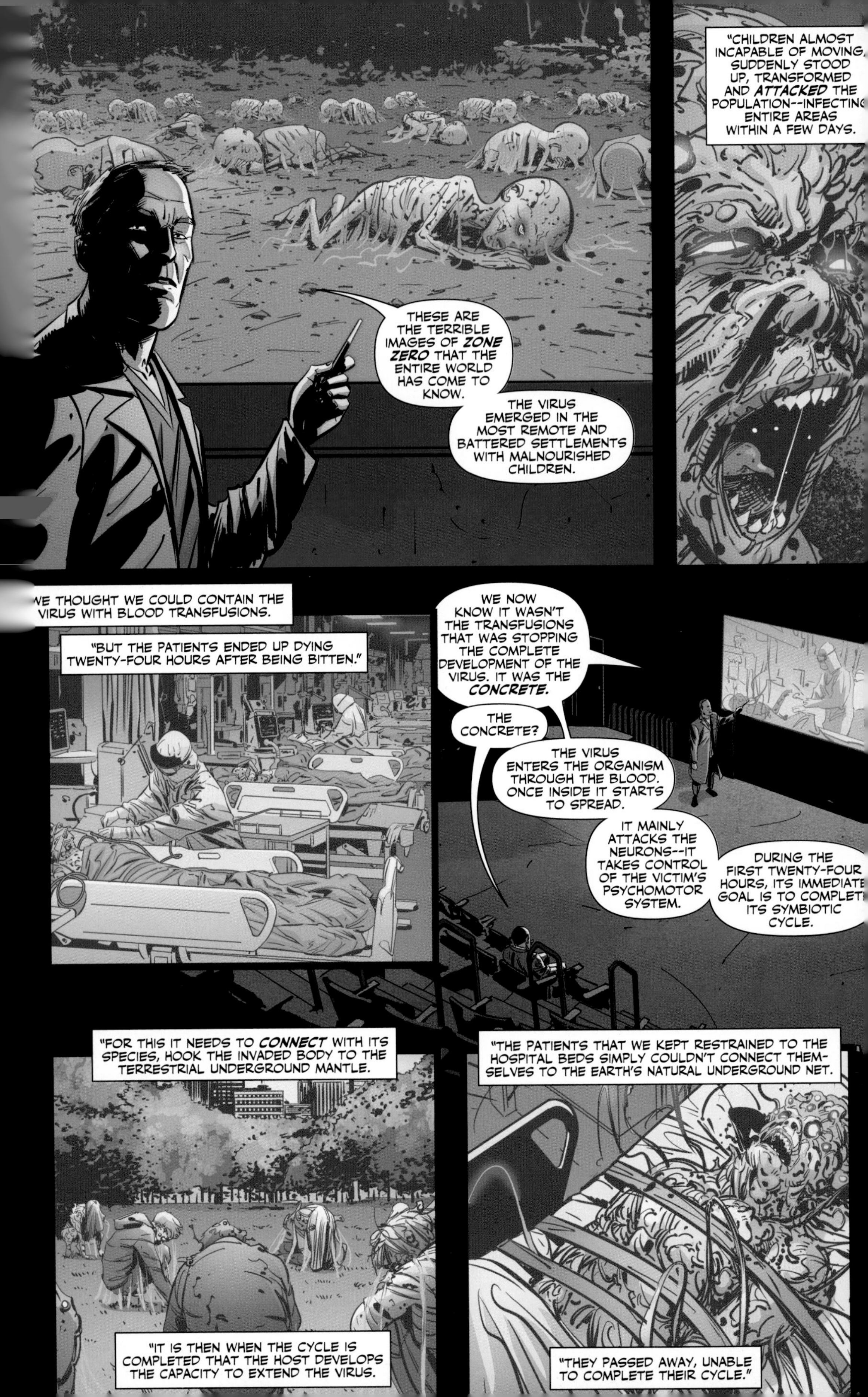
THESE ARE THE TERRIBLE IMAGES OF *ZONE ZERO* THAT THE ENTIRE WORLD HAS COME TO KNOW.
THE VIRUS EMERGED IN THE MOST REMOTE AND BATTERED SETTLEMENTS WITH MALNOURISHED CHILDREN.
"CHILDREN ALMOST INCAPABLE OF MOVING, SUDDENLY STOOD UP, TRANSFORMED AND *ATTACKED* THE POPULATION--INFECTING ENTIRE AREAS WITHIN A FEW DAYS.
WE THOUGHT WE COULD CONTAIN THE VIRUS WITH BLOOD TRANSFUSIONS.
"BUT THE PATIENTS ENDED UP DYING TWENTY-FOUR HOURS AFTER BEING BITTEN."
WE NOW KNOW IT WASN'T THE TRANSFUSIONS THAT WAS STOPPING THE COMPLETE DEVELOPMENT OF THE VIRUS. IT WAS THE *CONCRETE.*
THE CONCRETE?
THE VIRUS ENTERS THE ORGANISM THROUGH THE BLOOD. ONCE INSIDE IT STARTS TO SPREAD.
IT MAINLY ATTACKS THE NEURONS--IT TAKES CONTROL OF THE VICTIM'S PSYCHOMOTOR SYSTEM.
DURING THE FIRST TWENTY-FOUR HOURS, ITS IMMEDIATE GOAL IS TO COMPLETE ITS SYMBIOTIC CYCLE.
"FOR THIS IT NEEDS TO *CONNECT* WITH ITS SPECIES, HOOK THE INVADED BODY TO THE TERRESTRIAL UNDERGROUND MANTLE.
"IT IS THEN WHEN THE CYCLE IS COMPLETED THAT THE HOST DEVELOPS THE CAPACITY TO EXTEND THE VIRUS.
"THE PATIENTS THAT WE KEPT RESTRAINED TO THE HOSPITAL BEDS SIMPLY COULDN'T CONNECT THEMSELVES TO THE EARTH'S NATURAL UNDERGROUND NET.
"THEY PASSED AWAY, UNABLE TO COMPLETE THEIR CYCLE."

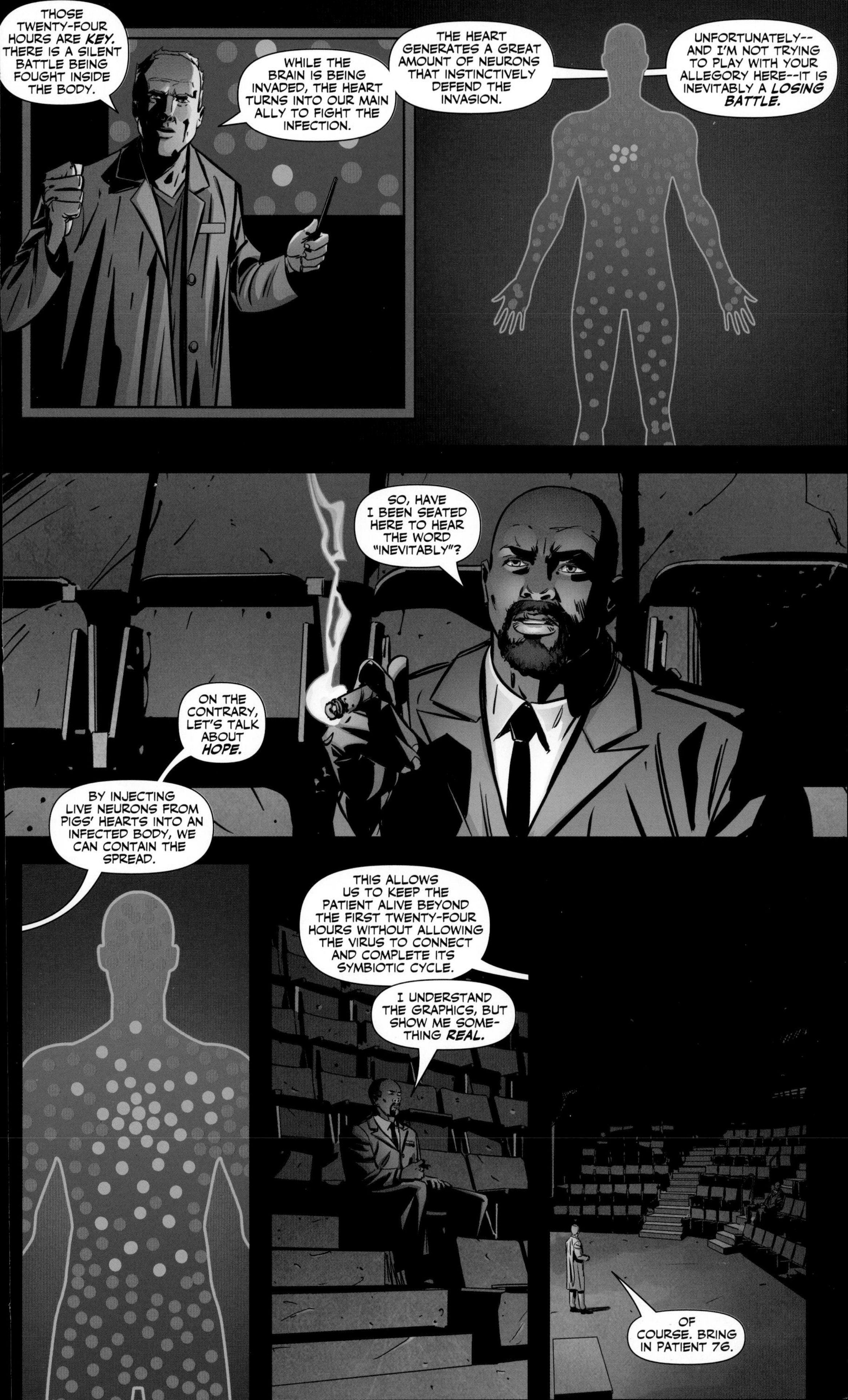
THOSE TWENTY-FOUR HOURS ARE KEY. THERE IS A SILENT BATTLE BEING FOUGHT INSIDE THE BODY.
WHILE THE BRAIN IS BEING INVADED, THE HEART TURNS INTO OUR MAIN ALLY TO FIGHT THE INFECTION.
THE HEART GENERATES A GREAT AMOUNT OF NEURONS THAT INSTINCTIVELY DEFEND THE INVASION.
UNFORTUNATELY-- AND I'M NOT TRYING TO PLAY WITH YOUR ALLEGORY HERE--IT IS INEVITABLY A LOSING BATTLE.
SO, HAVE I BEEN SEATED HERE TO HEAR THE WORD "INEVITABLY"?
ON THE CONTRARY, LET'S TALK ABOUT HOPE.
BY INJECTING LIVE NEURONS FROM PIGS' HEARTS INTO AN INFECTED BODY, WE CAN CONTAIN THE SPREAD.
THIS ALLOWS US TO KEEP THE PATIENT ALIVE BEYOND THE FIRST TWENTY-FOUR HOURS WITHOUT ALLOWING THE VIRUS TO CONNECT AND COMPLETE ITS SYMBIOTIC CYCLE.
I UNDERSTAND THE GRAPHICS, BUT SHOW ME SOME-THING REAL.
OF COURSE. BRING IN PATIENT 76.

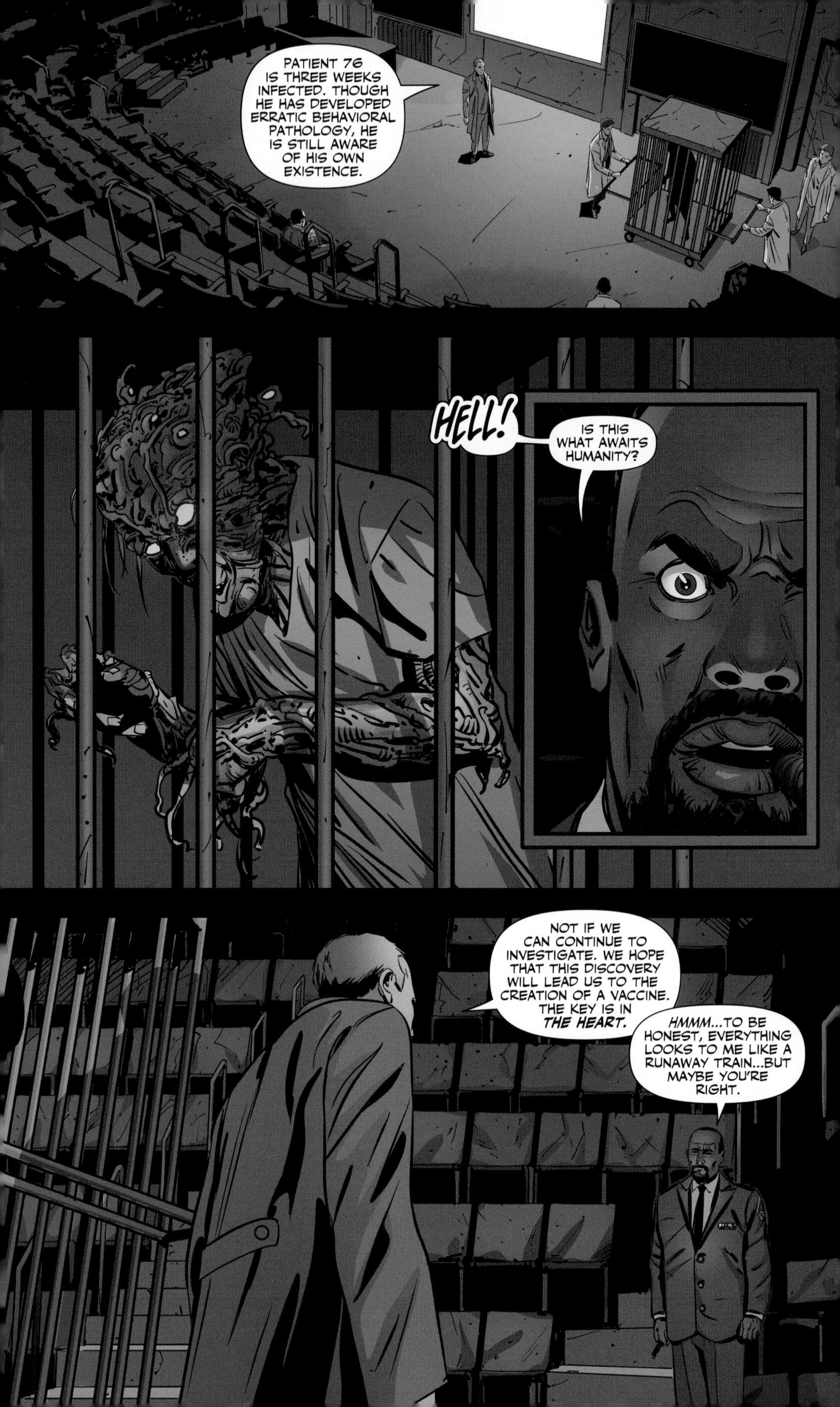
PATIENT 76 IS THREE WEEKS INFECTED. THOUGH HE HAS DEVELOPED ERRATIC BEHAVIORAL PATHOLOGY, HE IS STILL AWARE OF HIS OWN EXISTENCE.
HELL!
IS THIS WHAT AWAITS HUMANITY?
NOT IF WE CAN CONTINUE TO INVESTIGATE. WE HOPE THAT THIS DISCOVERY WILL LEAD US TO THE CREATION OF A VACCINE. THE KEY IS IN *THE HEART.*
HMMM...TO BE HONEST, EVERYTHING LOOKS TO ME LIKE A RUNAWAY TRAIN...BUT MAYBE YOU'RE RIGHT.

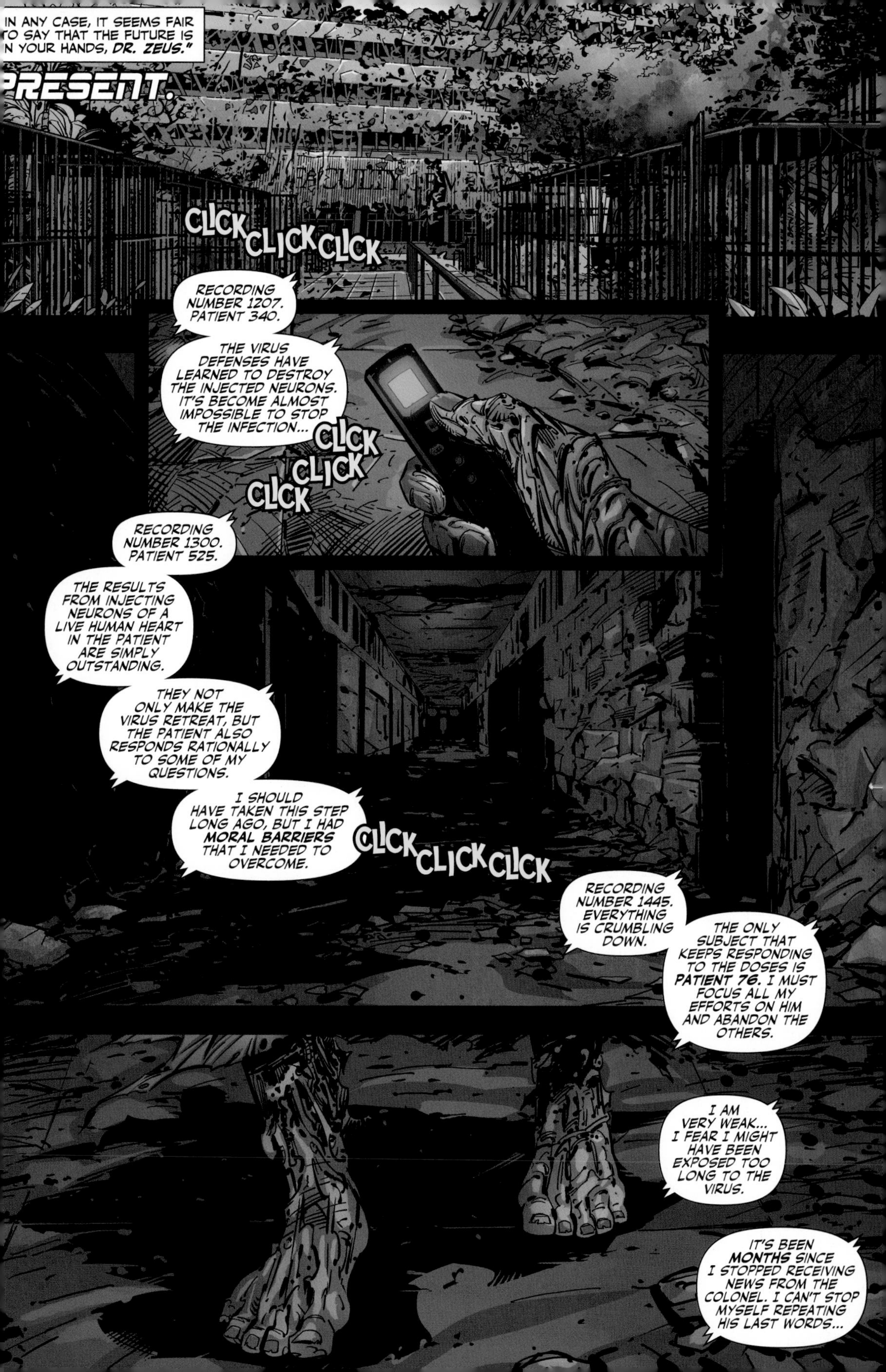
IN ANY CASE, IT SEEMS FAIR TO SAY THAT THE FUTURE IS IN YOUR HANDS, DR. ZEUS."
PRESENT.
CLICK CLICK CLICK
RECORDING NUMBER 1207. PATIENT 340.
THE VIRUS DEFENSES HAVE LEARNED TO DESTROY THE INJECTED NEURONS. IT'S BECOME ALMOST IMPOSSIBLE TO STOP THE INFECTION...
CLICK CLICK CLICK
RECORDING NUMBER 1300. PATIENT 525.
THE RESULTS FROM INJECTING NEURONS OF A LIVE HUMAN HEART IN THE PATIENT ARE SIMPLY OUTSTANDING.
THEY NOT ONLY MAKE THE VIRUS RETREAT, BUT THE PATIENT ALSO RESPONDS RATIONALLY TO SOME OF MY QUESTIONS.
I SHOULD HAVE TAKEN THIS STEP LONG AGO, BUT I HAD MORAL BARRIERS THAT I NEEDED TO OVERCOME.
CLICK CLICK CLICK
RECORDING NUMBER 1445. EVERYTHING IS CRUMBLING DOWN.
THE ONLY SUBJECT THAT KEEPS RESPONDING TO THE DOSES IS PATIENT 76. I MUST FOCUS ALL MY EFFORTS ON HIM AND ABANDON THE OTHERS.
I AM VERY WEAK... I FEAR I MIGHT HAVE BEEN EXPOSED TOO LONG TO THE VIRUS.
IT'S BEEN MONTHS SINCE I STOPPED RECEIVING NEWS FROM THE COLONEL. I CAN'T STOP MYSELF REPEATING HIS LAST WORDS...

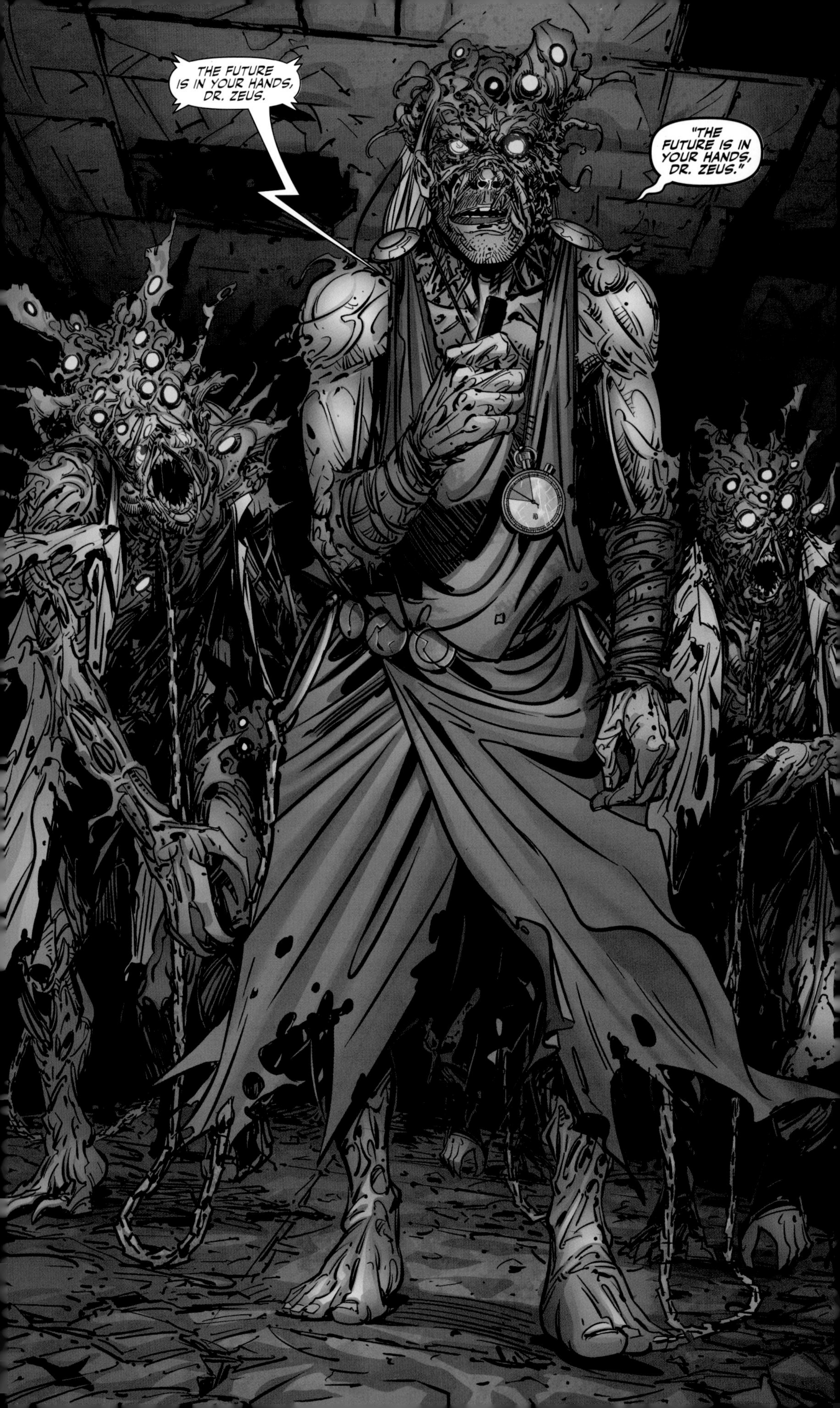
THE FUTURE IS IN YOUR HANDS, DR. ZEUS.
"THE FUTURE IS IN YOUR HANDS, DR. ZEUS."

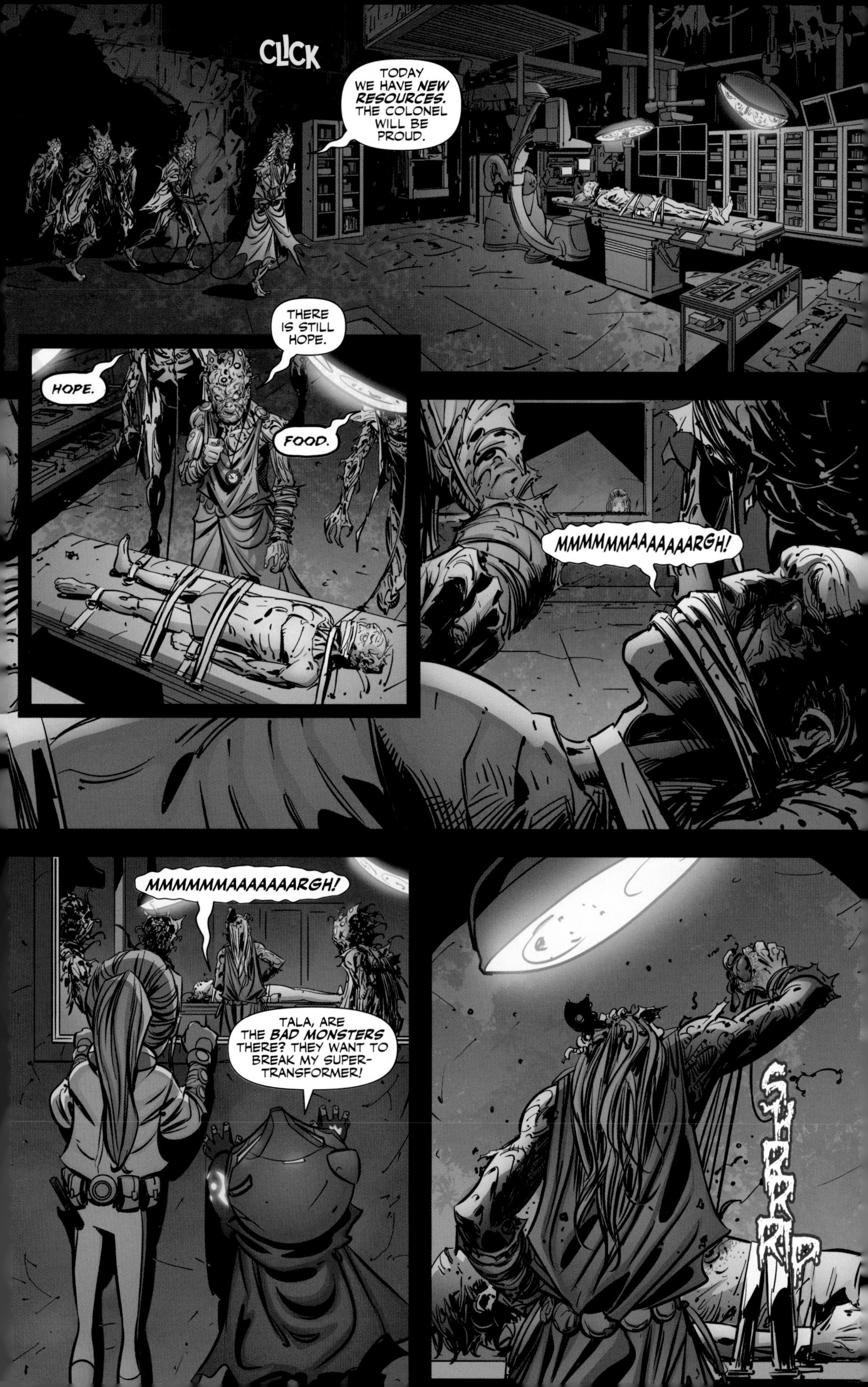

CLICK
TODAY WE HAVE NEW RESOURCES. THE COLONEL WILL BE PROUD.
THERE IS STILL HOPE.
HOPE.
FOOD.
MMMMMMAAAAAAARGH!
MMMMMMAAAAAAARGH!
TALA, ARE THE BAD MONSTERS THERE? THEY WANT TO BREAK MY SUPER-TRANSFORMER!

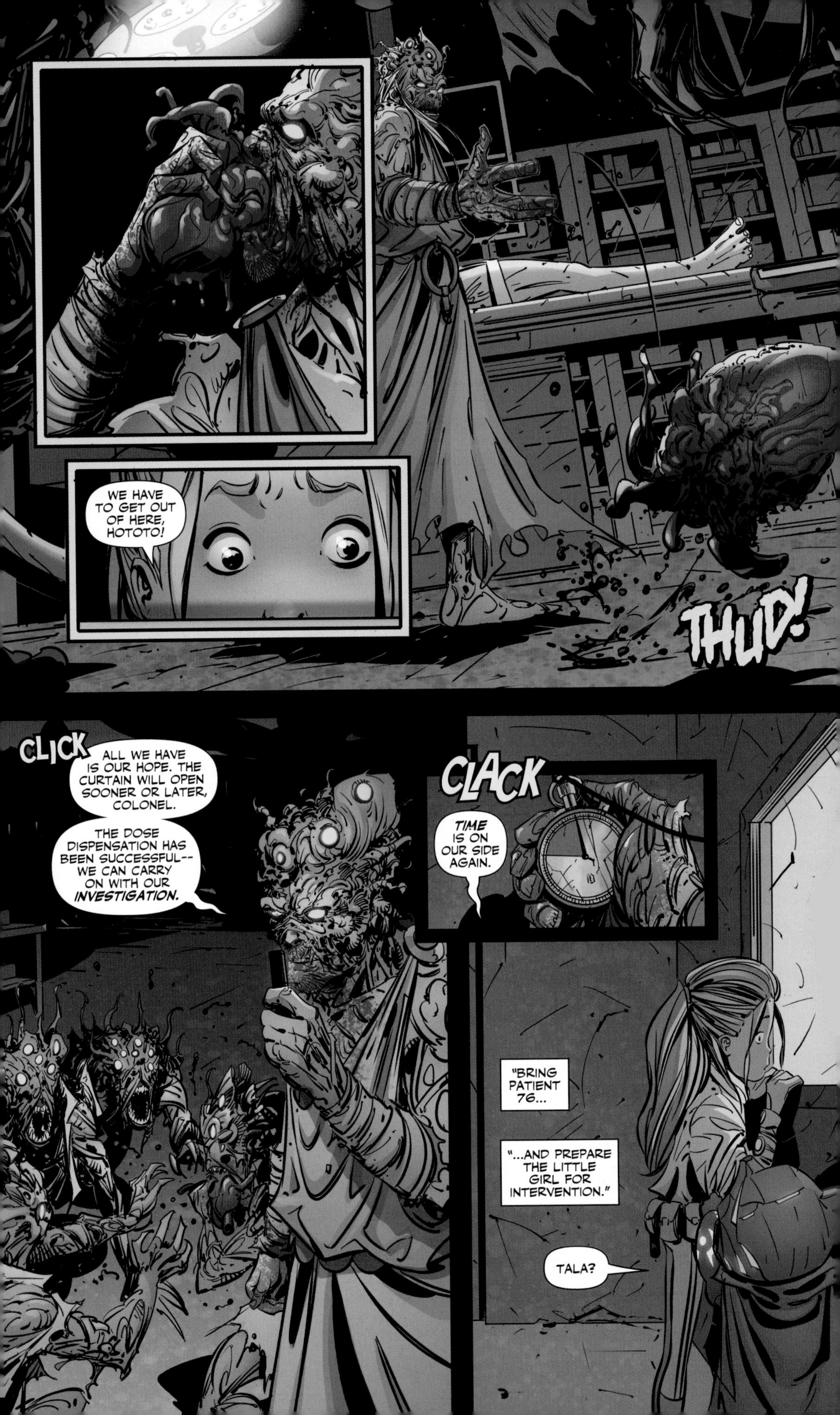
WE HAVE TO GET OUT OF HERE, HOTOTO!
THUD!
CLICK
ALL WE HAVE IS OUR HOPE. THE CURTAIN WILL OPEN SOONER OR LATER, COLONEL.
THE DOSE DISPENSATION HAS BEEN SUCCESSFUL-- WE CAN CARRY ON WITH OUR *INVESTIGATION.*
CLACK
TIME IS ON OUR SIDE AGAIN.
"BRING PATIENT 76...
"...AND PREPARE THE LITTLE GIRL FOR INTERVENTION."
TALA?

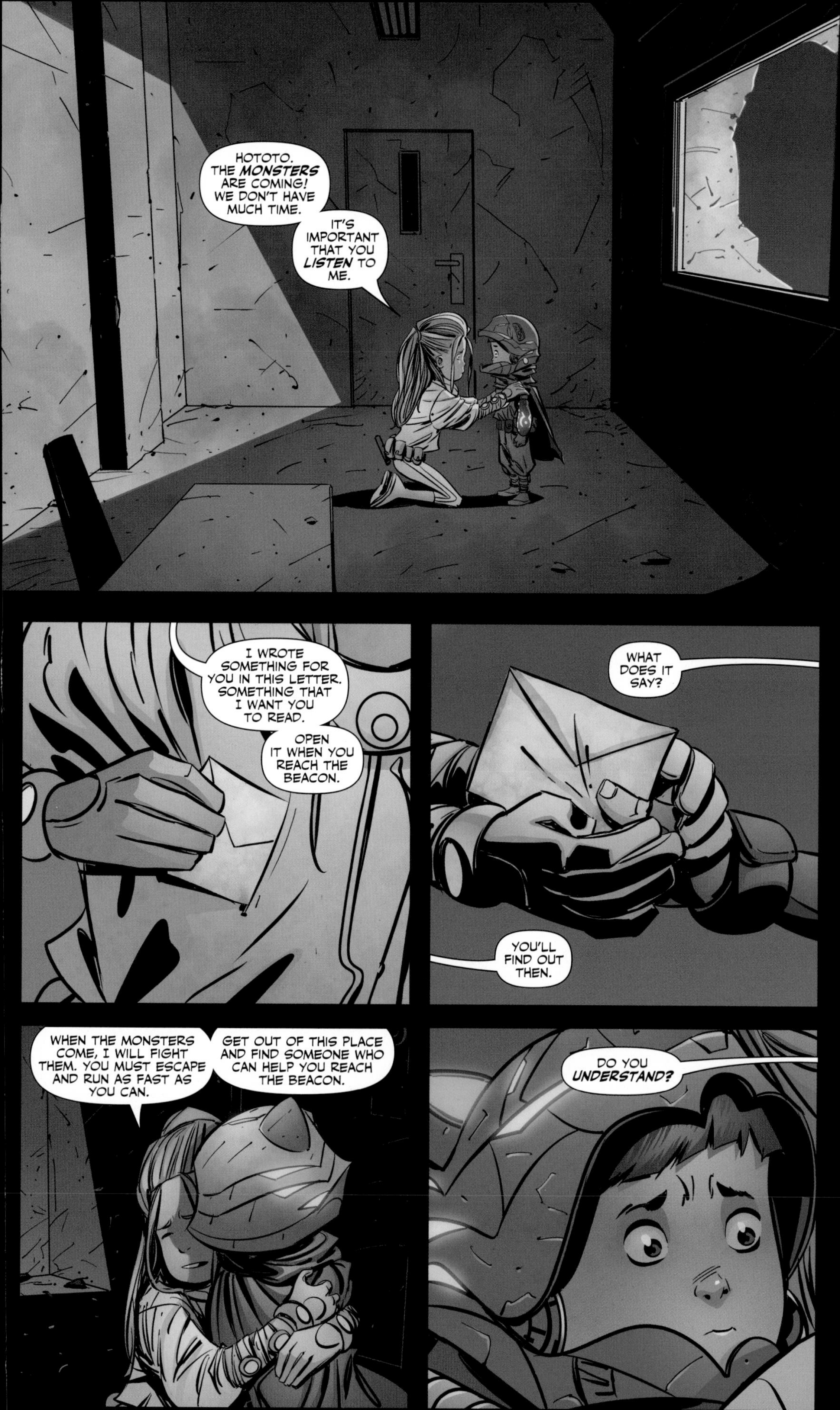
HOTOTO. THE MONSTERS ARE COMING! WE DON'T HAVE MUCH TIME.
IT'S IMPORTANT THAT YOU LISTEN TO ME.
I WROTE SOMETHING FOR YOU IN THIS LETTER. SOMETHING THAT I WANT YOU TO READ.
OPEN IT WHEN YOU REACH THE BEACON.
WHAT DOES IT SAY?
YOU'LL FIND OUT THEN.
WHEN THE MONSTERS COME, I WILL FIGHT THEM. YOU MUST ESCAPE AND RUN AS FAST AS YOU CAN.
GET OUT OF THIS PLACE AND FIND SOMEONE WHO CAN HELP YOU REACH THE BEACON.
DO YOU UNDERSTAND?

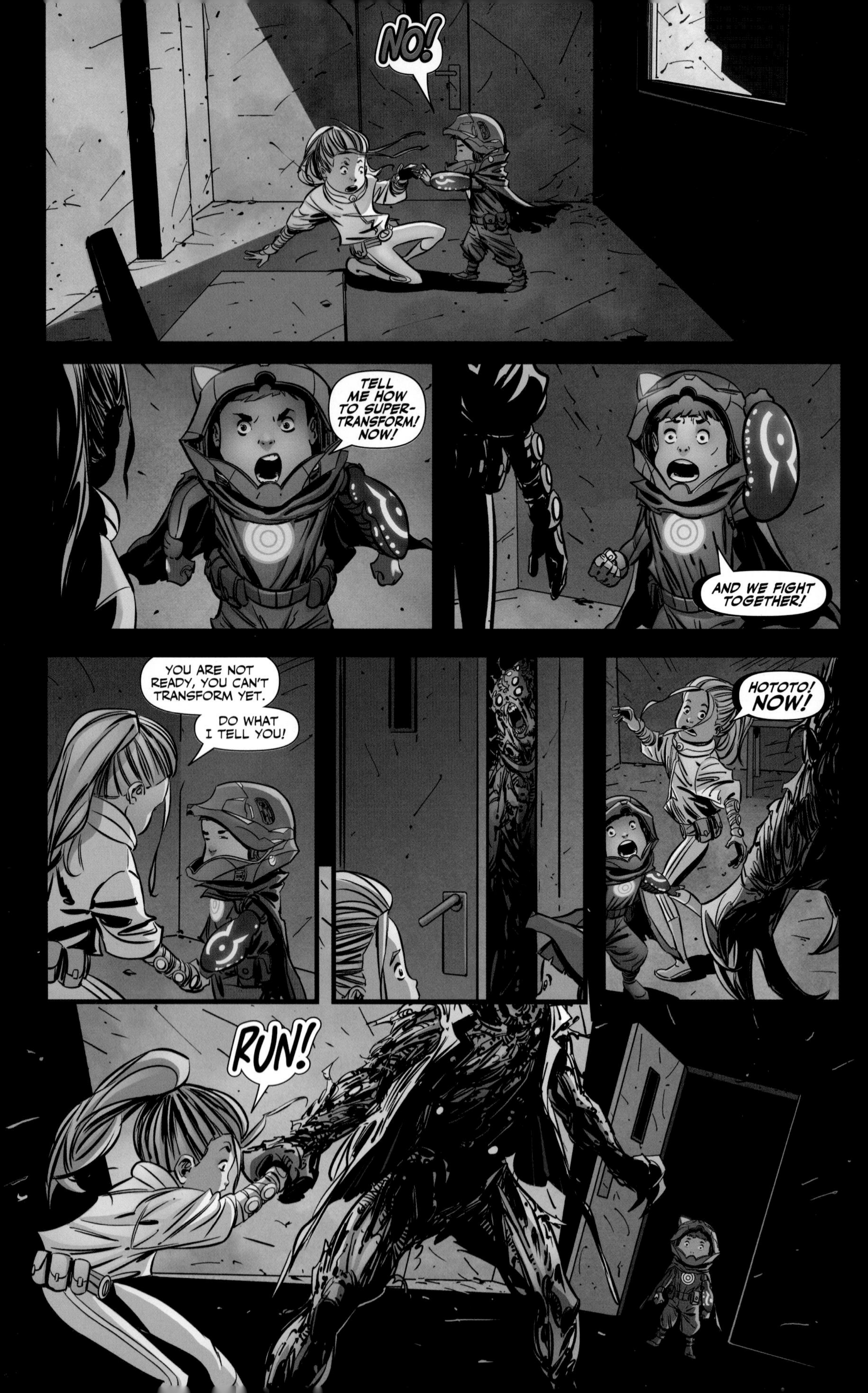
NO!
TELL ME HOW TO SUPER-TRANSFORM! NOW!
AND WE FIGHT TOGETHER!
YOU ARE NOT READY, YOU CAN'T TRANSFORM YET.
DO WHAT I TELL YOU!
HOTOTO! NOW!
RUN!

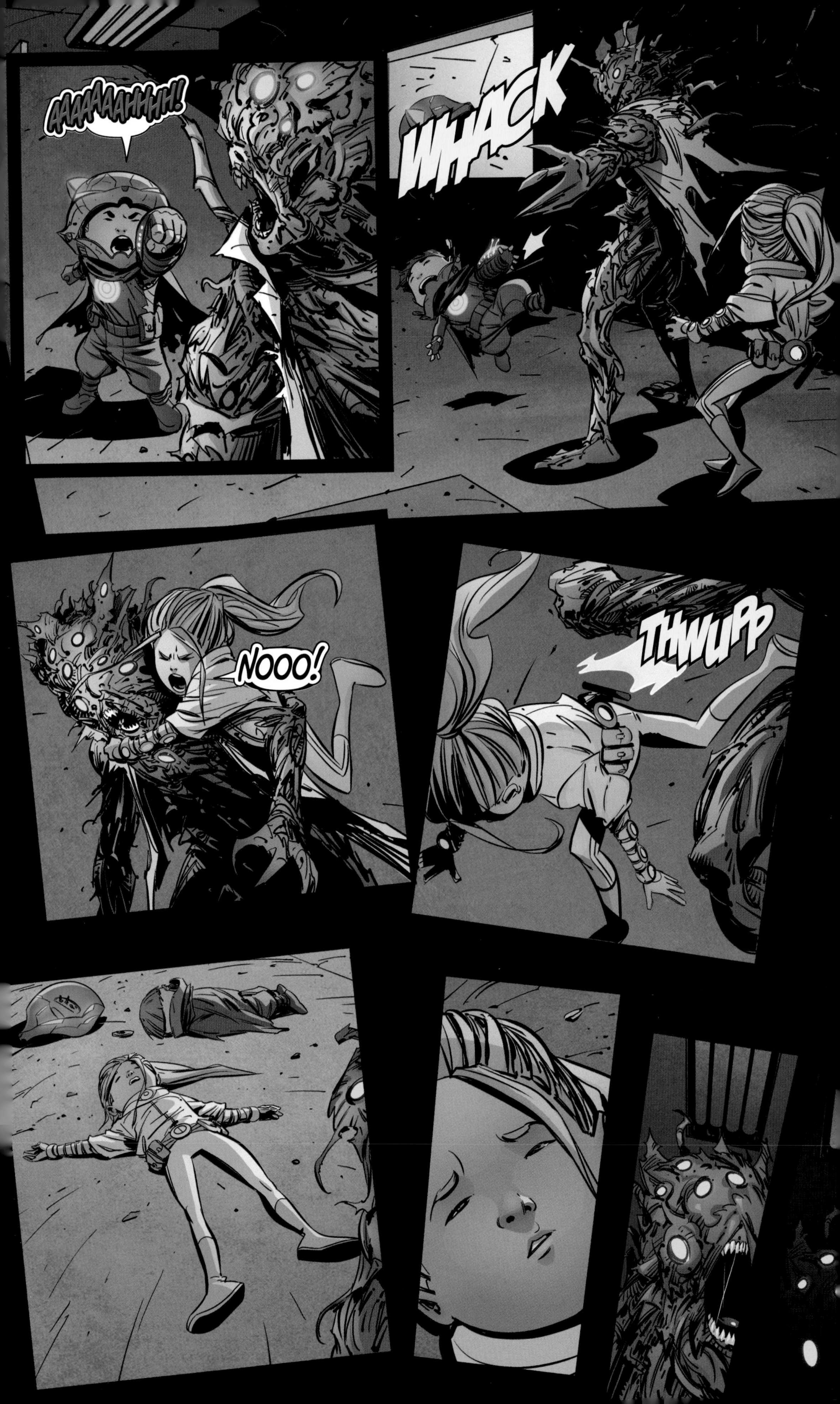
AAAAAAAHHHH!
WHACK
NOOO!
THWUPP

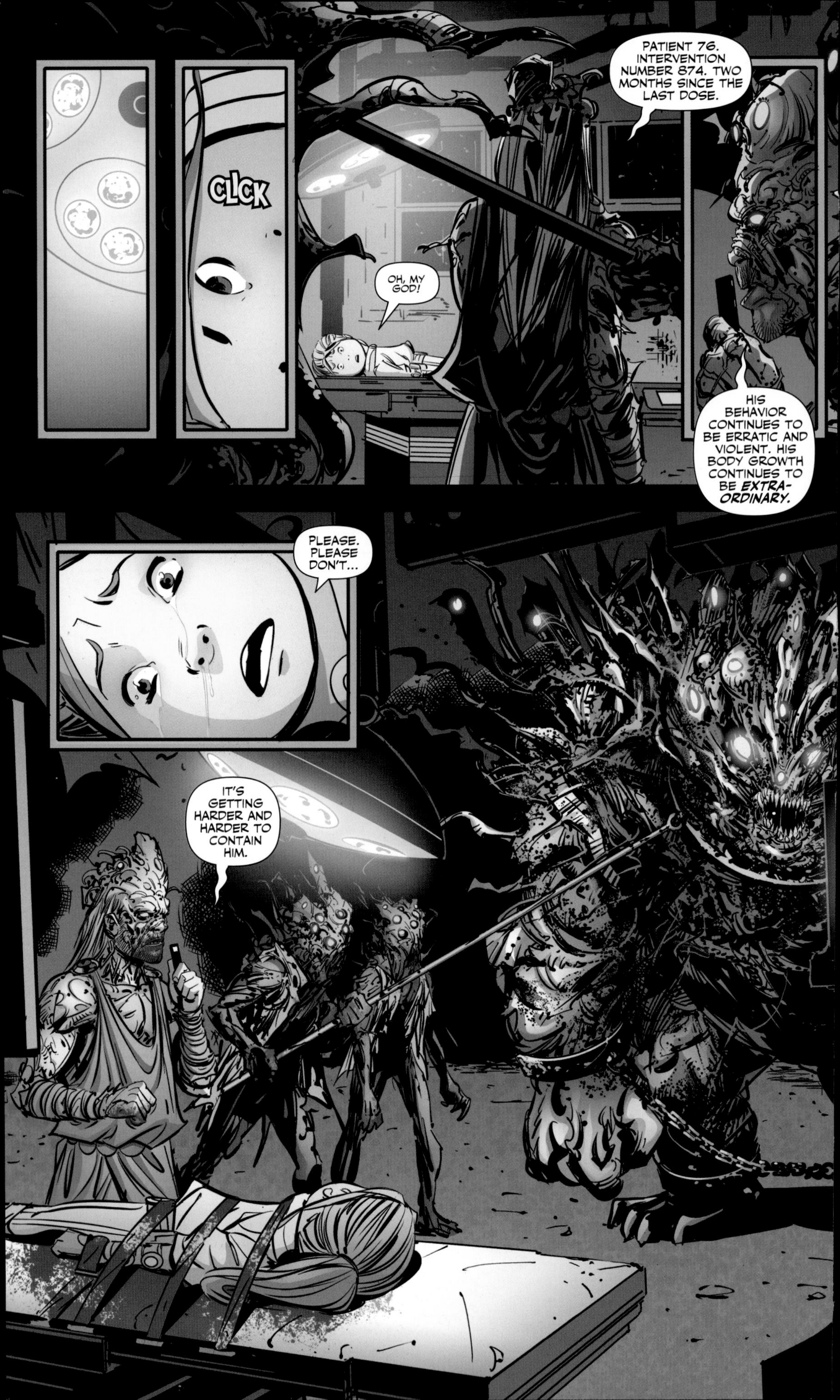
CLICK
PATIENT 76. INTERVENTION NUMBER 874. TWO MONTHS SINCE THE LAST DOSE.
OH, MY GOD!
HIS BEHAVIOR CONTINUES TO BE ERRATIC AND VIOLENT. HIS BODY GROWTH CONTINUES TO BE EXTRA-ORDINARY.
PLEASE. PLEASE DON'T...
IT'S GETTING HARDER AND HARDER TO CONTAIN HIM.

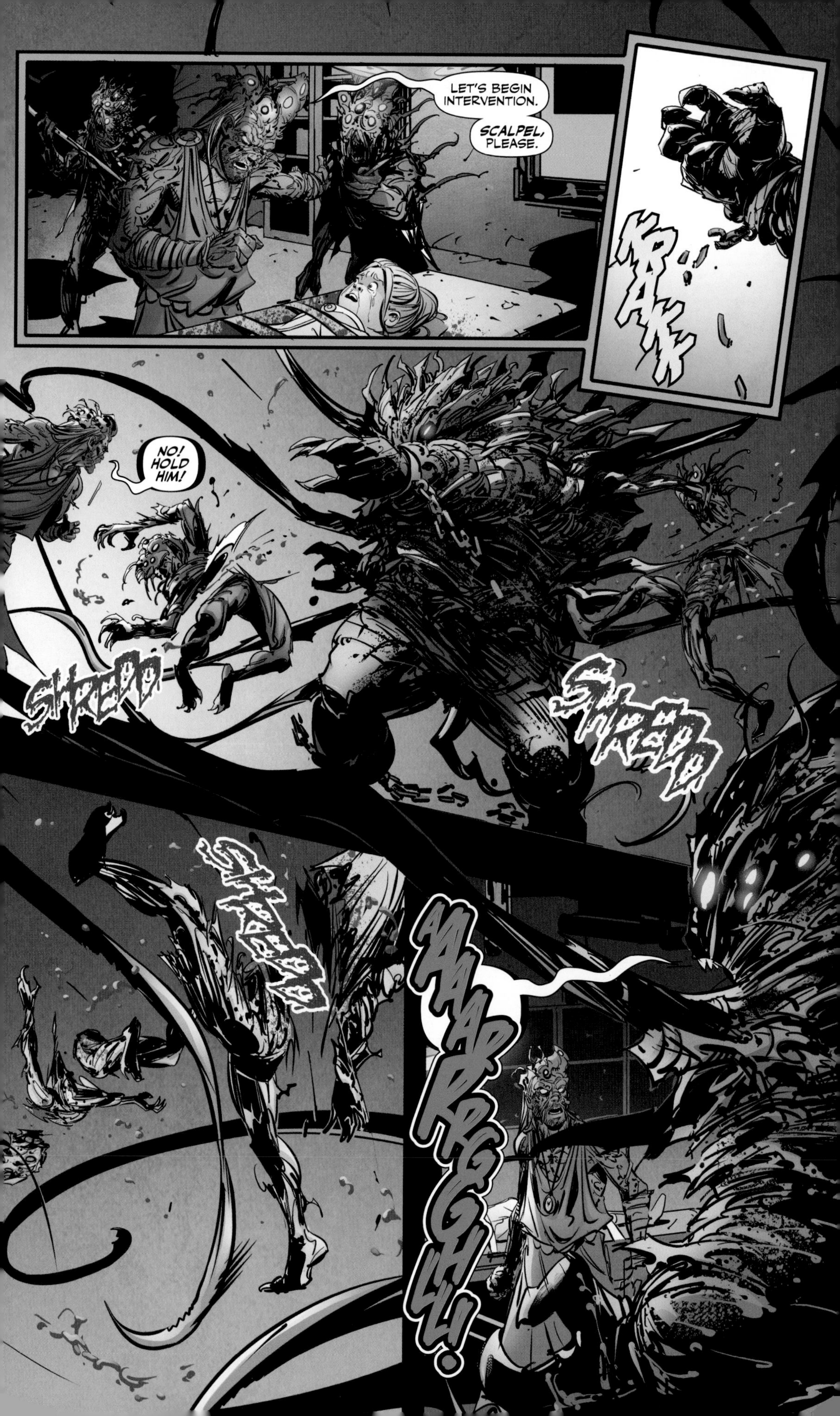
LET'S BEGIN INTERVENTION.
SCALPEL, PLEASE.
KRAKK
NO! HOLD HIM!
SHREDD
SHREDD
SHREDD
AAAAARRRGGHHLLL!

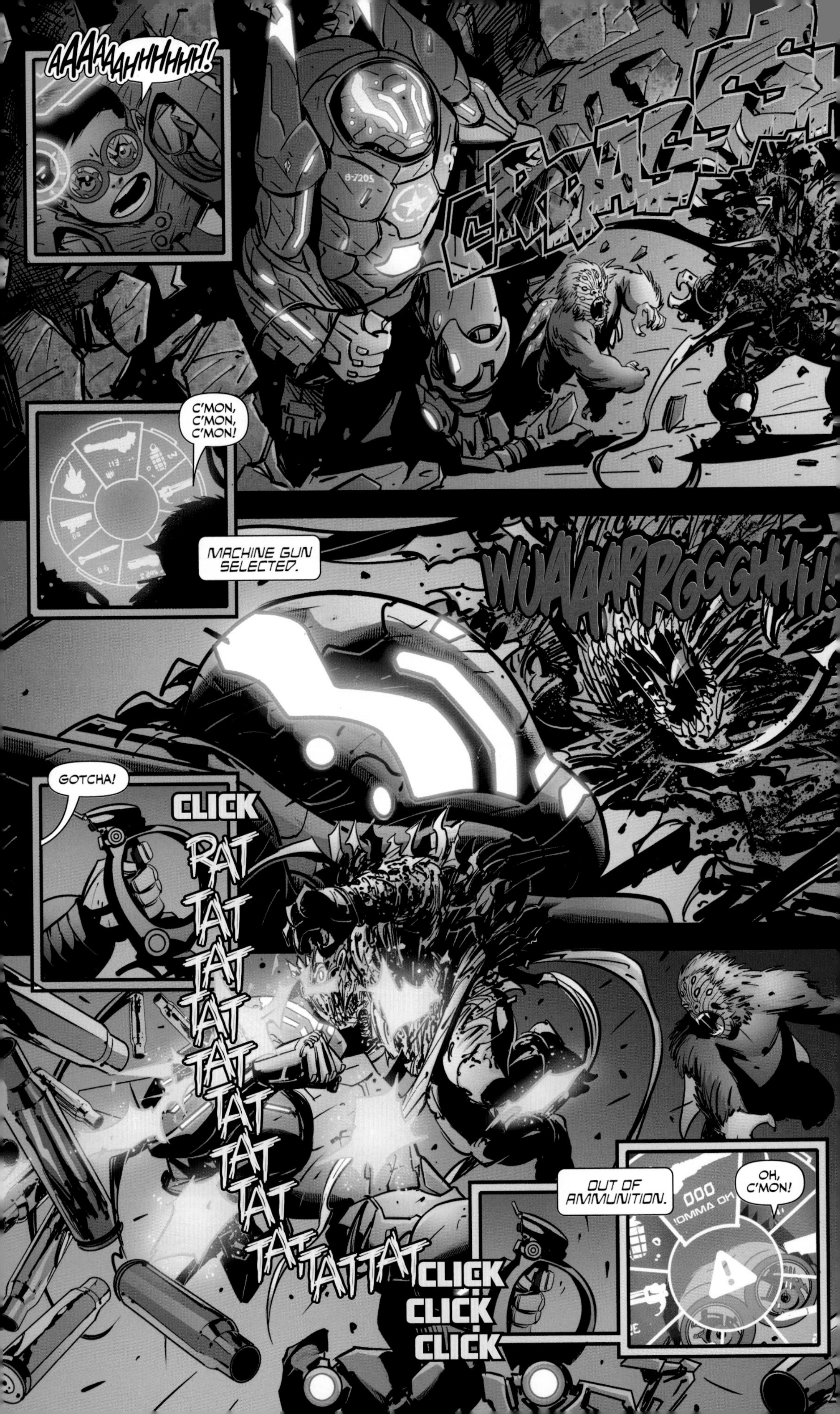
AAAAAAHHHHHH!
8-7205
C'MON, C'MON, C'MON!
MACHINE GUN SELECTED.
WUAAARRGGGHHH!
GOTCHA!
CLICK
RAT TAT TAT TAT TAT TAT TAT TAT TAT TAT TATTATTAT
CLICK CLICK CLICK
OUT OF AMMUNITION.
NO AMMO!
OH, C'MON!

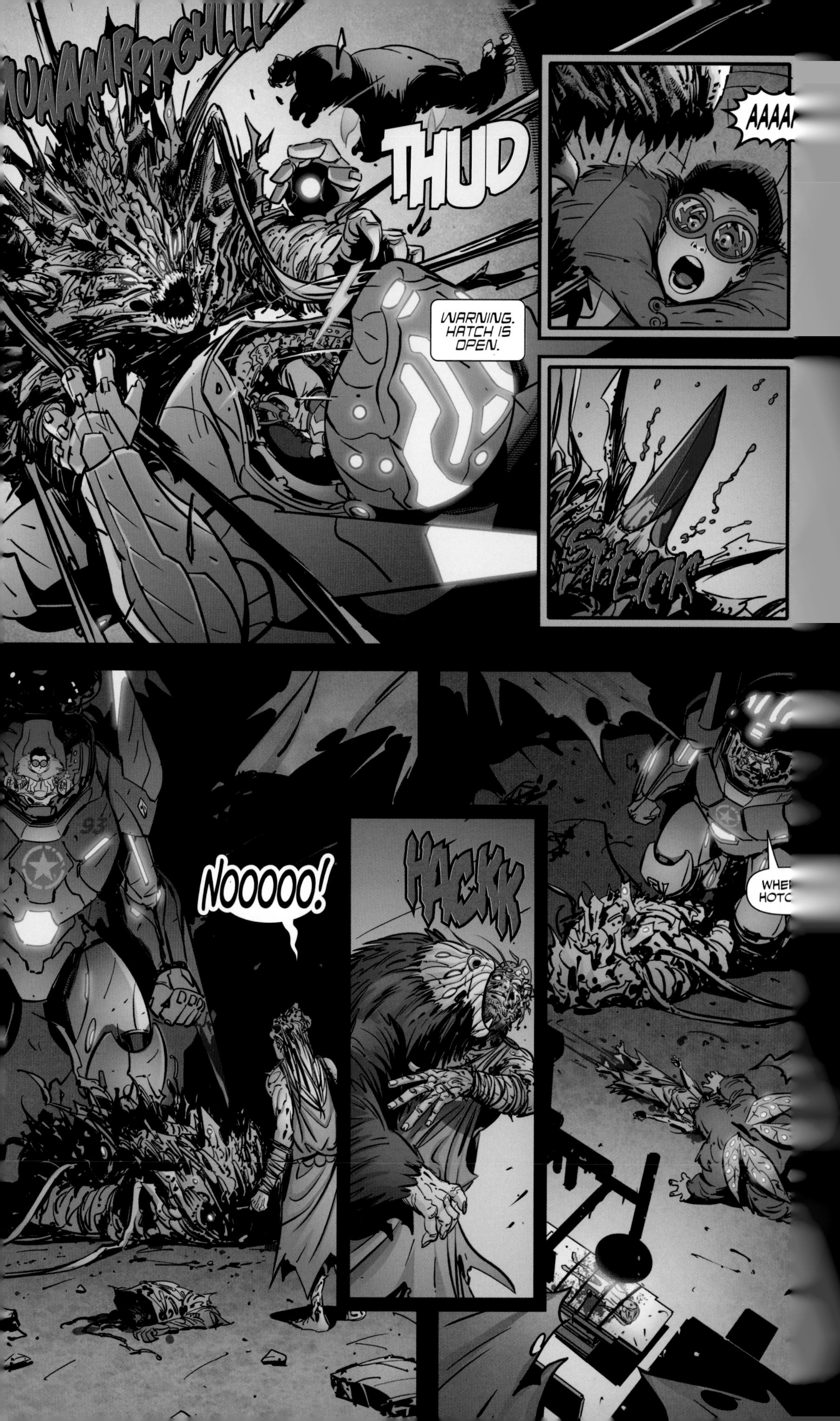
MUAAAARRRGHLLL
THUD
AAAA
WARNING. HATCH IS OPEN.
SHLICK
NOOOOO!
HACKK

THE INVISIBLE
KINGDOM

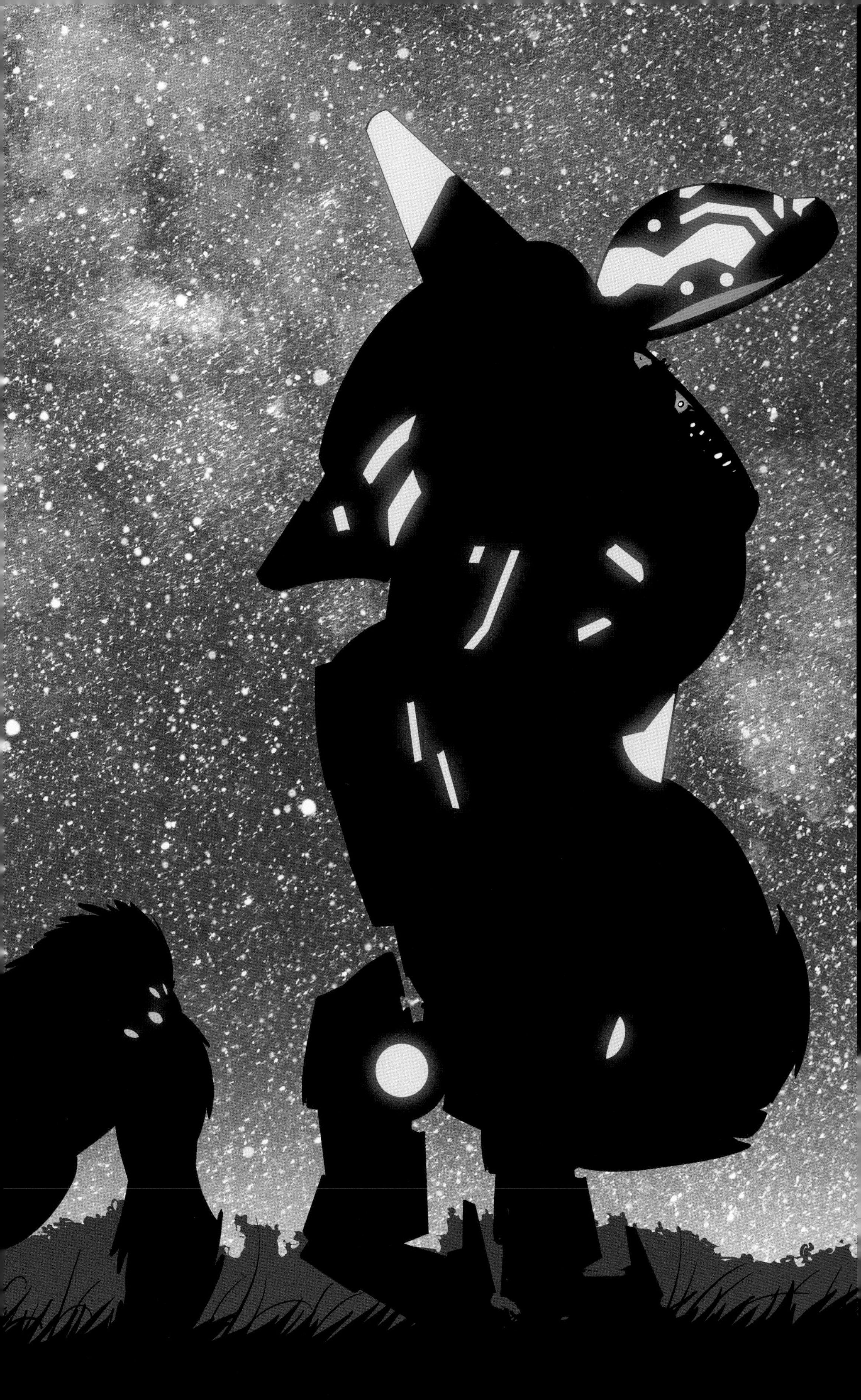

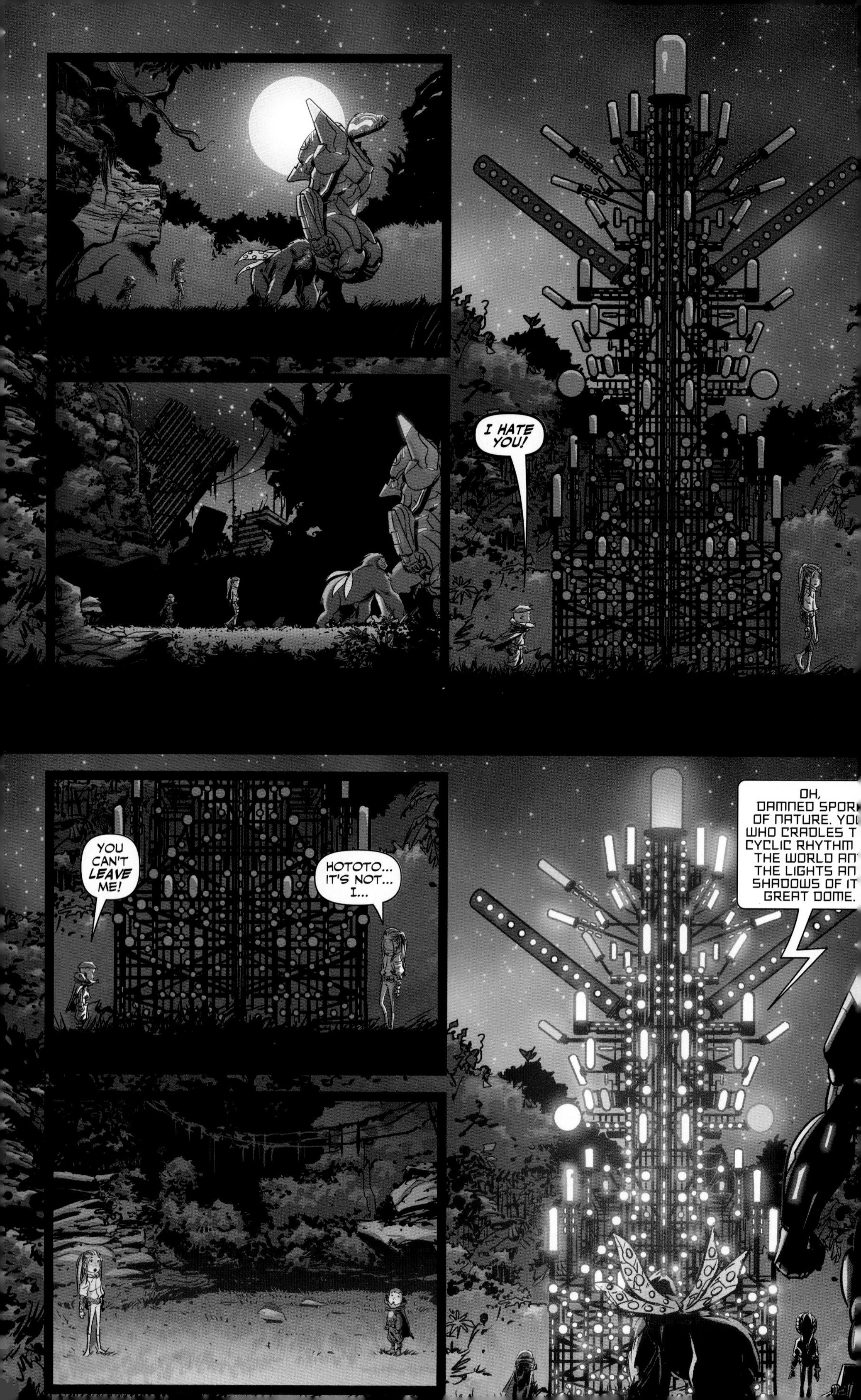
I HATE YOU!
YOU CAN'T LEAVE ME!
HOTOTO... IT'S NOT... I...
OH, DAMNED SPOR
OF NATURE. YO
WHO CRADLES T
CYCLIC RHYTHM
THE WORLD AN
THE LIGHTS AN
SHADOWS OF IT
GREAT DOME.

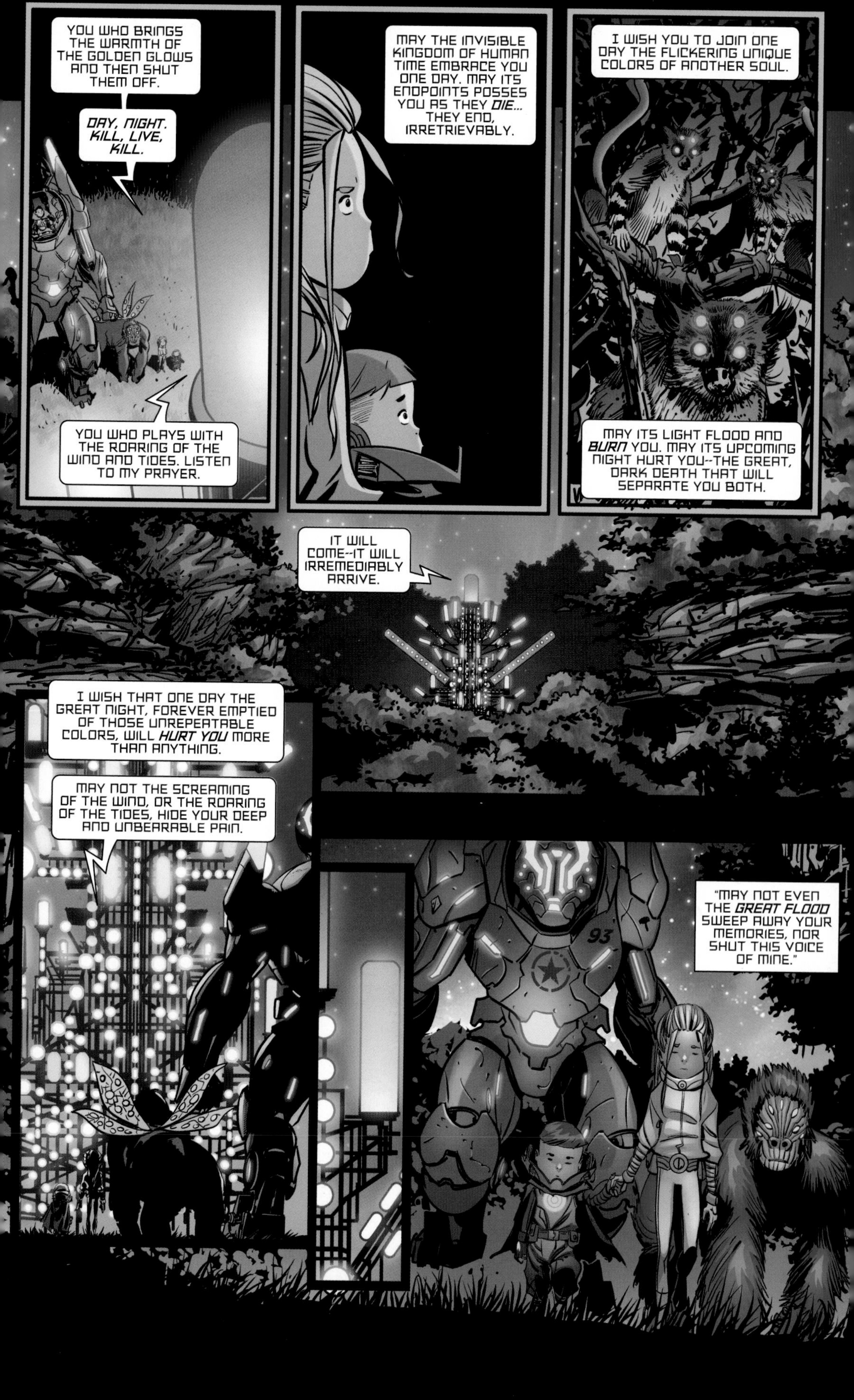
YOU WHO BRINGS THE WARMTH OF THE GOLDEN GLOWS AND THEN SHUT THEM OFF.
DAY, NIGHT. KILL, LIVE, KILL.
YOU WHO PLAYS WITH THE ROARING OF THE WIND AND TIDES. LISTEN TO MY PRAYER.
MAY THE INVISIBLE KINGDOM OF HUMAN TIME EMBRACE YOU ONE DAY. MAY ITS ENDPOINTS POSSES YOU AS THEY DIE... THEY END, IRRETRIEVABLY.
I WISH YOU TO JOIN ONE DAY THE FLICKERING UNIQUE COLORS OF ANOTHER SOUL.
MAY ITS LIGHT FLOOD AND BURN YOU. MAY ITS UPCOMING NIGHT HURT YOU--THE GREAT, DARK DEATH THAT WILL SEPARATE YOU BOTH.
IT WILL COME--IT WILL IRREMEDIABLY ARRIVE.
I WISH THAT ONE DAY THE GREAT NIGHT, FOREVER EMPTIED OF THOSE UNREPEATABLE COLORS, WILL HURT YOU MORE THAN ANYTHING.
MAY NOT THE SCREAMING OF THE WIND, OR THE ROARING OF THE TIDES, HIDE YOUR DEEP AND UNBEARABLE PAIN.
"MAY NOT EVEN THE GREAT FLOOD SWEEP AWAY YOUR MEMORIES, NOR SHUT THIS VOICE OF MINE."

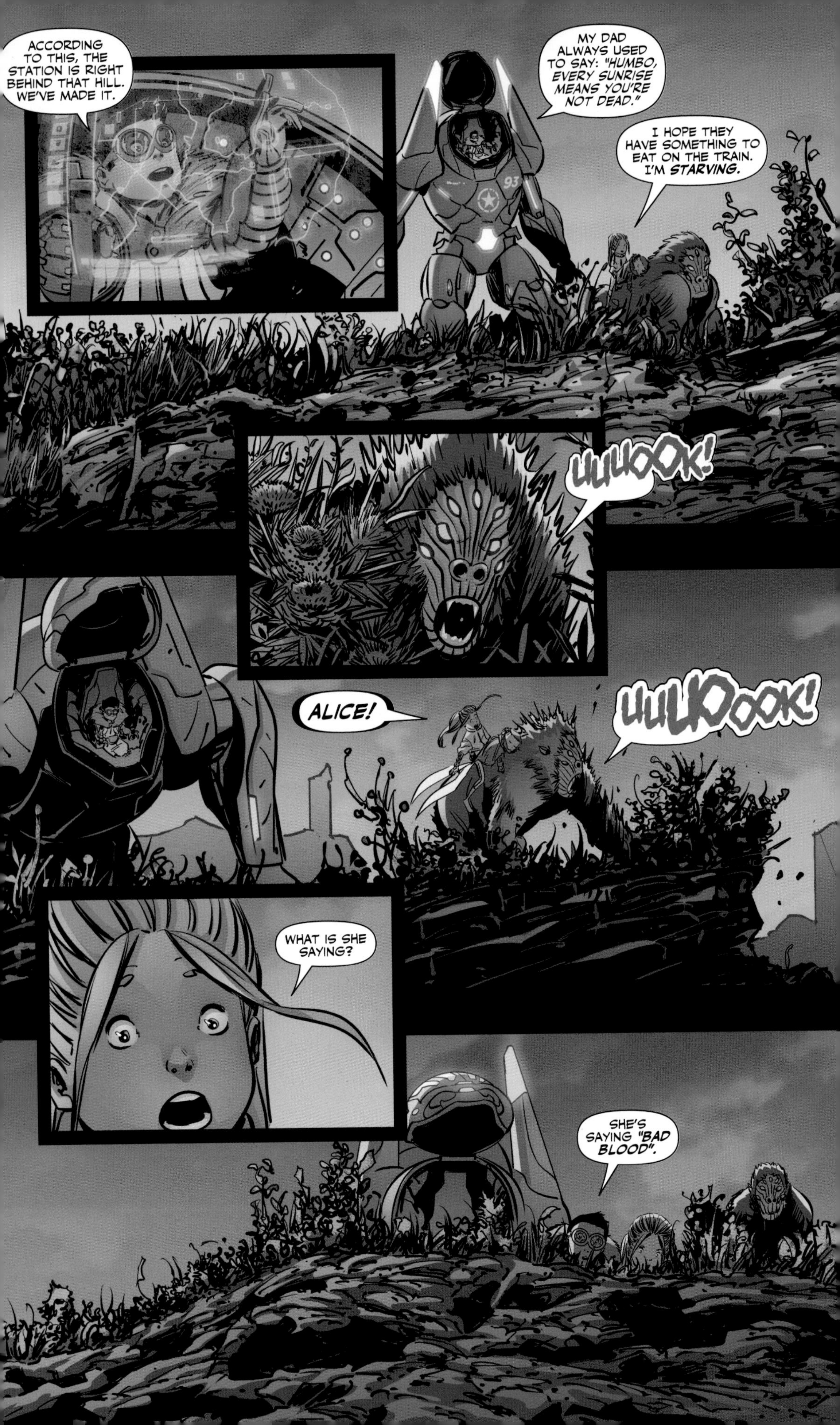
ACCORDING TO THIS, THE STATION IS RIGHT BEHIND THAT HILL. WE'VE MADE IT.
MY DAD ALWAYS USED TO SAY: "HUMBO, EVERY SUNRISE MEANS YOU'RE NOT DEAD."
I HOPE THEY HAVE SOMETHING TO EAT ON THE TRAIN. I'M STARVING.
UULLOOK!
ALICE!
UULLOOOK!
WHAT IS SHE SAYING?
SHE'S SAYING "BAD BLOOD".

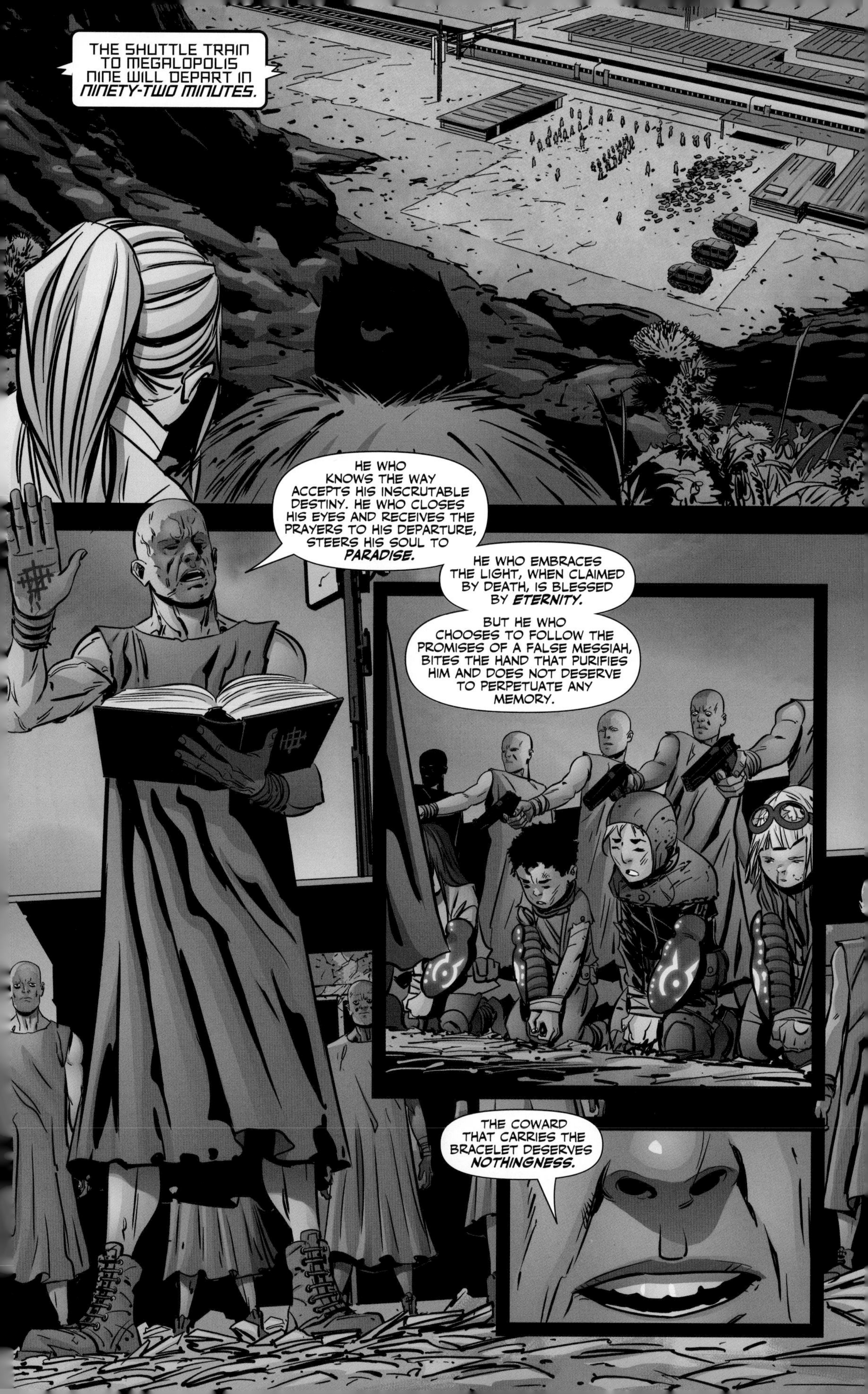
THE SHUTTLE TRAIN TO MEGALOPOLIS NINE WILL DEPART IN NINETY-TWO MINUTES.
HE WHO KNOWS THE WAY ACCEPTS HIS INSCRUTABLE DESTINY. HE WHO CLOSES HIS EYES AND RECEIVES THE PRAYERS TO HIS DEPARTURE, STEERS HIS SOUL TO PARADISE.
HE WHO EMBRACES THE LIGHT, WHEN CLAIMED BY DEATH, IS BLESSED BY ETERNITY.
BUT HE WHO CHOOSES TO FOLLOW THE PROMISES OF A FALSE MESSIAH, BITES THE HAND THAT PURIFIES HIM AND DOES NOT DESERVE TO PERPETUATE ANY MEMORY.
THE COWARD THAT CARRIES THE BRACELET DESERVES NOTHINGNESS.

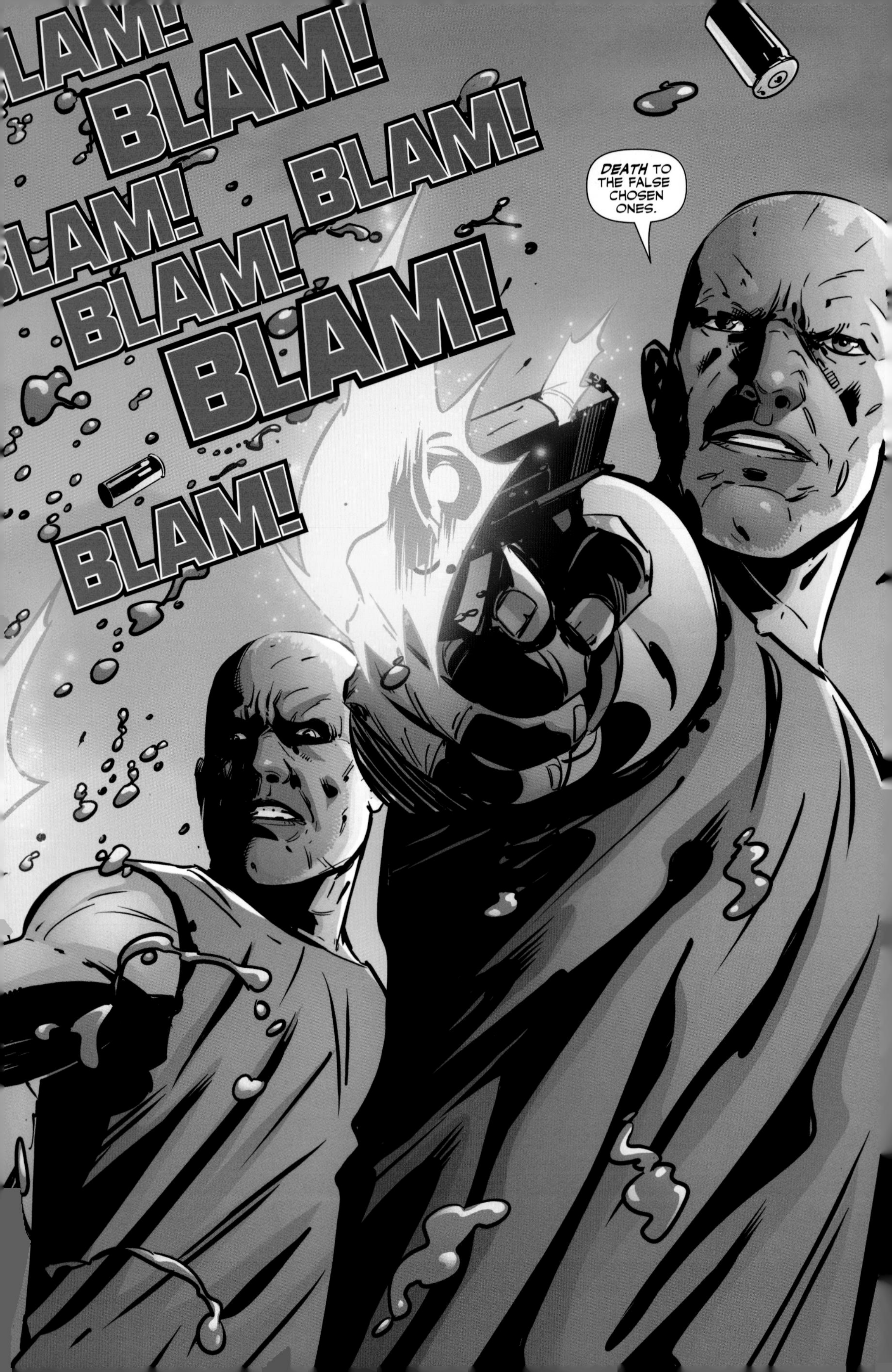

BLAM!
BLAM!
BLAM!
BLAM!
BLAM!
BLAM!
BLAM!
DEATH TO THE FALSE CHOSEN ONES.

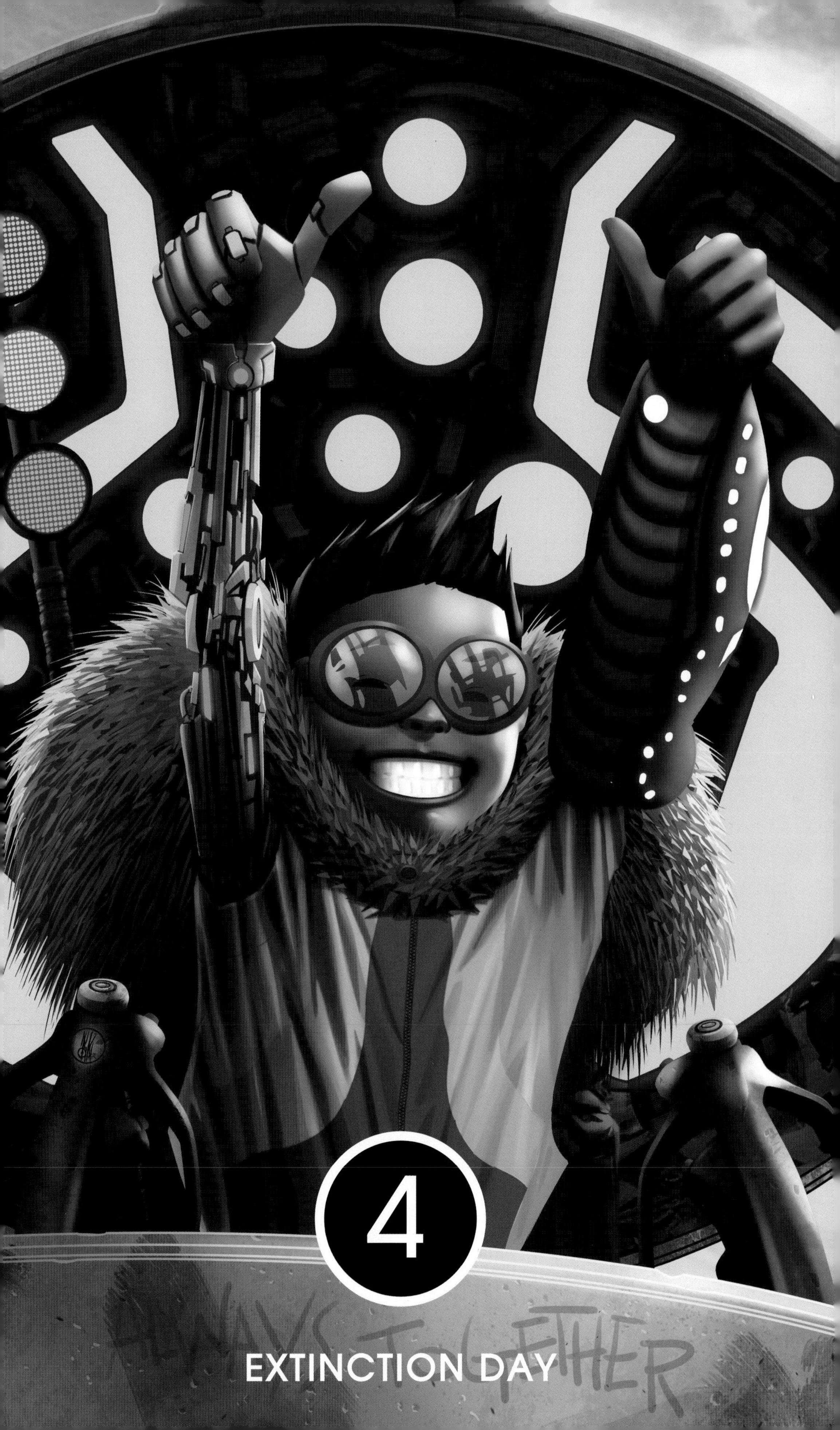

4

EXTINCTION DAY

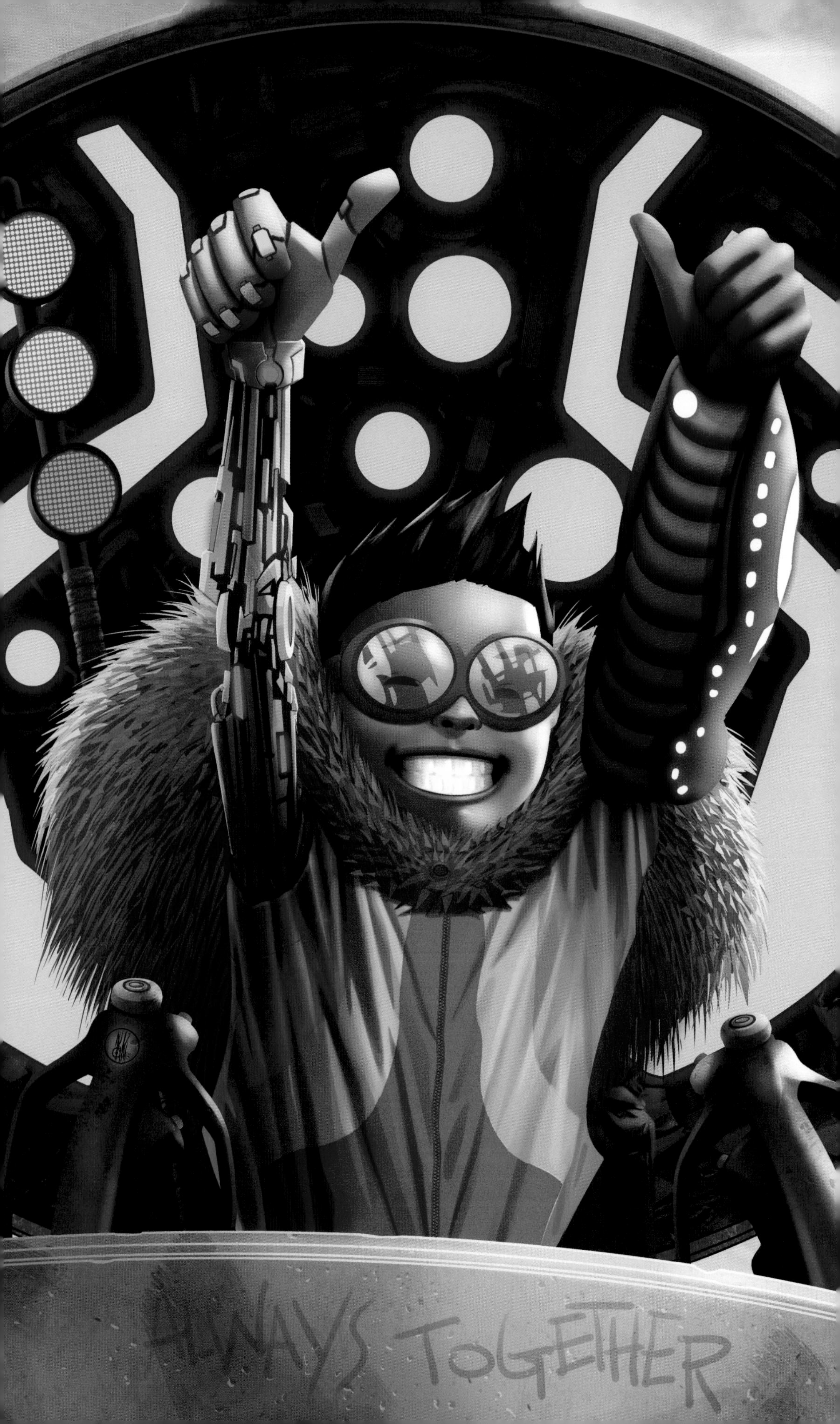
ALWAYS TOGETHER

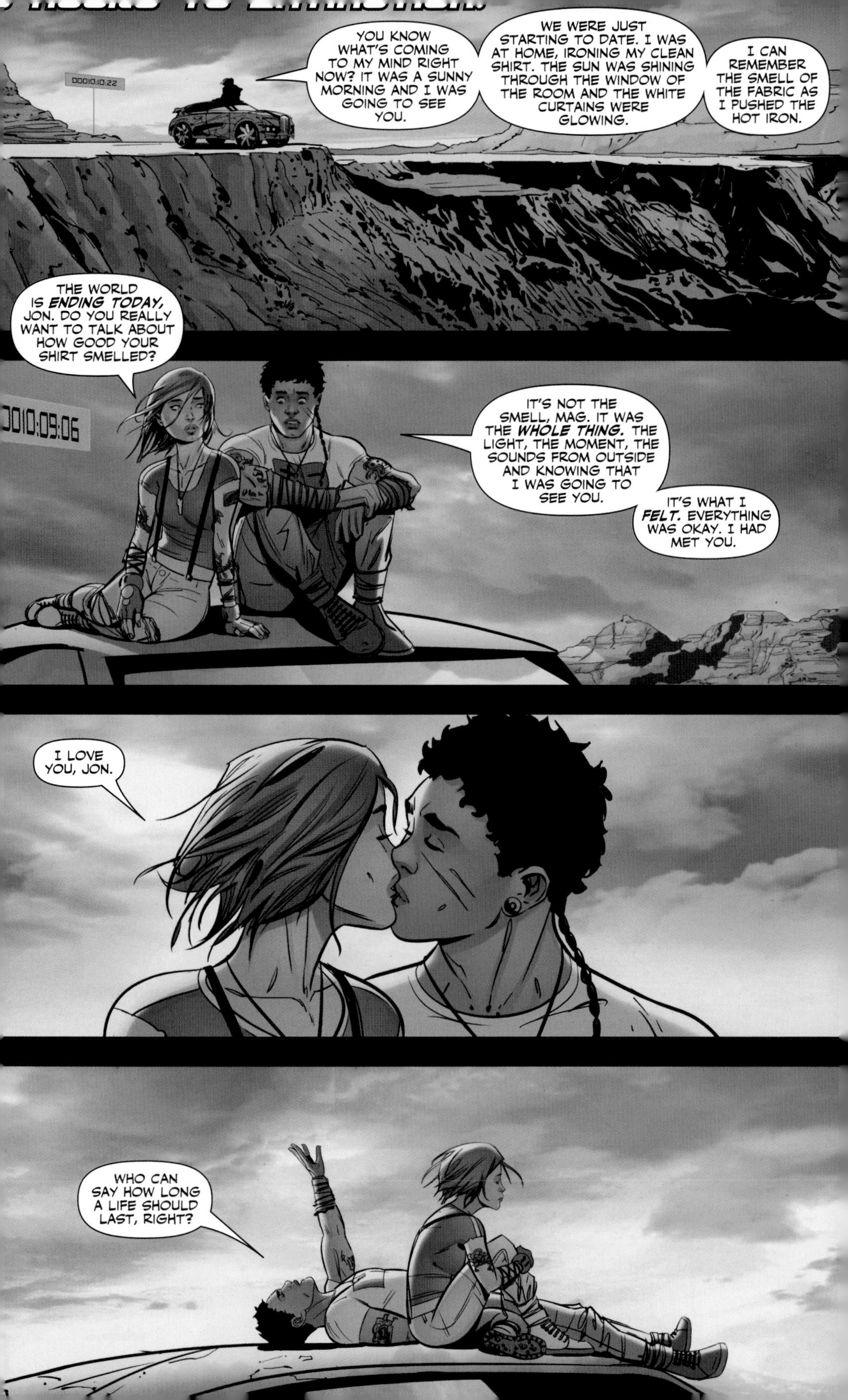

00010:10:22
YOU KNOW WHAT'S COMING TO MY MIND RIGHT NOW? IT WAS A SUNNY MORNING AND I WAS GOING TO SEE YOU.
WE WERE JUST STARTING TO DATE. I WAS AT HOME, IRONING MY CLEAN SHIRT. THE SUN WAS SHINING THROUGH THE WINDOW OF THE ROOM AND THE WHITE CURTAINS WERE GLOWING.
I CAN REMEMBER THE SMELL OF THE FABRIC AS I PUSHED THE HOT IRON.
THE WORLD IS *ENDING TODAY,* JON. DO YOU REALLY WANT TO TALK ABOUT HOW GOOD YOUR SHIRT SMELLED?
0010:09:06
IT'S NOT THE SMELL, MAG. IT WAS THE *WHOLE THING.* THE LIGHT, THE MOMENT, THE SOUNDS FROM OUTSIDE AND KNOWING THAT I WAS GOING TO SEE YOU.
IT'S WHAT I *FELT.* EVERYTHING WAS OKAY. I HAD MET YOU.
I LOVE YOU, JON.
WHO CAN SAY HOW LONG A LIFE SHOULD LAST, RIGHT?

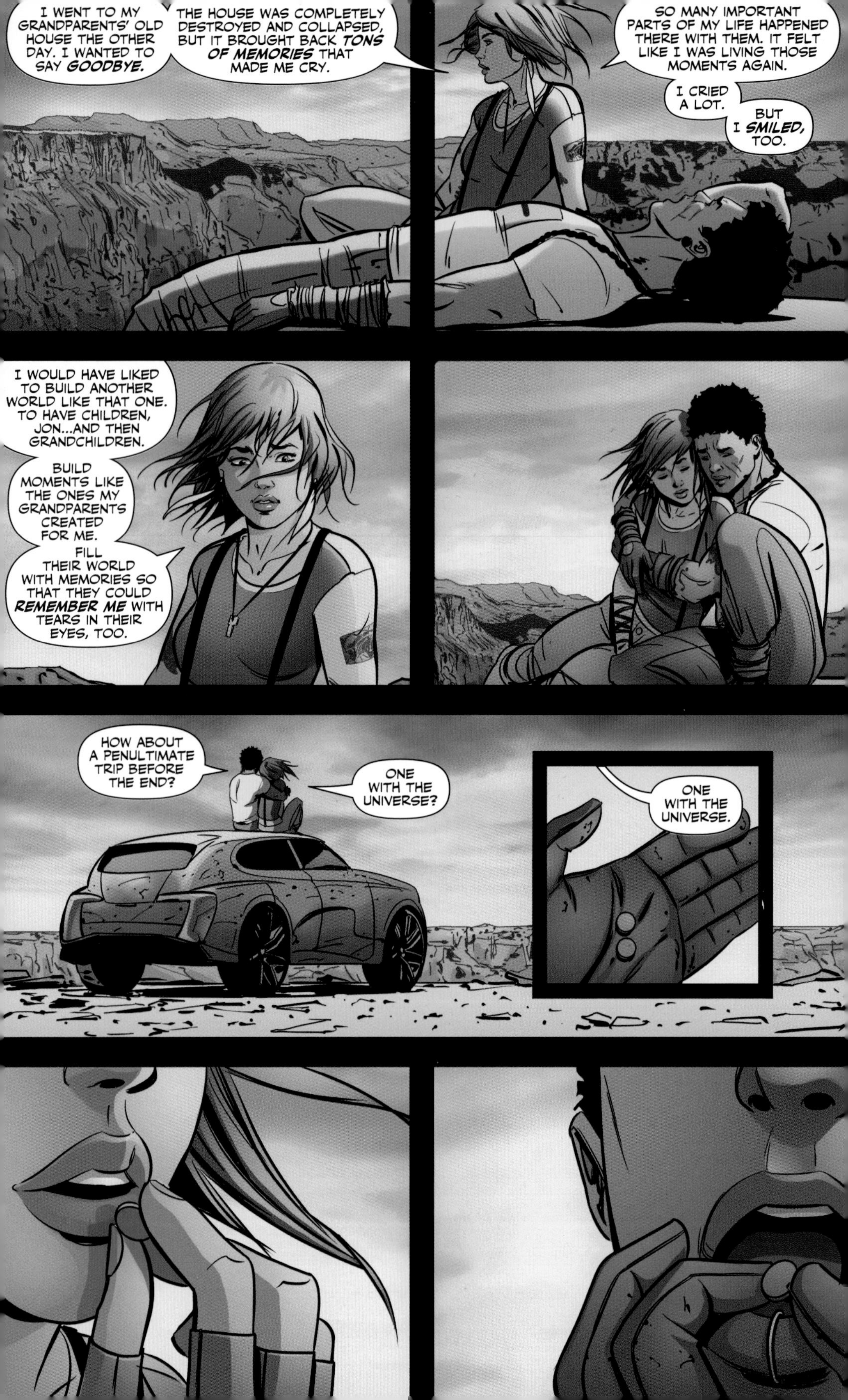
I WENT TO MY GRANDPARENTS' OLD HOUSE THE OTHER DAY. I WANTED TO SAY GOODBYE.
THE HOUSE WAS COMPLETELY DESTROYED AND COLLAPSED, BUT IT BROUGHT BACK TONS OF MEMORIES THAT MADE ME CRY.
SO MANY IMPORTANT PARTS OF MY LIFE HAPPENED THERE WITH THEM. IT FELT LIKE I WAS LIVING THOSE MOMENTS AGAIN.
I CRIED A LOT.
BUT I SMILED, TOO.
I WOULD HAVE LIKED TO BUILD ANOTHER WORLD LIKE THAT ONE. TO HAVE CHILDREN, JON...AND THEN GRANDCHILDREN.
BUILD MOMENTS LIKE THE ONES MY GRANDPARENTS CREATED FOR ME.
FILL THEIR WORLD WITH MEMORIES SO THAT THEY COULD REMEMBER ME WITH TEARS IN THEIR EYES, TOO.
HOW ABOUT A PENULTIMATE TRIP BEFORE THE END?
ONE WITH THE UNIVERSE?
ONE WITH THE UNIVERSE.

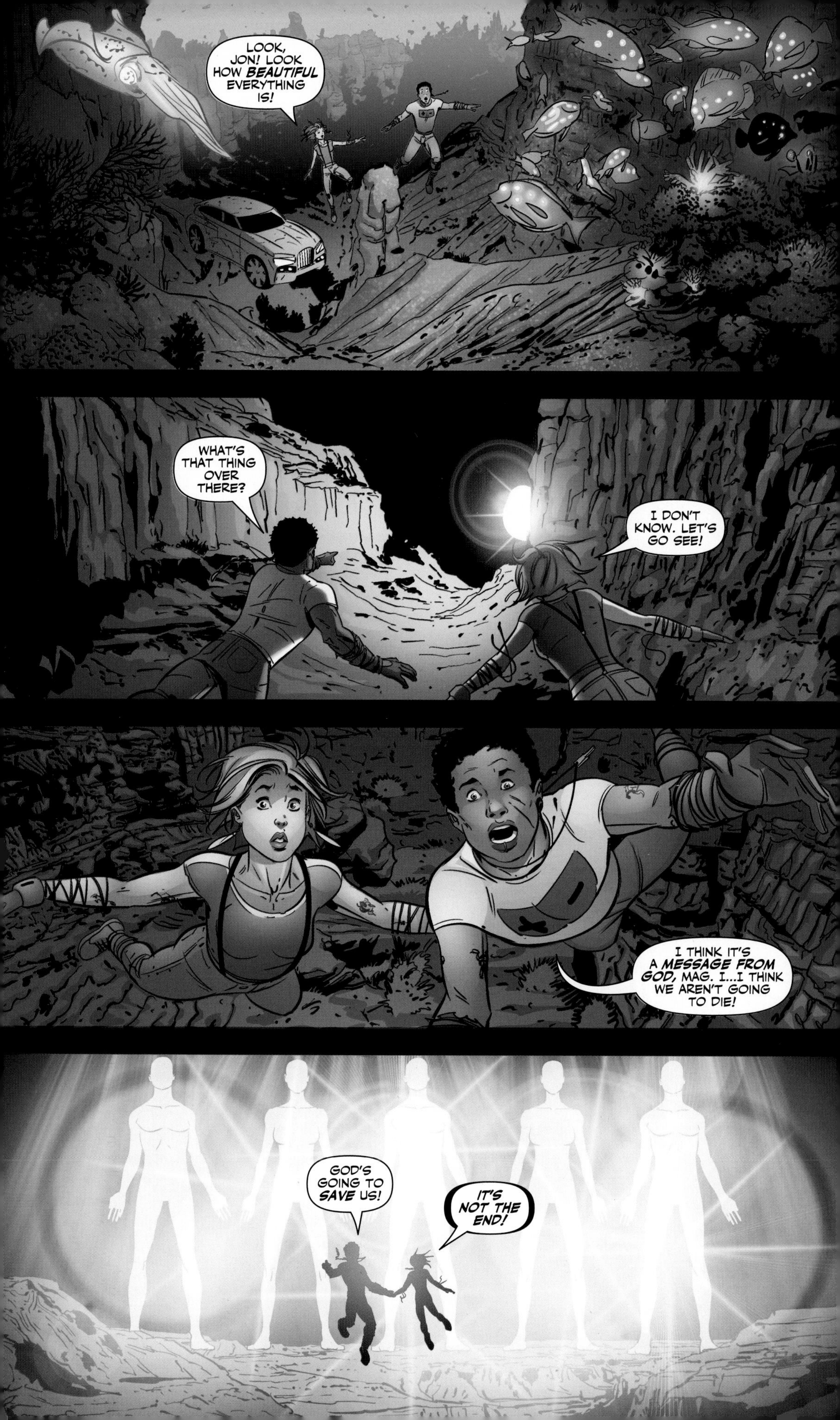
LOOK, JON! LOOK HOW BEAUTIFUL EVERYTHING IS!
WHAT'S THAT THING OVER THERE?
I DON'T KNOW. LET'S GO SEE!
I THINK IT'S A MESSAGE FROM GOD, MAG. I...I THINK WE AREN'T GOING TO DIE!
GOD'S GOING TO SAVE US!
IT'S NOT THE END!

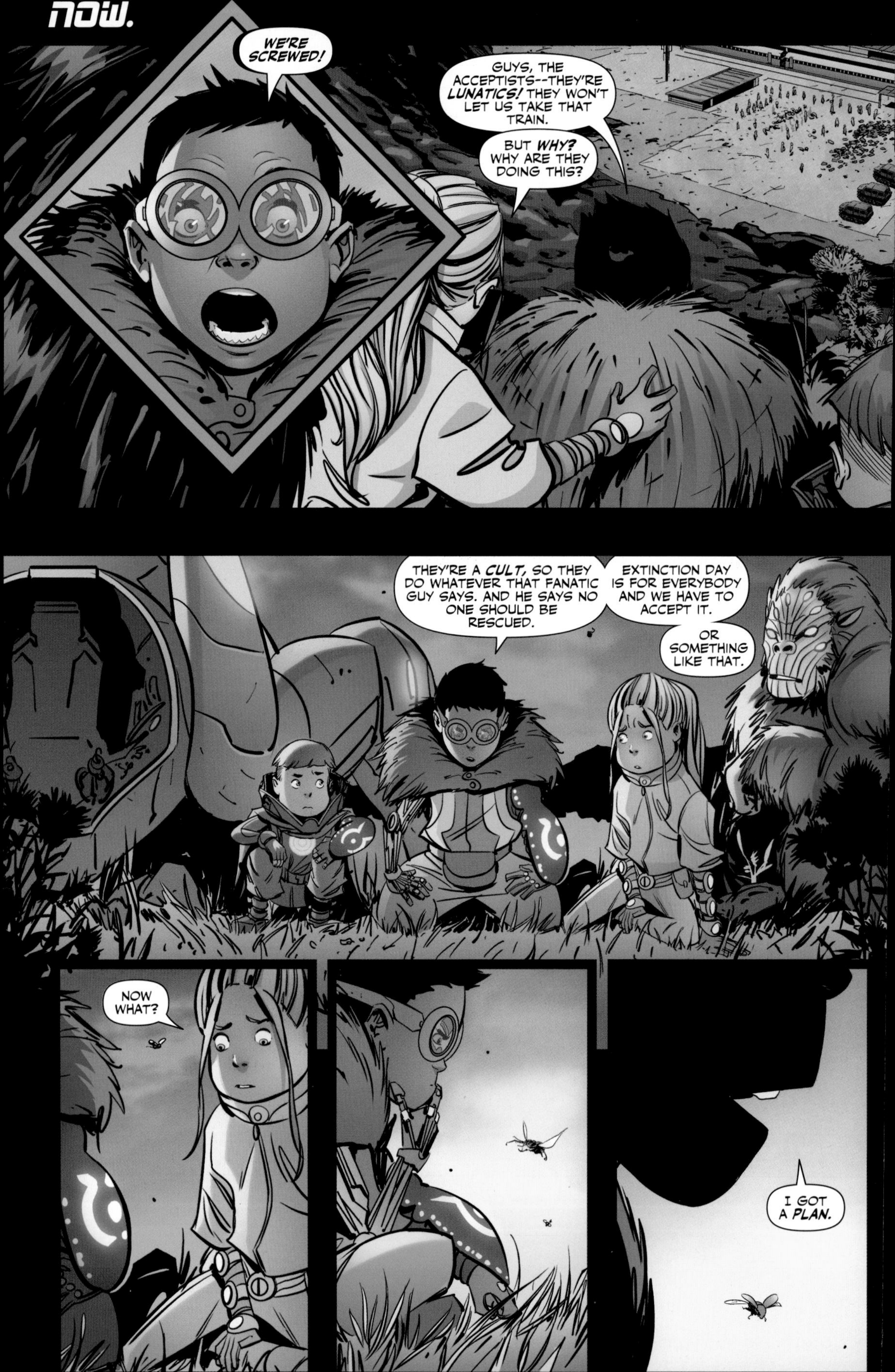
NOW.
WE'RE SCREWED!
GUYS, THE ACCEPTISTS--THEY'RE LUNATICS! THEY WON'T LET US TAKE THAT TRAIN.
BUT WHY? WHY ARE THEY DOING THIS?
THEY'RE A CULT, SO THEY DO WHATEVER THAT FANATIC GUY SAYS. AND HE SAYS NO ONE SHOULD BE RESCUED.
EXTINCTION DAY IS FOR EVERYBODY AND WE HAVE TO ACCEPT IT.
OR SOMETHING LIKE THAT.
NOW WHAT?
I GOT A PLAN.

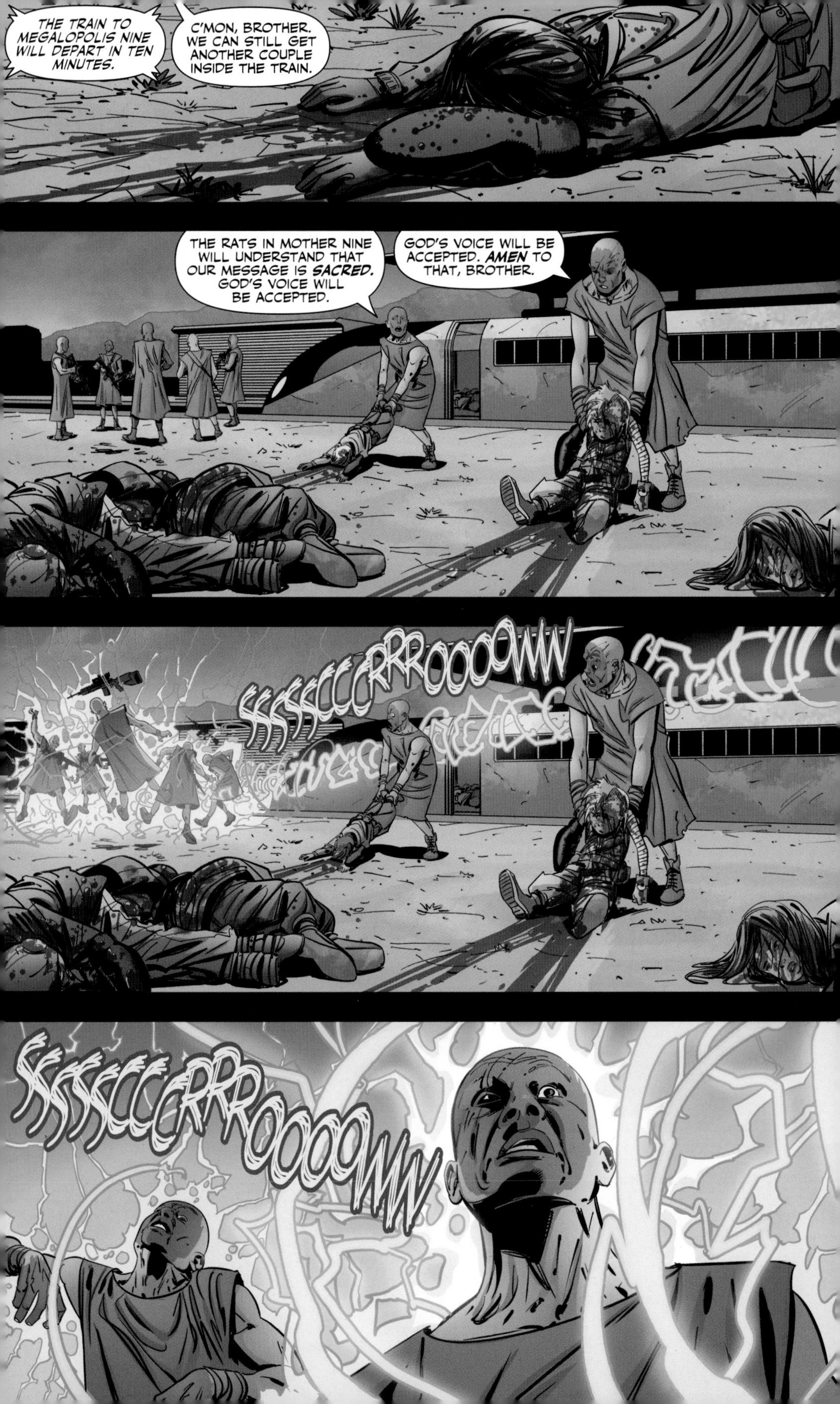
THE TRAIN TO MEGALOPOLIS NINE WILL DEPART IN TEN MINUTES.
C'MON, BROTHER. WE CAN STILL GET ANOTHER COUPLE INSIDE THE TRAIN.
THE RATS IN MOTHER NINE WILL UNDERSTAND THAT OUR MESSAGE IS SACRED. GOD'S VOICE WILL BE ACCEPTED.
GOD'S VOICE WILL BE ACCEPTED. AMEN TO THAT, BROTHER.
SSSSSCCCRRROOOOOWW
SSSSSCCCRRROOOOOWW

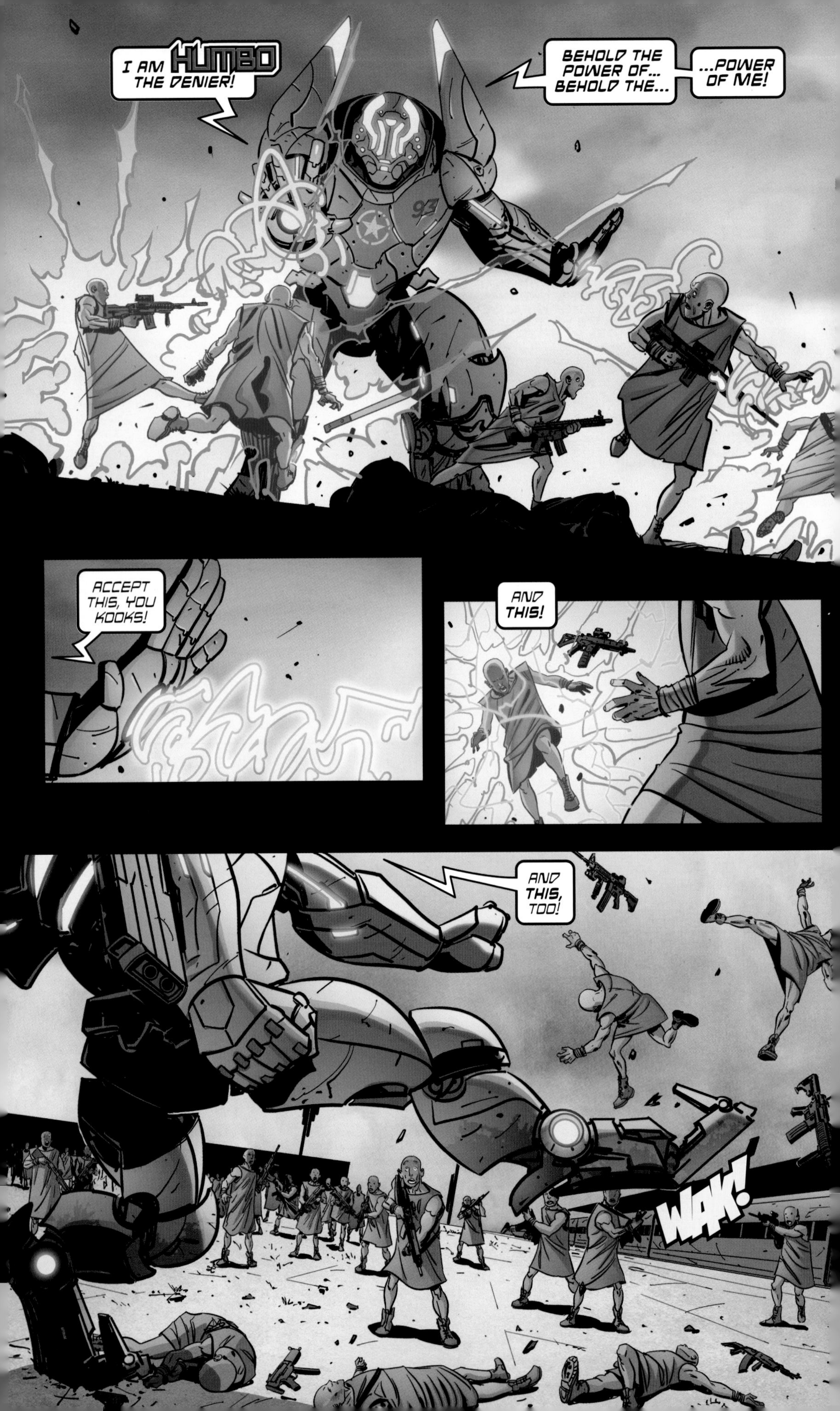
I AM HUMBO THE DENIER!
BEHOLD THE POWER OF... BEHOLD THE...
...POWER OF ME!
ACCEPT THIS, YOU KOOKS!
AND THIS!
AND THIS, TOO!
WAK!

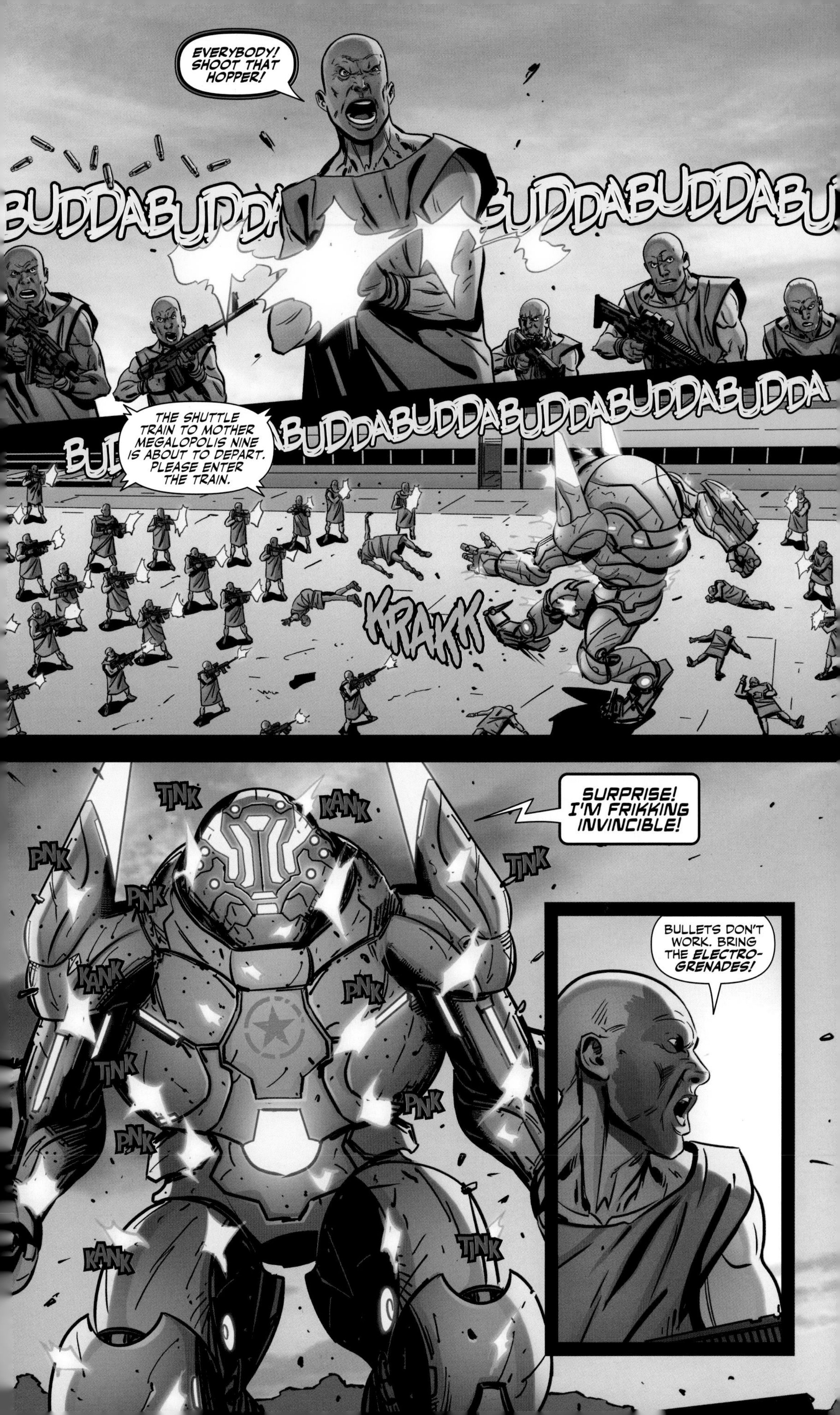

EVERYBODY! SHOOT THAT HOPPER!
BUDDABUDDA
BUDDABUDDABU
BUDDABUDDABUDDABUDDA
THE SHUTTLE TRAIN TO MOTHER MEGALOPOLIS NINE IS ABOUT TO DEPART. PLEASE ENTER THE TRAIN.
KRAKK
SURPRISE! I'M FRIKKING INVINCIBLE!
TINK
KANK
PNK
PNK
TINK
KANK
PNK
TINK
PNK
PNK
KANK
TINK
BULLETS DON'T WORK. BRING THE ELECTRO-GRENADES!

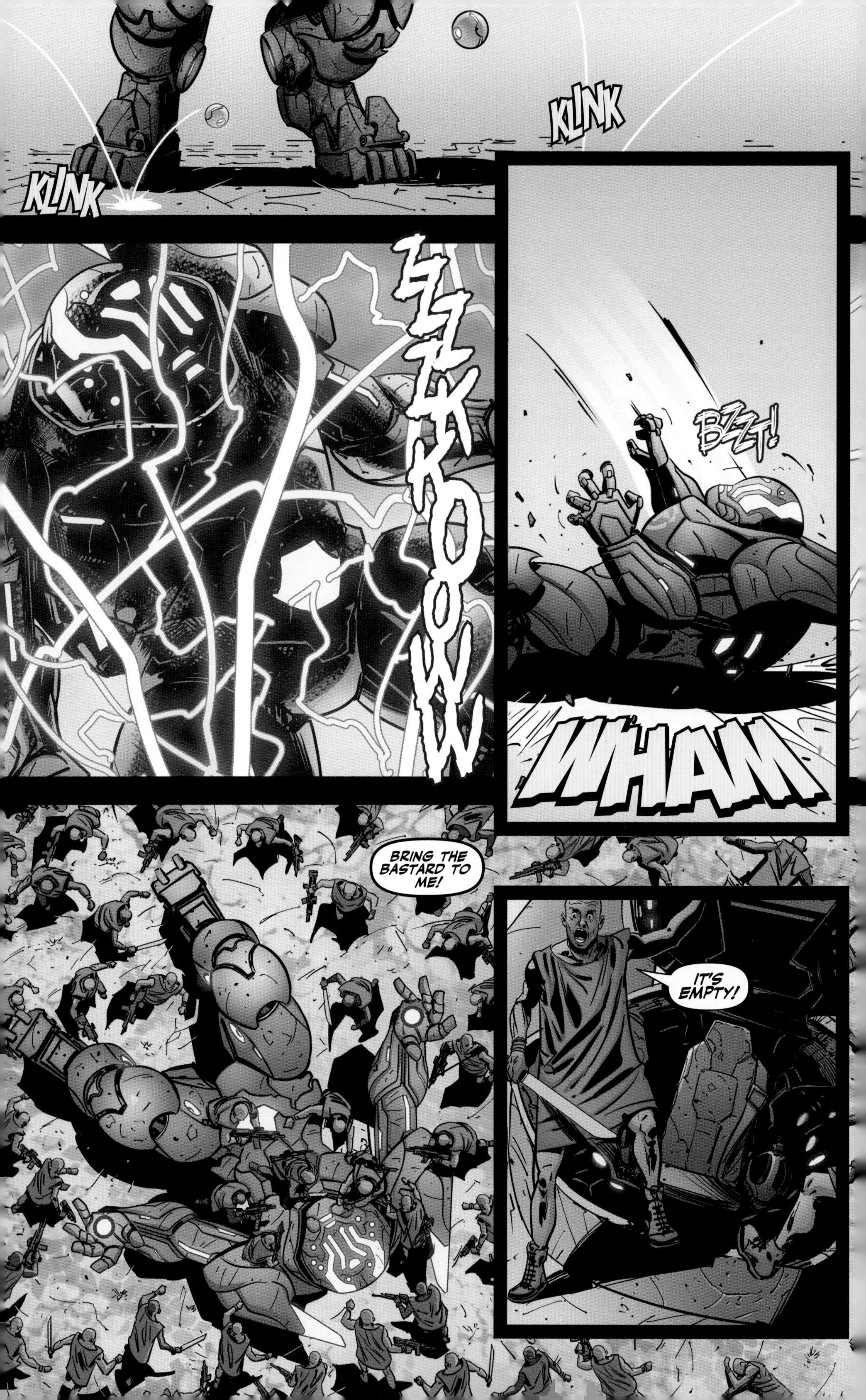

KLINK
KLINK
ZZZKKOOW
BZZT!
WHAM
BRING THE BASTARD TO ME!
IT'S EMPTY!

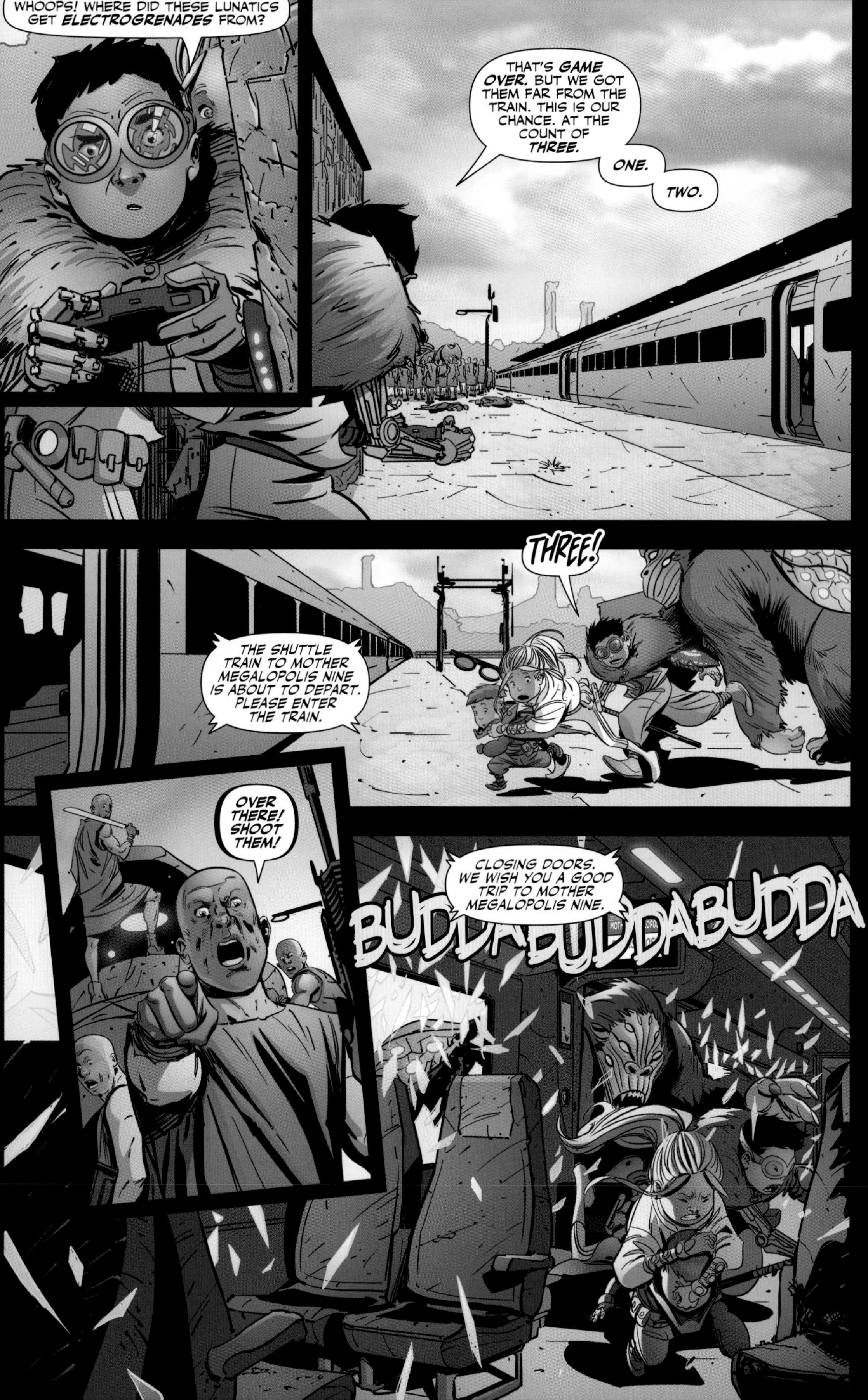
WHOOPS! WHERE DID THESE LUNATICS GET ELECTROGRENADES FROM?
THAT'S GAME OVER. BUT WE GOT THEM FAR FROM THE TRAIN. THIS IS OUR CHANCE. AT THE COUNT OF THREE.
ONE.
TWO.
THREE!
THE SHUTTLE TRAIN TO MOTHER MEGALOPOLIS NINE IS ABOUT TO DEPART. PLEASE ENTER THE TRAIN.
OVER THERE! SHOOT THEM!
CLOSING DOORS. WE WISH YOU A GOOD TRIP TO MOTHER MEGALOPOLIS NINE.
BUDDABUDDABUDDA

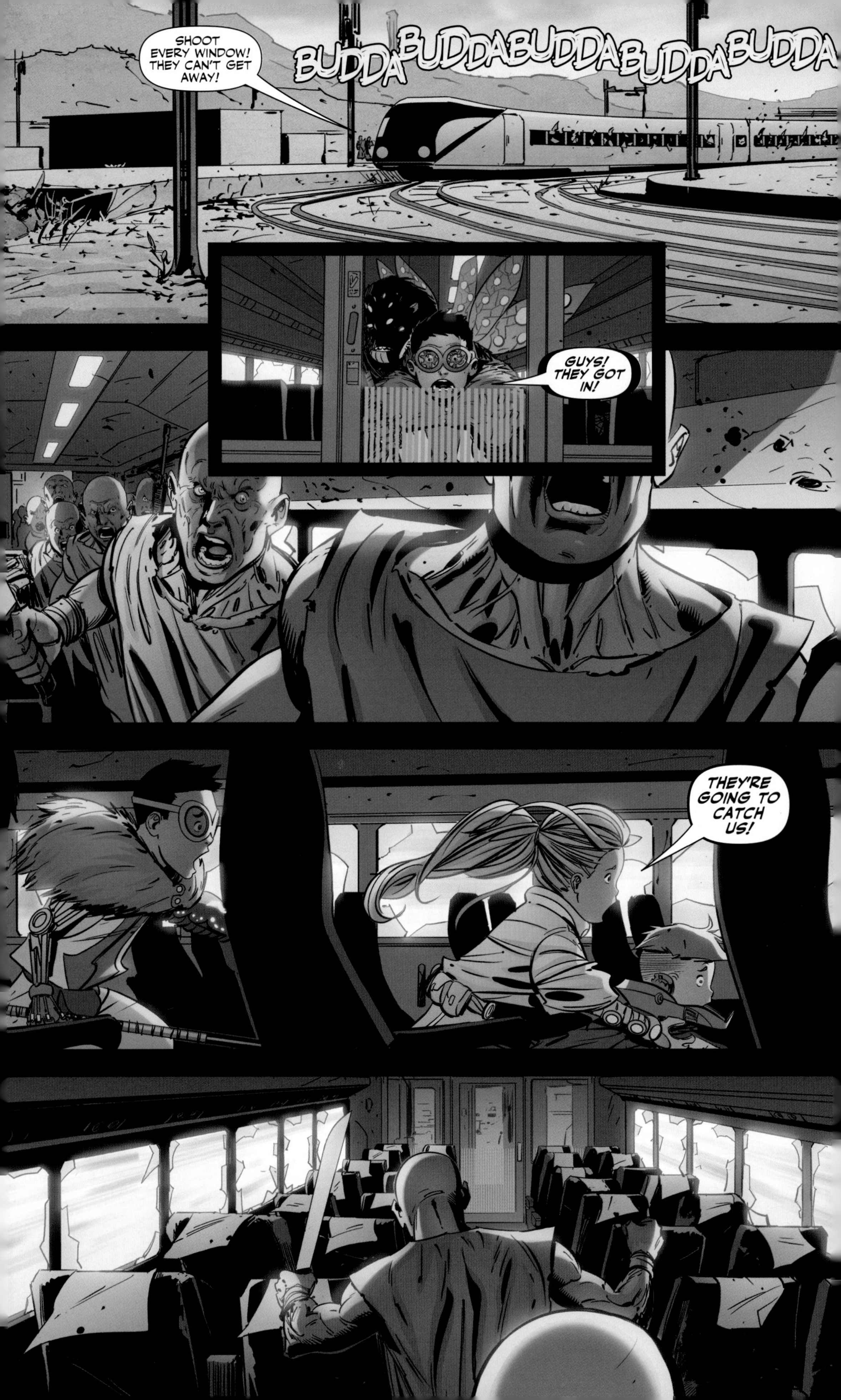
SHOOT EVERY WINDOW! THEY CAN'T GET AWAY!
BUDDABUDDABUDDABUDDABUDDA
GUYS! THEY GOT IN!
THEY'RE GOING TO CATCH US!

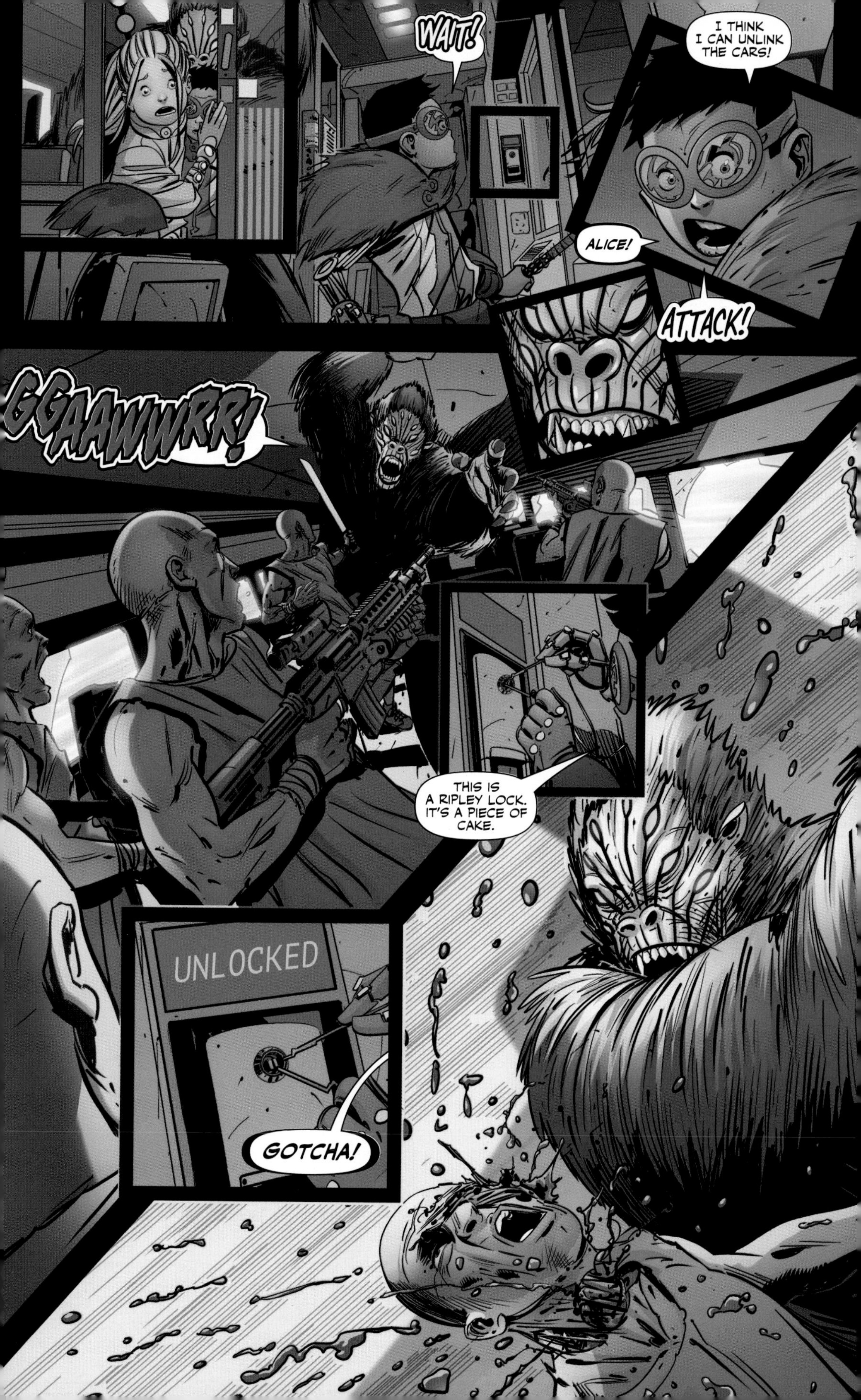
WAIT!
I THINK
I CAN UNLINK
THE CARS!
ALICE!
ATTACK!
GGAAWWRR!
THIS IS
A RIPLEY LOCK.
IT'S A PIECE OF
CAKE.
UNLOCKED
GOTCHA!

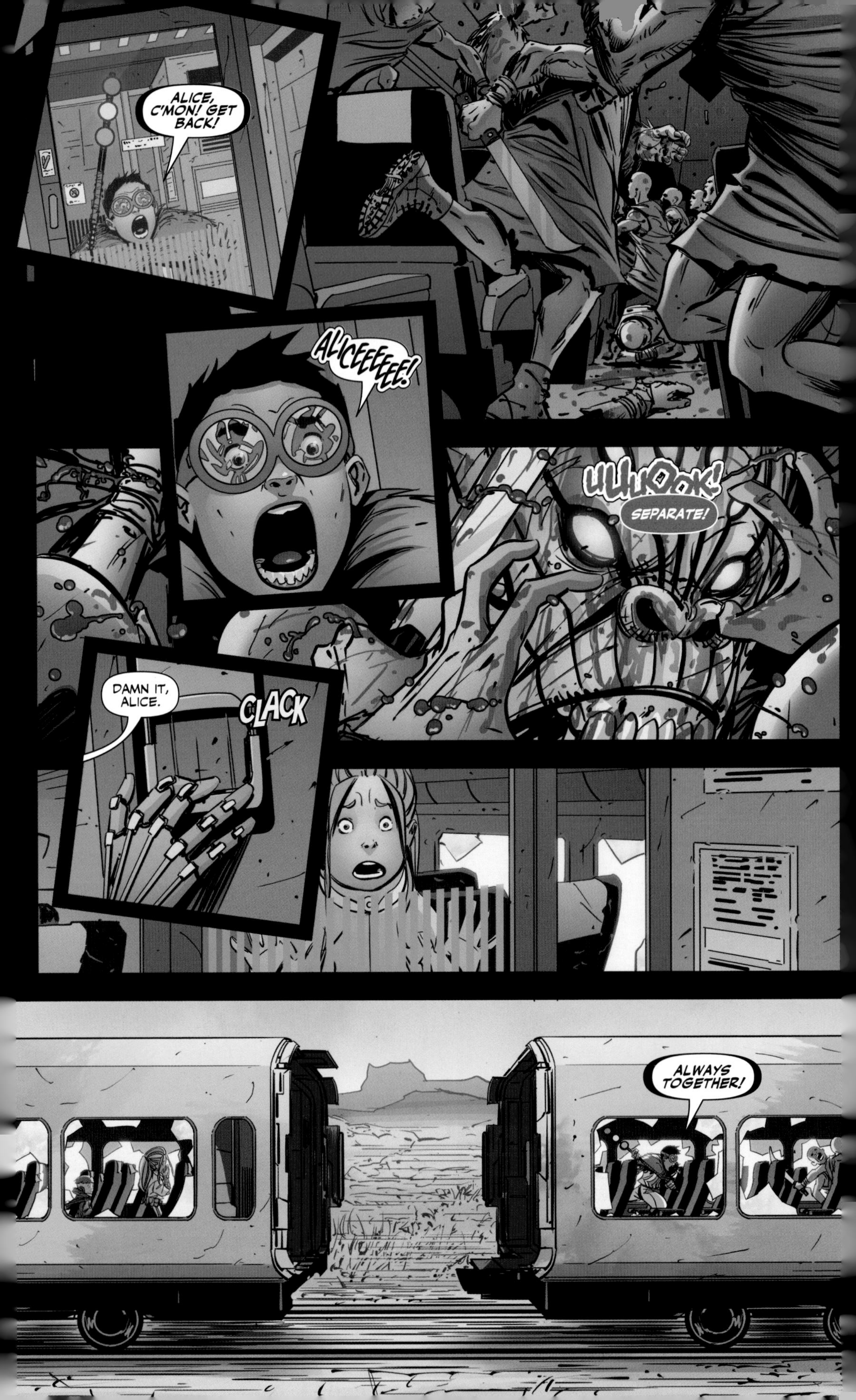
ALICE, C'MON! GET BACK!
ALICEEEEEEE!
UUUKOOK!
SEPARATE!
DAMN IT, ALICE.
CLACK
ALWAYS TOGETHER!

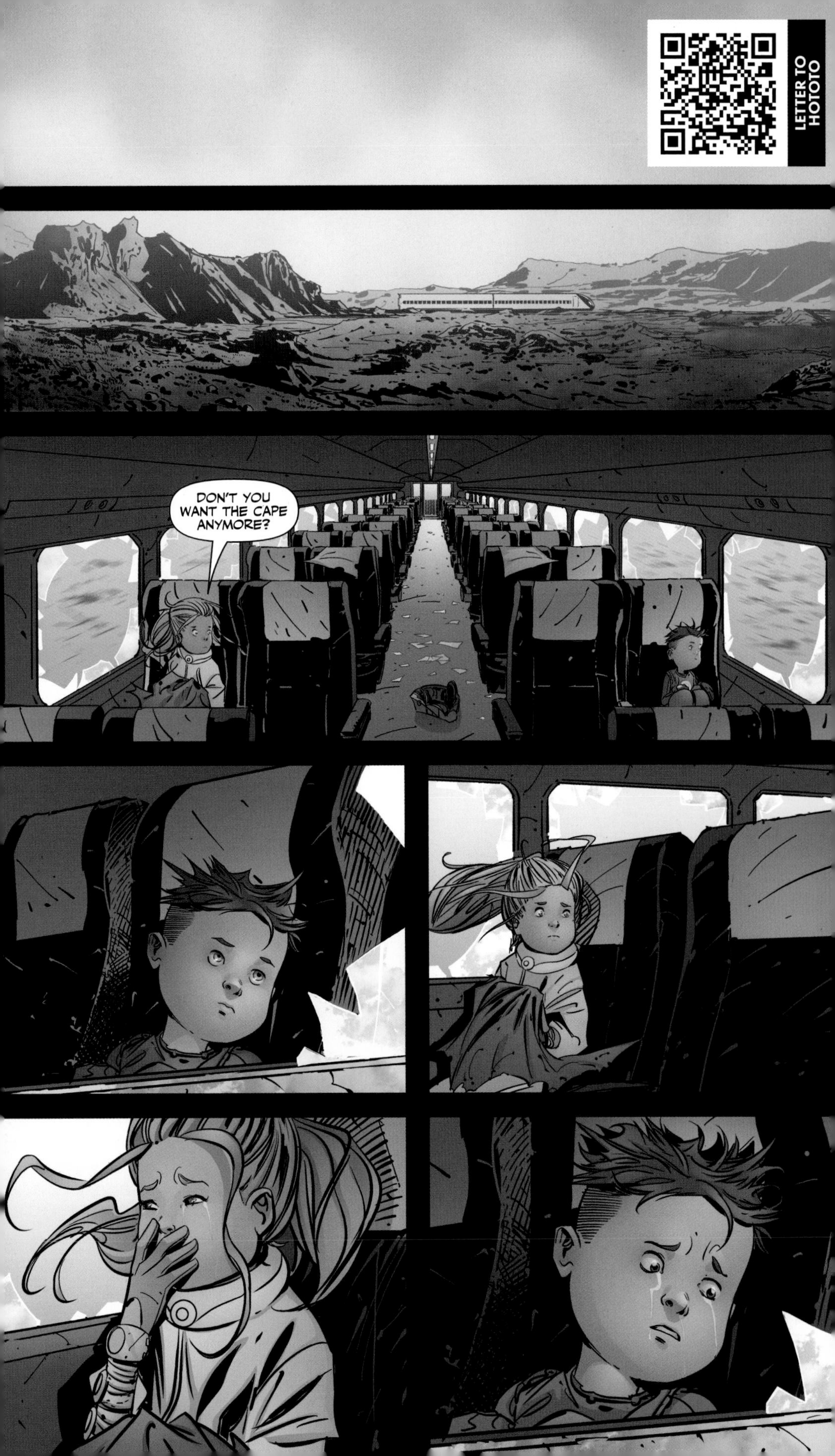
LETTER TO HOTOTO
DON'T YOU WANT THE CAPE ANYMORE?

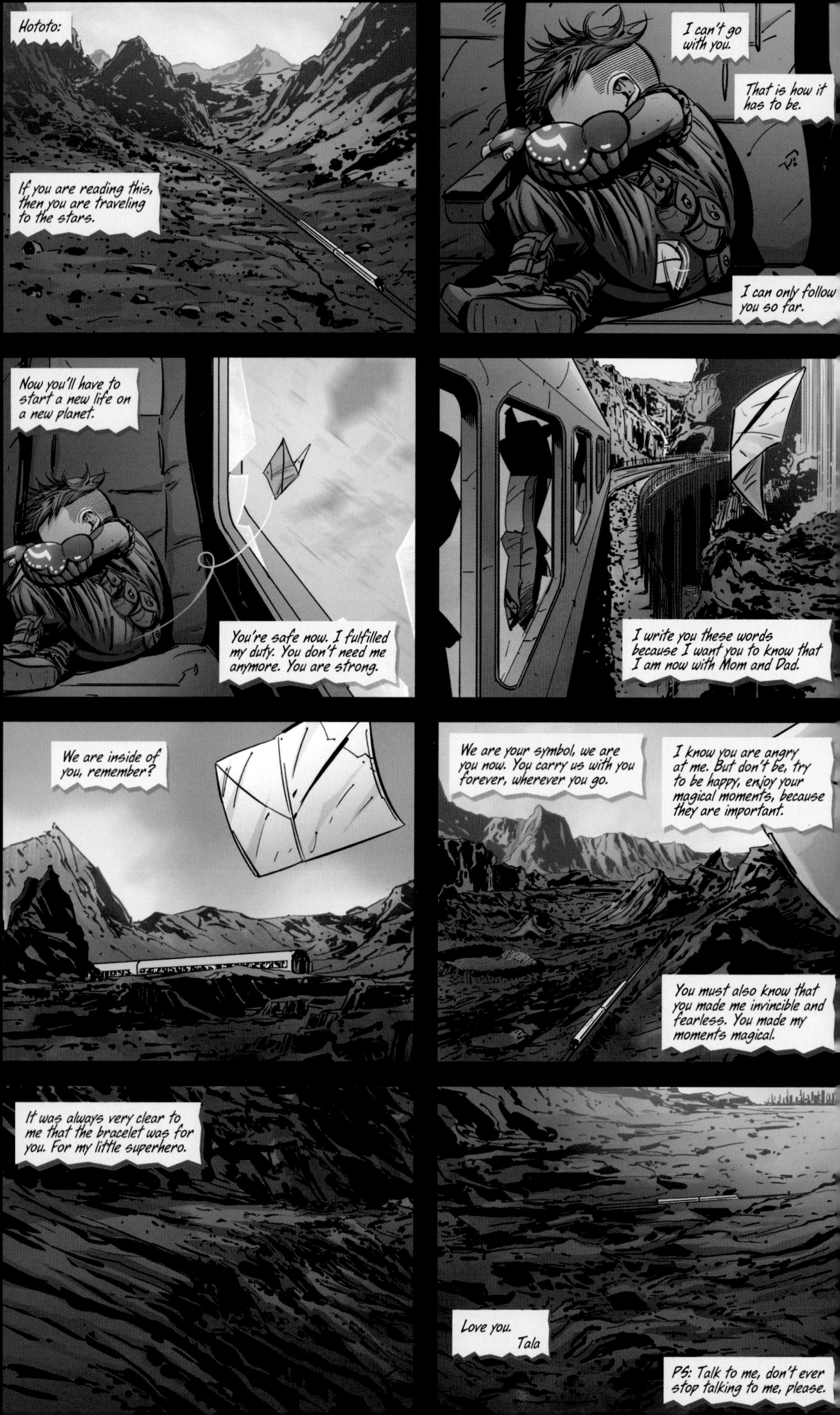

Hototo:
If you are reading this, then you are traveling to the stars.
I can't go with you.
That is how it has to be.
I can only follow you so far.
Now you'll have to start a new life on a new planet.
You're safe now. I fulfilled my duty. You don't need me anymore. You are strong.
I write you these words because I want you to know that I am now with Mom and Dad.
We are inside of you, remember?
We are your symbol, we are you now. You carry us with you forever, wherever you go.
I know you are angry at me. But don't be, try to be happy, enjoy your magical moments, because they are important.
You must also know that you made me invincible and fearless. You made my moments magical.
It was always very clear to me that the bracelet was for you. For my little superhero.
Love you.
Tala
PS: Talk to me, don't ever stop talking to me, please.

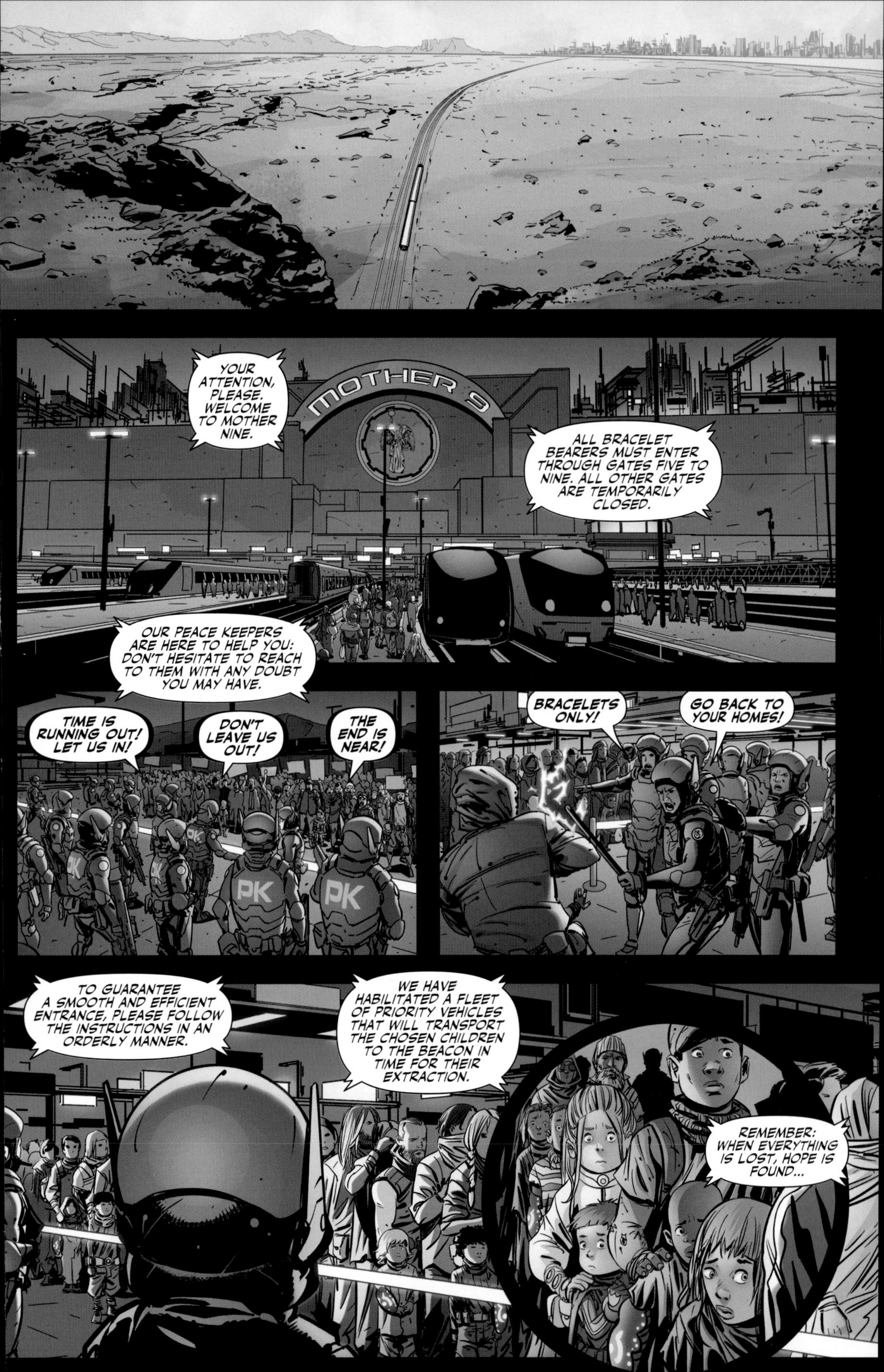

MOTHER 9
YOUR ATTENTION, PLEASE. WELCOME TO MOTHER NINE.
ALL BRACELET BEARERS MUST ENTER THROUGH GATES FIVE TO NINE. ALL OTHER GATES ARE TEMPORARILY CLOSED.
OUR PEACE KEEPERS ARE HERE TO HELP YOU: DON'T HESITATE TO REACH TO THEM WITH ANY DOUBT YOU MAY HAVE.
TIME IS RUNNING OUT! LET US IN!
DON'T LEAVE US OUT!
THE END IS NEAR!
PK
PK
PK
PK
BRACELETS ONLY!
GO BACK TO YOUR HOMES!
TO GUARANTEE A SMOOTH AND EFFICIENT ENTRANCE, PLEASE FOLLOW THE INSTRUCTIONS IN AN ORDERLY MANNER.
WE HAVE HABILITATED A FLEET OF PRIORITY VEHICLES THAT WILL TRANSPORT THE CHOSEN CHILDREN TO THE BEACON IN TIME FOR THEIR EXTRACTION.
REMEMBER: WHEN EVERYTHING IS LOST, HOPE IS FOUND...

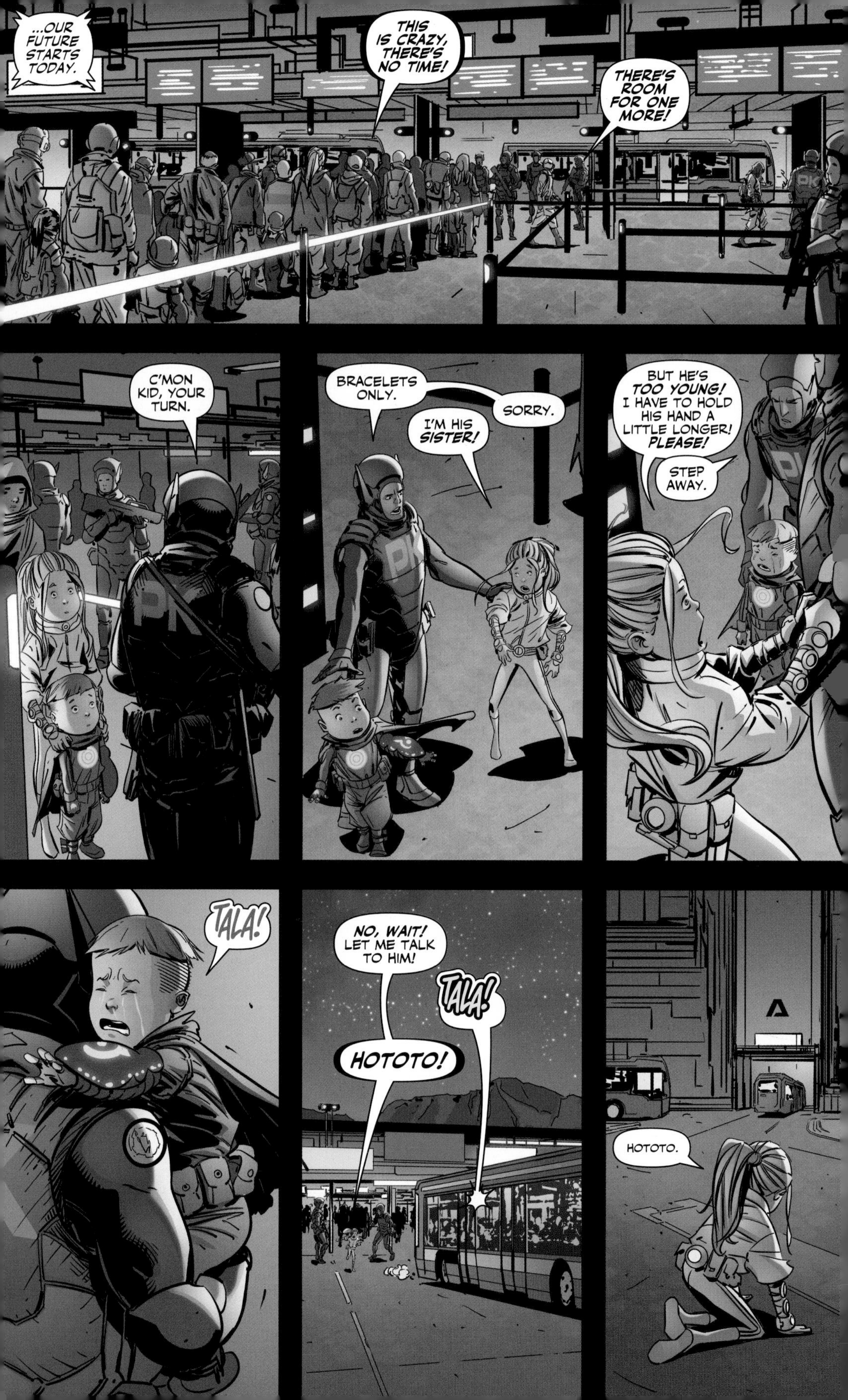
...OUR FUTURE STARTS TODAY.
THIS IS CRAZY, THERE'S NO TIME!
THERE'S ROOM FOR ONE MORE!
C'MON KID, YOUR TURN.
BRACELETS ONLY.
SORRY.
I'M HIS *SISTER!*
BUT HE'S *TOO YOUNG!* I HAVE TO HOLD HIS HAND A LITTLE LONGER! *PLEASE!*
STEP AWAY.
TALA!
NO, WAIT! LET ME TALK TO HIM!
HOTOTO!
TALA!
HOTOTO.

CRASSH!

AAAHHH!

BASTARDS!

NOW!

THE HELL WITH YOU!

MONSTERS!

LIARS!

THUNKK!

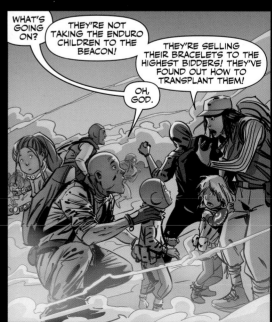

WHAT'S GOING ON?

THEY'RE NOT TAKING THE ENDURO CHILDREN TO THE BEACON!

THEY'RE SELLING THEIR BRACELETS TO THE HIGHEST BIDDERS! THEY'VE FOUND OUT HOW TO TRANSPLANT THEM!

OH, GOD.

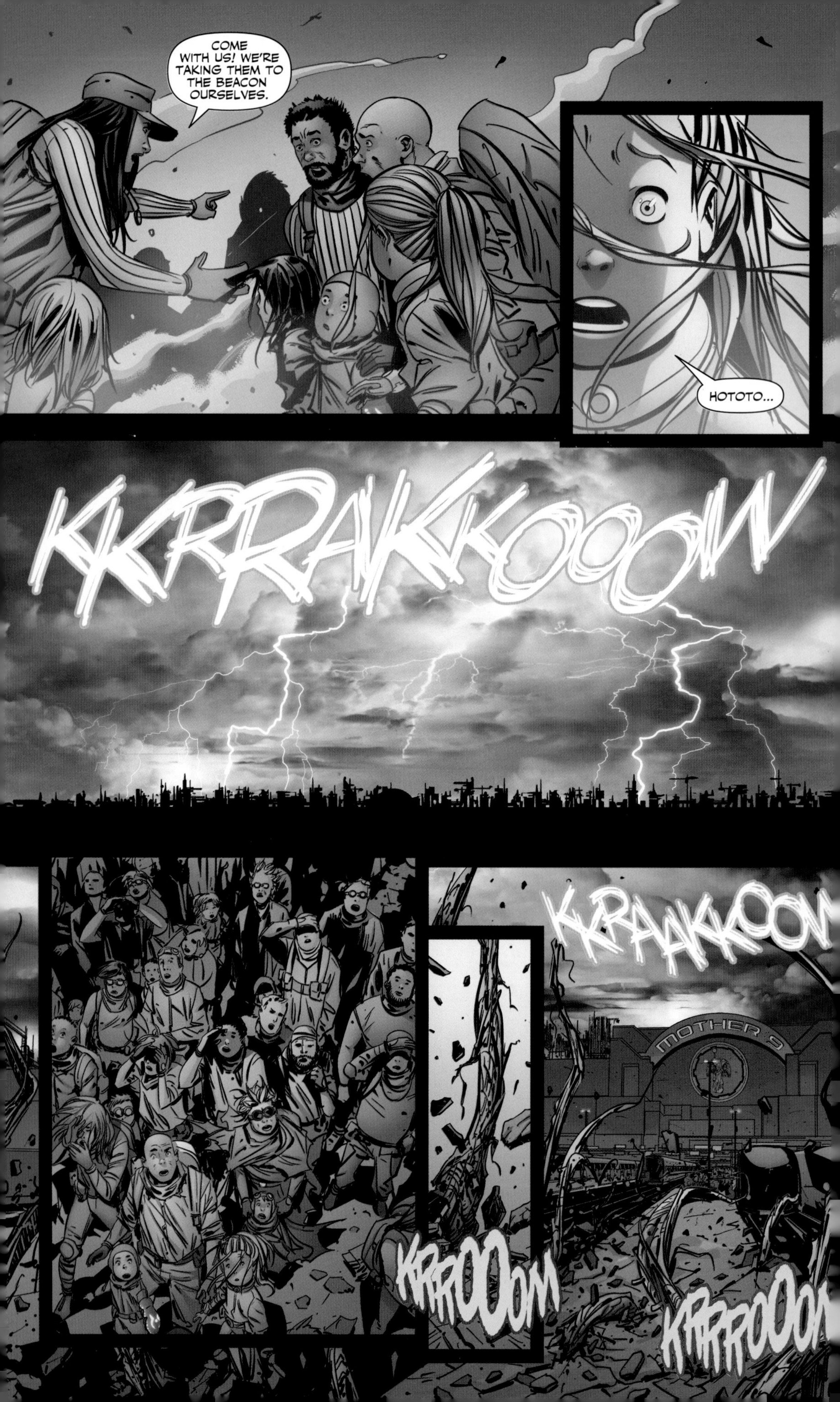
COME WITH US! WE'RE TAKING THEM TO THE BEACON OURSELVES.
HOTOTO...
KKRRAKKOOOOW
KKRAAKKOOM
MOTHER 9
KRROOOM
KRRROOOM

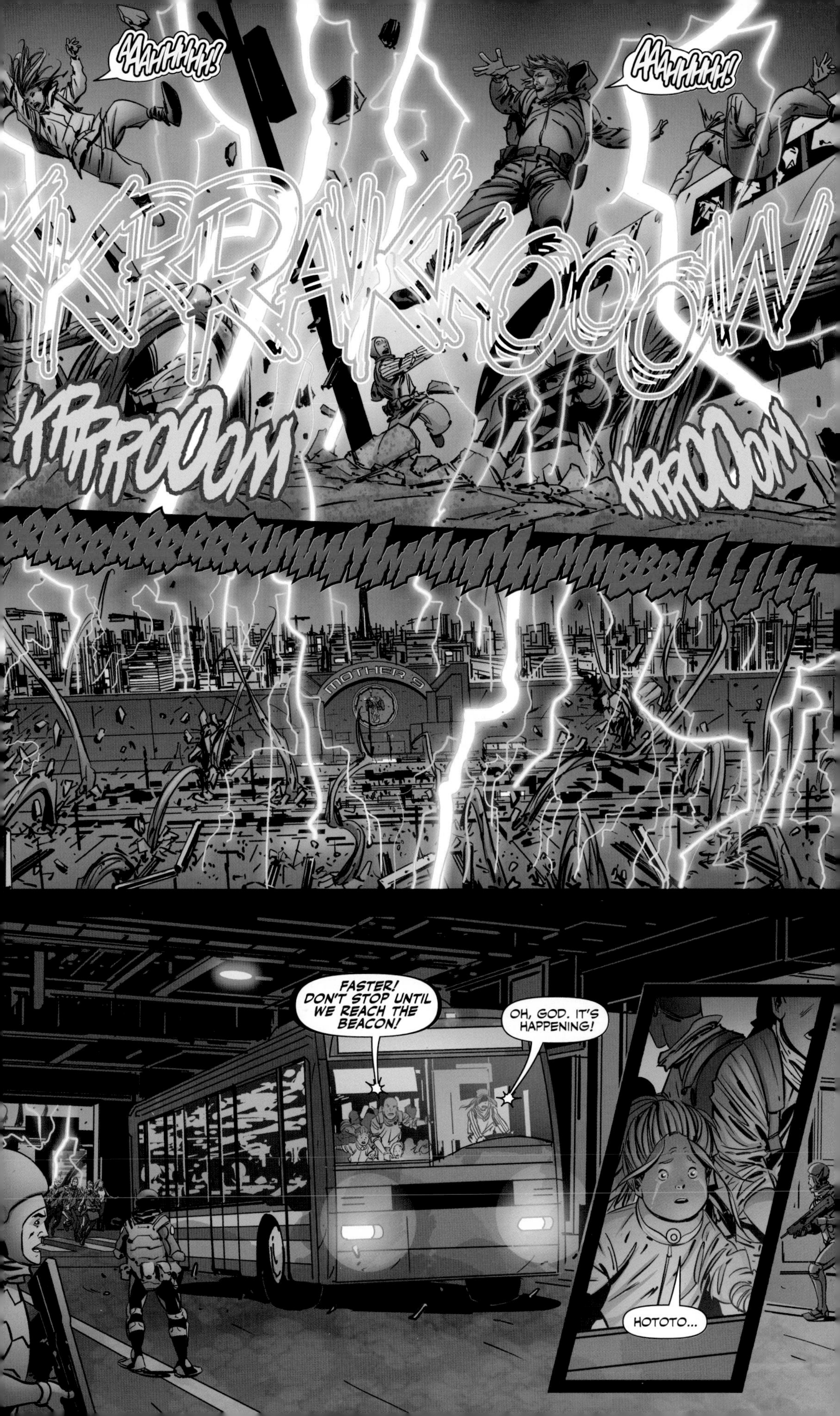
AAAHHHHH!
AAAHHHHH!
FASTER! DON'T STOP UNTIL WE REACH THE BEACON!
OH, GOD. IT'S HAPPENING!
HOTOTO...

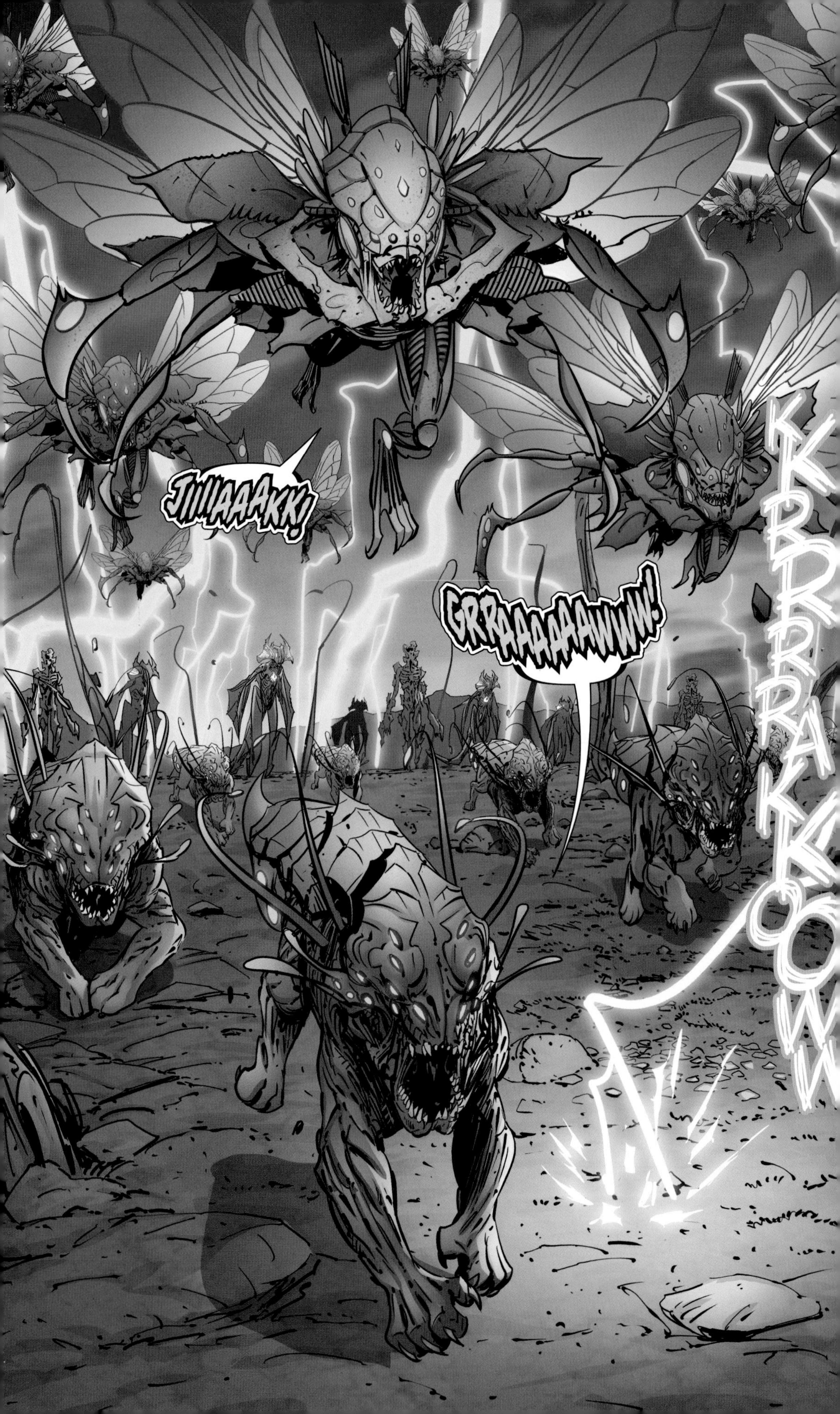
JIIIAAAKK!
GRRAAAAAAWWW!
KKRRRRAKKOOOW

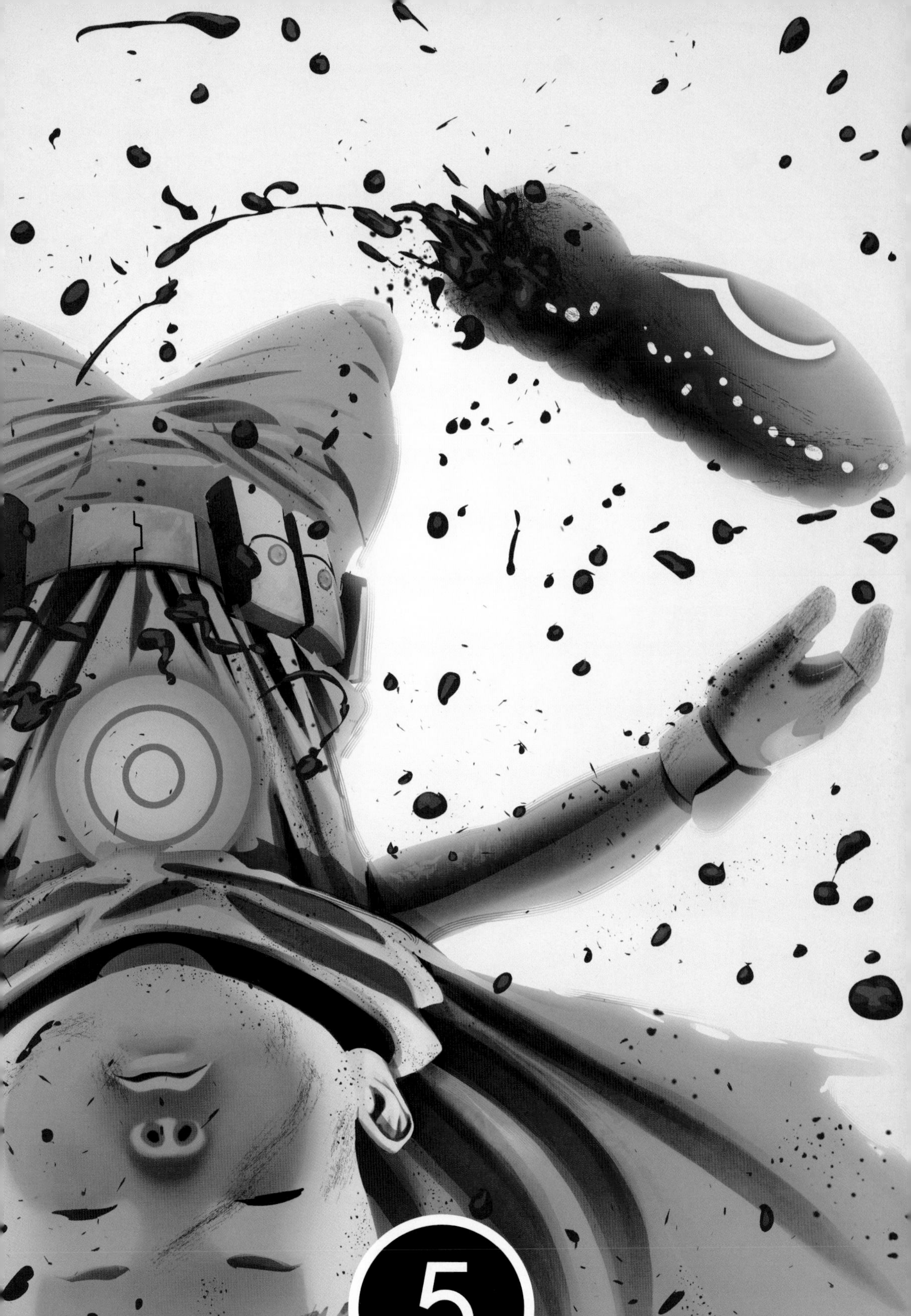

5

THE ERA OF THE PALLADIONS

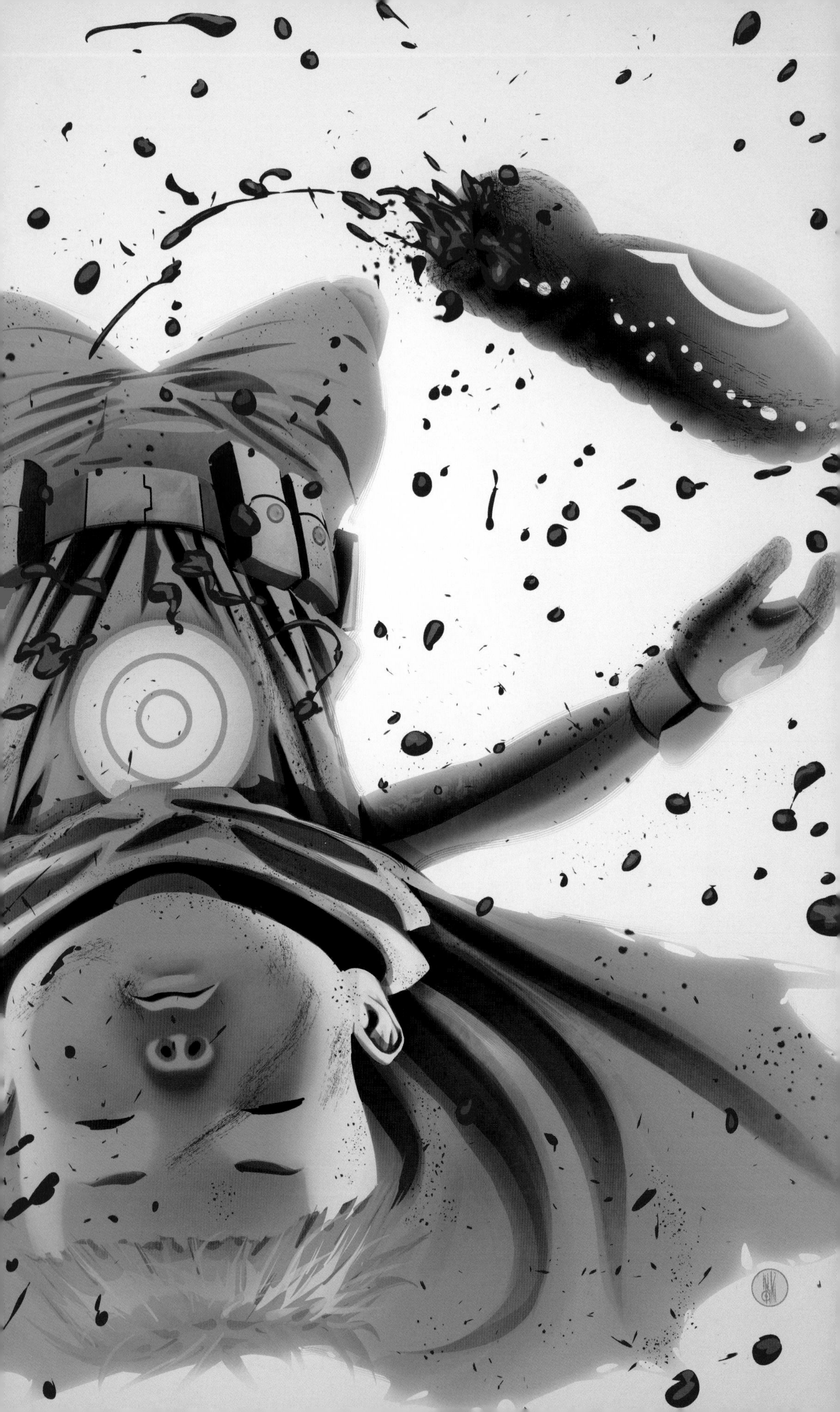

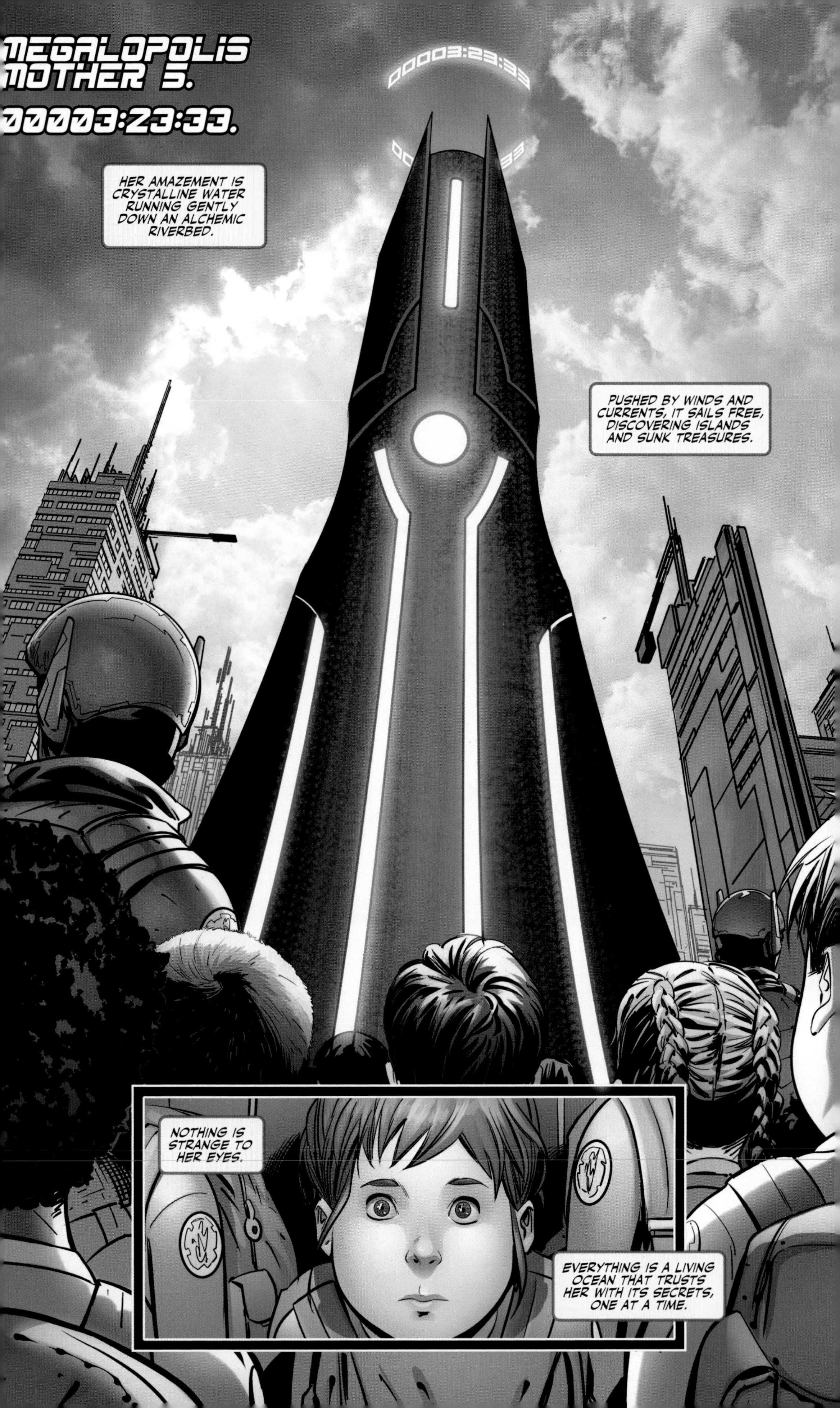
MEGALOPOLIS MOTHER 5.
00003:23:33.
00003:23:33
HER AMAZEMENT IS CRYSTALLINE WATER RUNNING GENTLY DOWN AN ALCHEMIC RIVERBED.
PUSHED BY WINDS AND CURRENTS, IT SAILS FREE, DISCOVERING ISLANDS AND SUNK TREASURES.
NOTHING IS STRANGE TO HER EYES.
EVERYTHING IS A LIVING OCEAN THAT TRUSTS HER WITH ITS SECRETS, ONE AT A TIME.

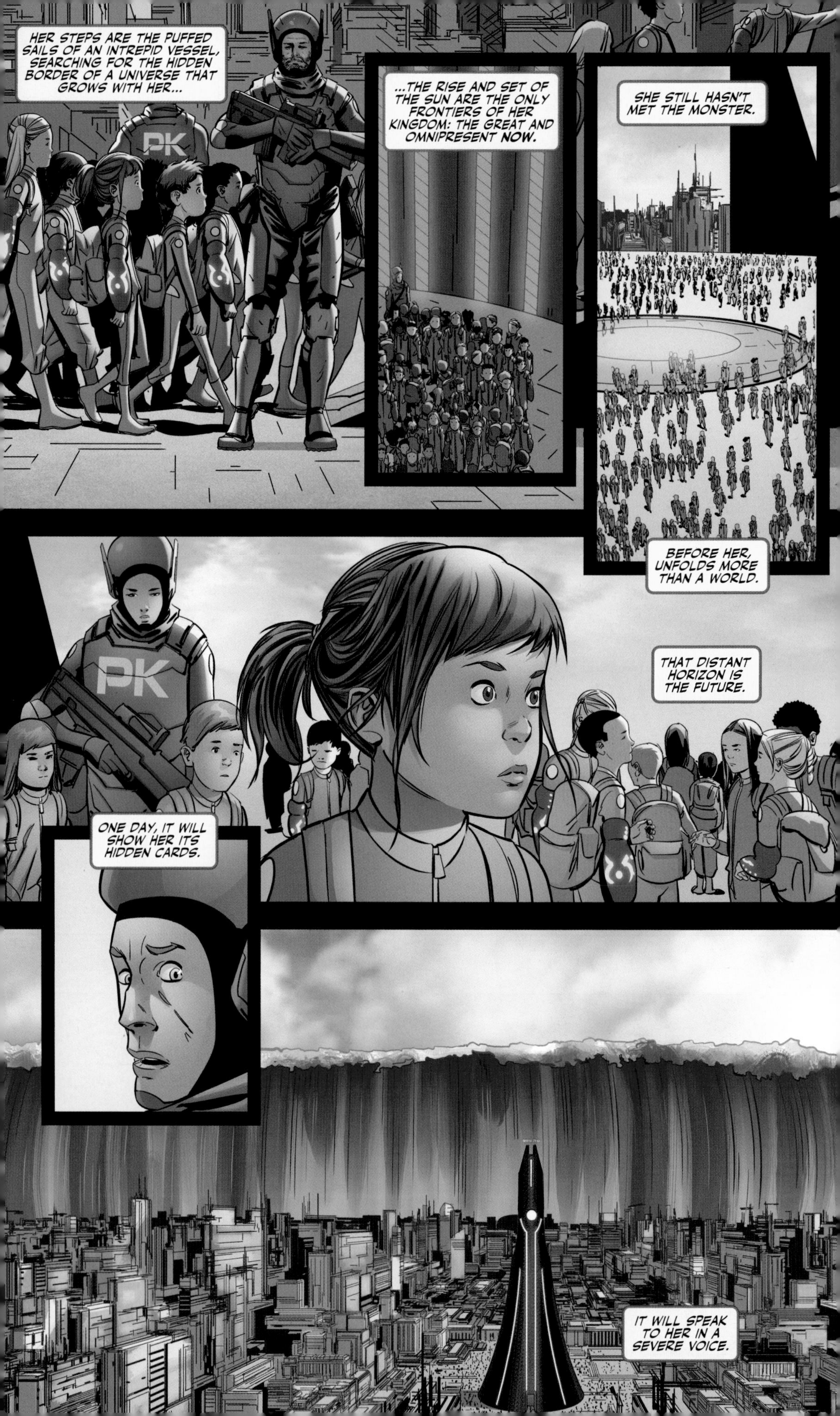
HER STEPS ARE THE PUFFED SAILS OF AN INTREPID VESSEL, SEARCHING FOR THE HIDDEN BORDER OF A UNIVERSE THAT GROWS WITH HER...
...THE RISE AND SET OF THE SUN ARE THE ONLY FRONTIERS OF HER KINGDOM: THE GREAT AND OMNIPRESENT NOW.
SHE STILL HASN'T MET THE MONSTER.
BEFORE HER, UNFOLDS MORE THAN A WORLD.
PK
PK
THAT DISTANT HORIZON IS THE FUTURE.
ONE DAY, IT WILL SHOW HER ITS HIDDEN CARDS.
IT WILL SPEAK TO HER IN A SEVERE VOICE.

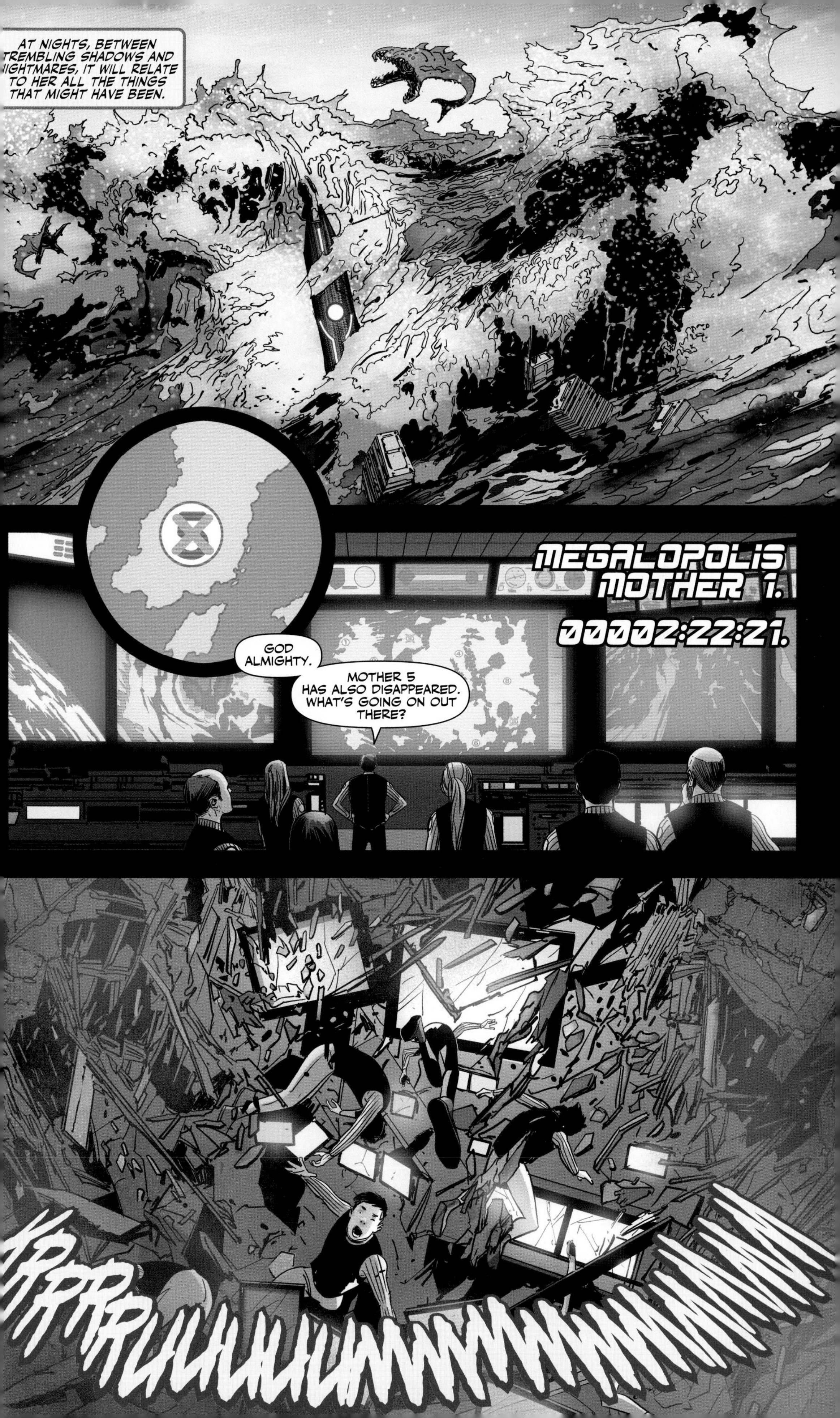
AT NIGHTS, BETWEEN TREMBLING SHADOWS AND NIGHTMARES, IT WILL RELATE TO HER ALL THE THINGS THAT MIGHT HAVE BEEN.
MEGALOPOLIS MOTHER 1.
00002:22:21.
GOD ALMIGHTY.
MOTHER 5 HAS ALSO DISAPPEARED. WHAT'S GOING ON OUT THERE?
KRRRRUUUUMMMMMMMM

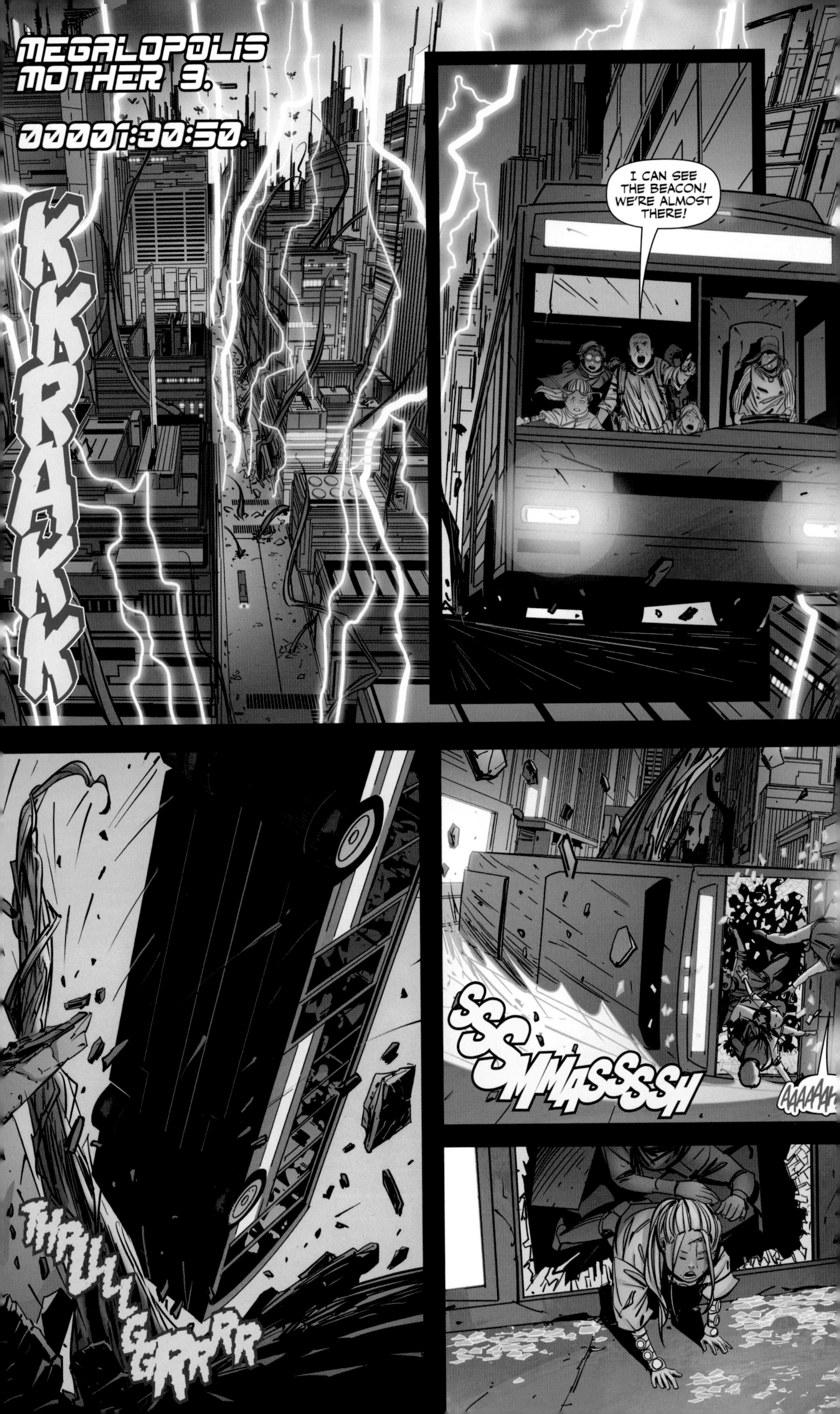
MEGALOPOLIS MOTHER 9.
00001:30:50.
KKRAKK
I CAN SEE THE BEACON! WE'RE ALMOST THERE!
THRULLGRRR
SSSMMASSSSH
AAAAAH

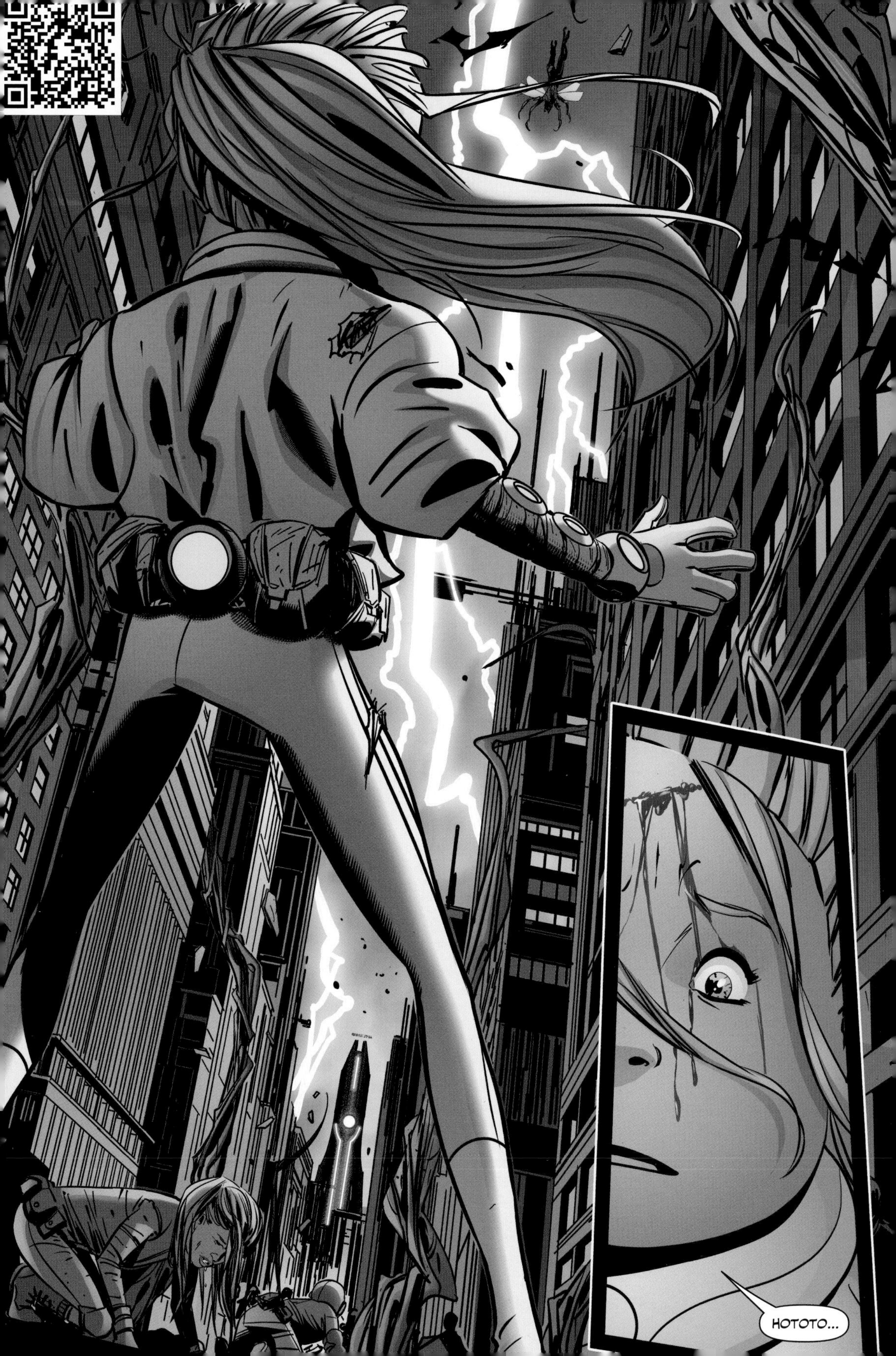
HOTOTO...

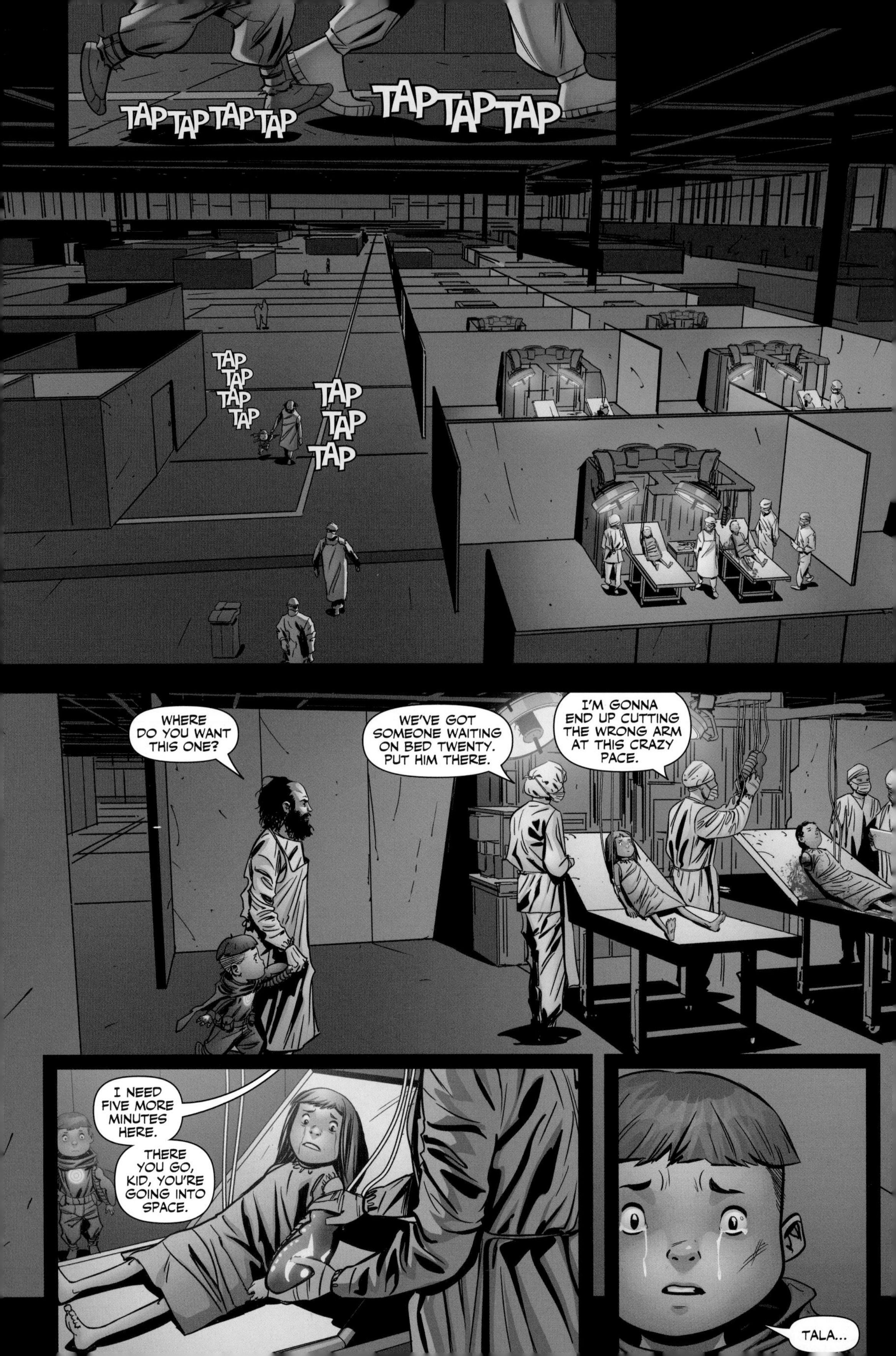
TAP TAP TAP TAP
TAP TAP TAP
TAP
TAP
TAP
TAP
TAP
TAP
TAP
WHERE DO YOU WANT THIS ONE?
WE'VE GOT SOMEONE WAITING ON BED TWENTY. PUT HIM THERE.
I'M GONNA END UP CUTTING THE WRONG ARM AT THIS CRAZY PACE.
I NEED FIVE MORE MINUTES HERE.
THERE YOU GO, KID, YOU'RE GOING INTO SPACE.
TALA...

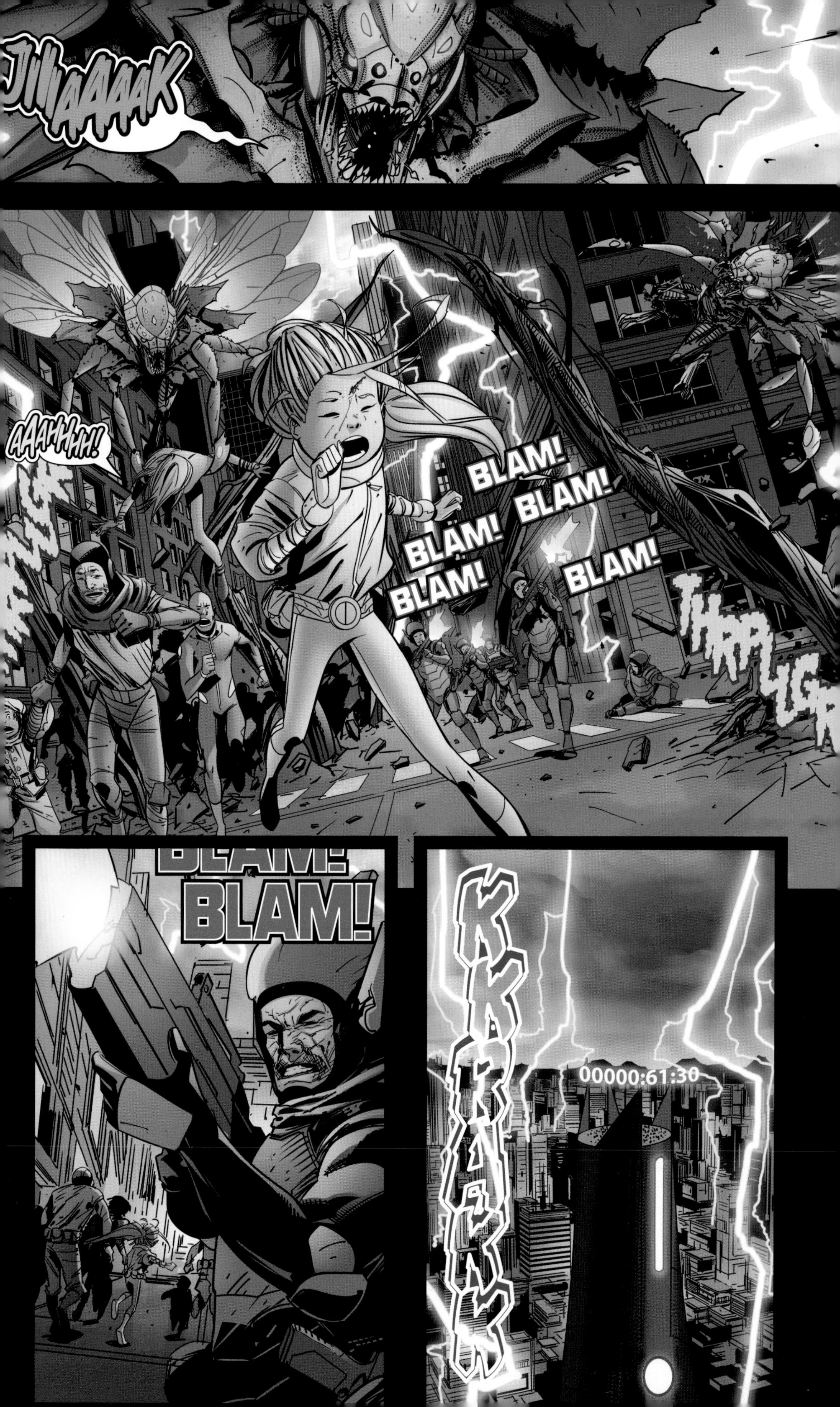
JIIIAAAAAK
AAAHHHH!
BLAM!
BLAM! BLAM!
BLAM!
BLAM!
BLAM!
BLAM!
00000:61:30

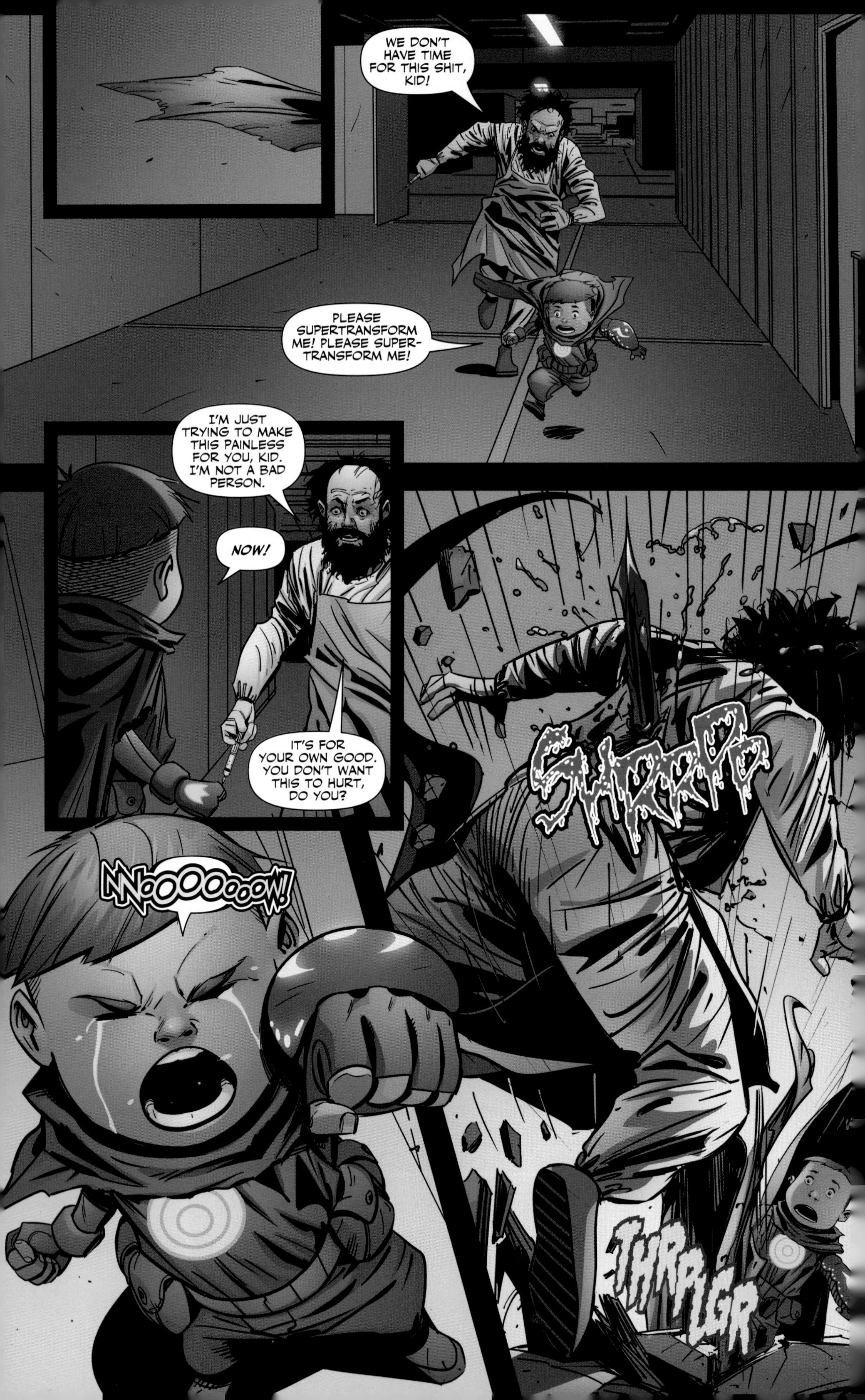
WE DON'T HAVE TIME FOR THIS SHIT, KID!
PLEASE SUPERTRANSFORM ME! PLEASE SUPER-TRANSFORM ME!
I'M JUST TRYING TO MAKE THIS PAINLESS FOR YOU, KID. I'M NOT A BAD PERSON.
NOW!
IT'S FOR YOUR OWN GOOD. YOU DON'T WANT THIS TO HURT, DO YOU?
NNOOOOOOOOOW!
SHTRRPP
THRRLGR

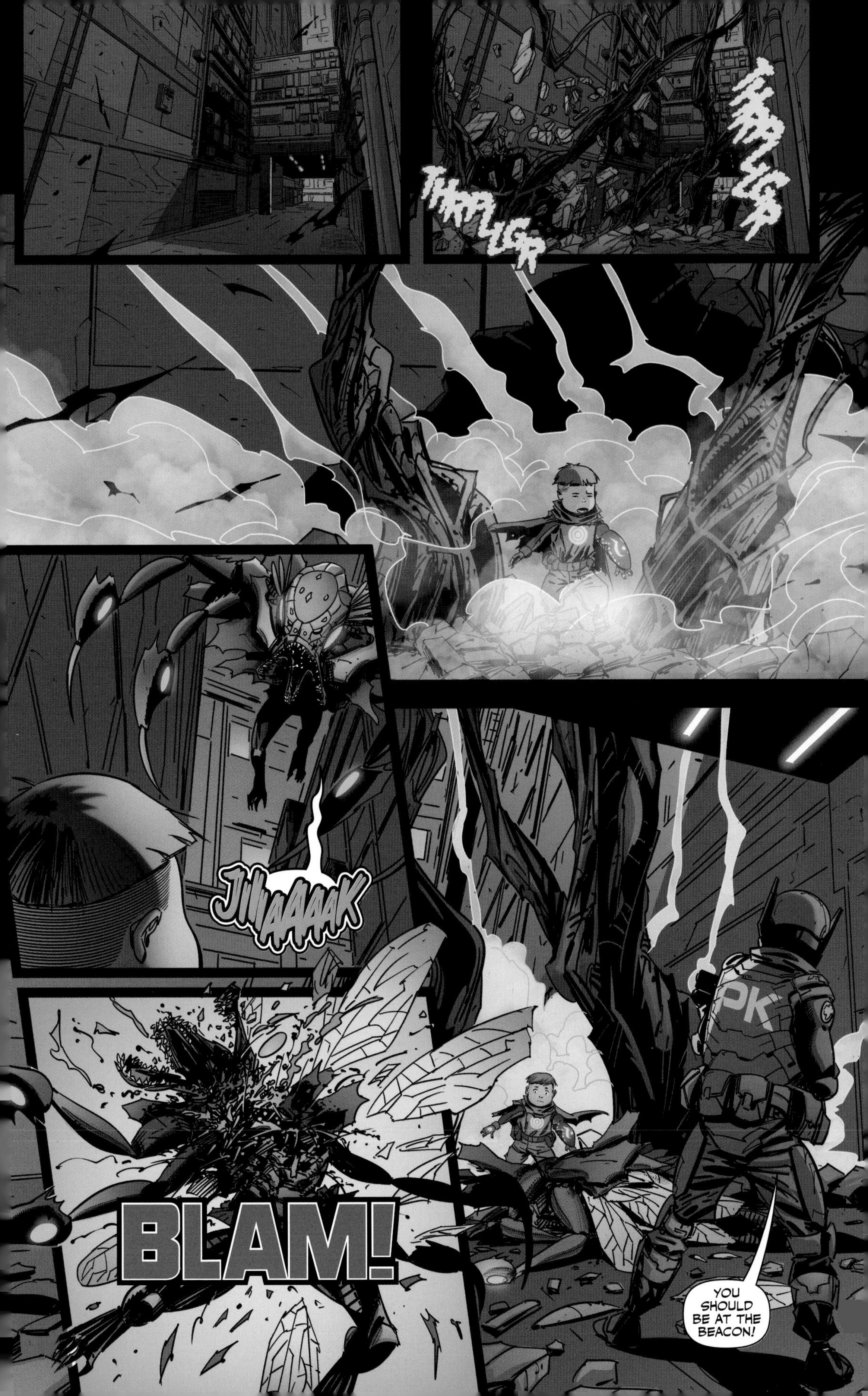
THRFLLGR
THRFLLGR
JIIIAAAAK
BLAM!
YOU SHOULD BE AT THE BEACON!

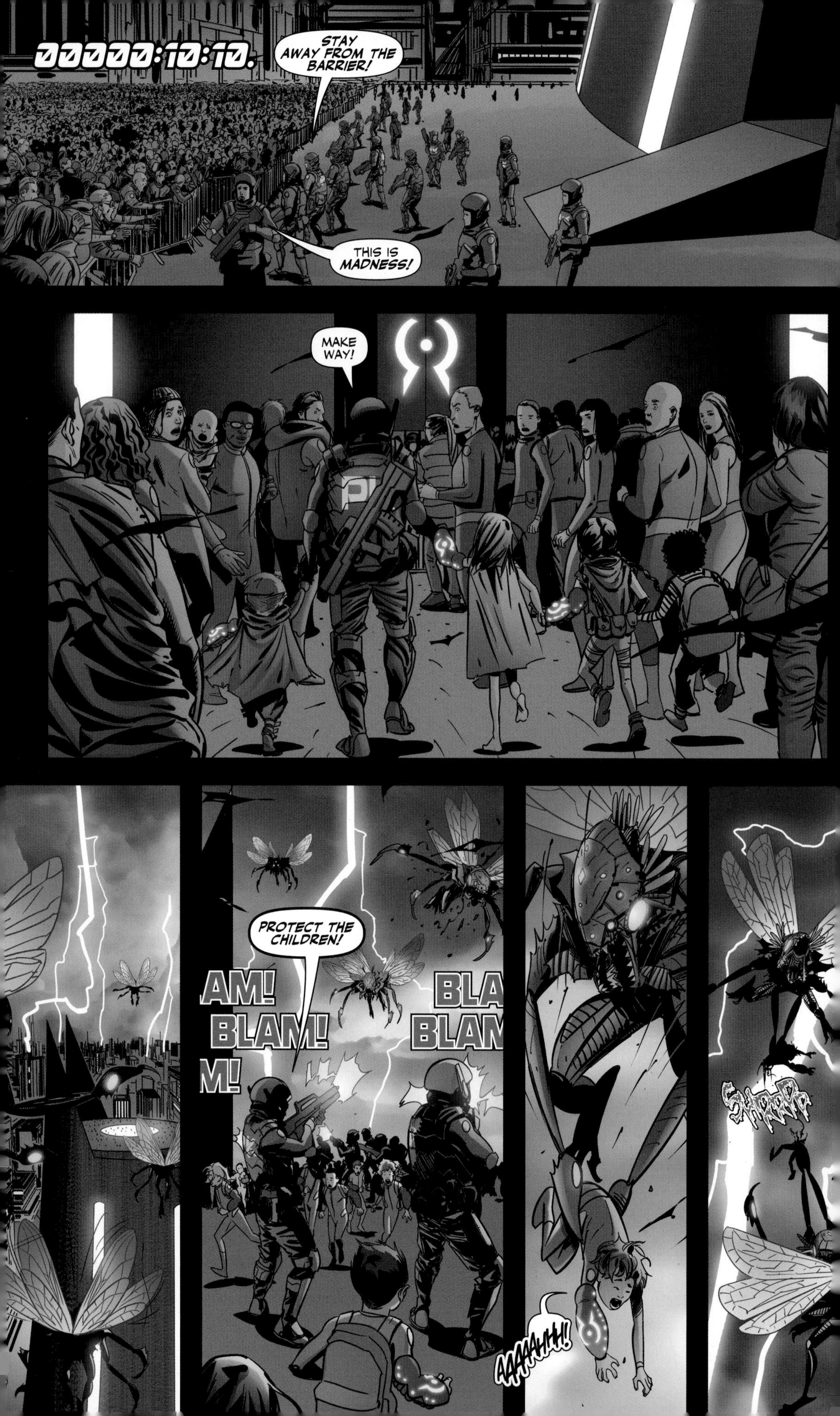
00000:10:10.
STAY AWAY FROM THE BARRIER!
THIS IS MADNESS!
MAKE WAY!
PROTECT THE CHILDREN!
AM! BLAM! M!
BLA BLAM
AAAAAHHH!

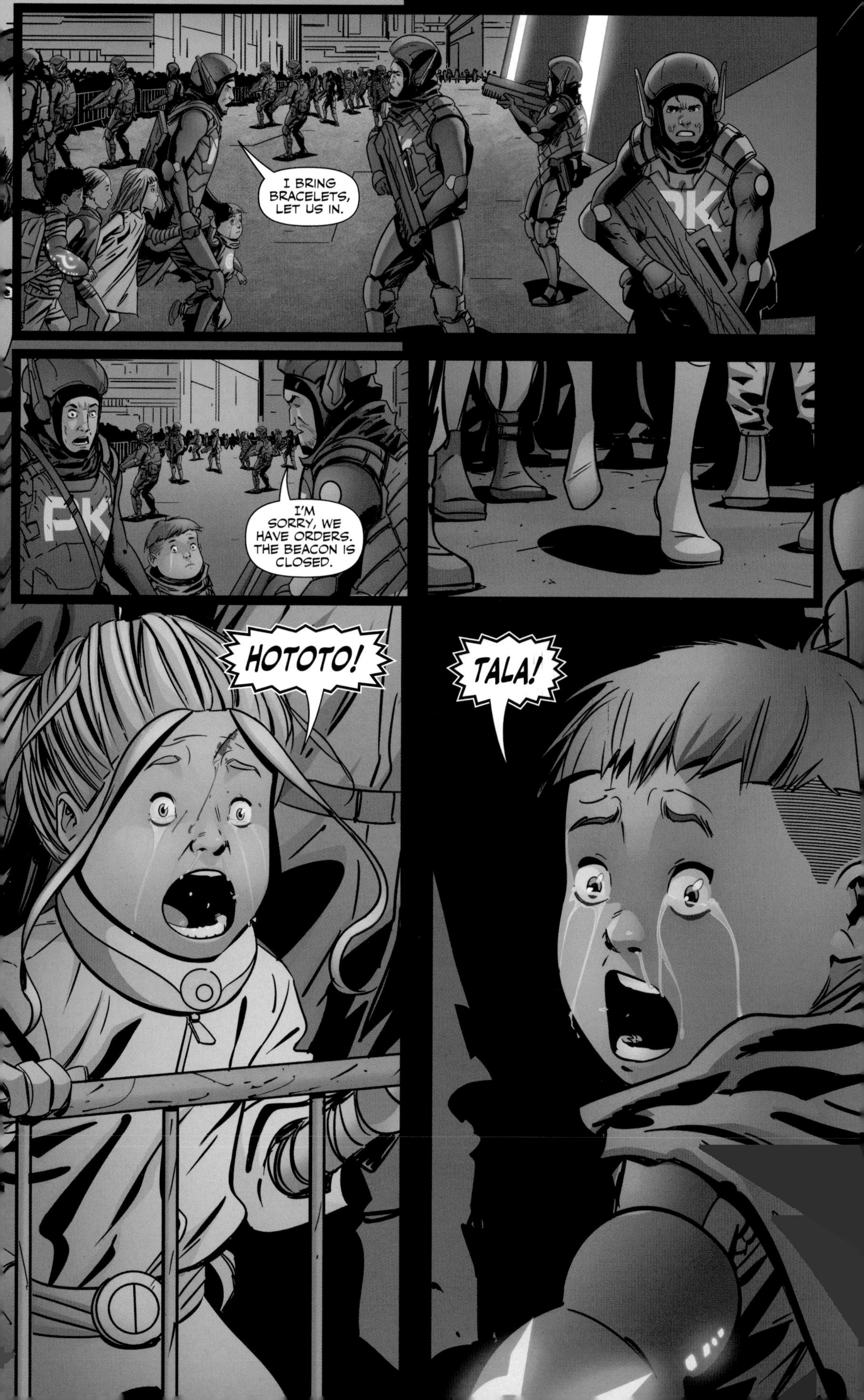
I BRING BRACELETS, LET US IN.
I'M SORRY, WE HAVE ORDERS. THE BEACON IS CLOSED.
HOTOTO!
TALA!

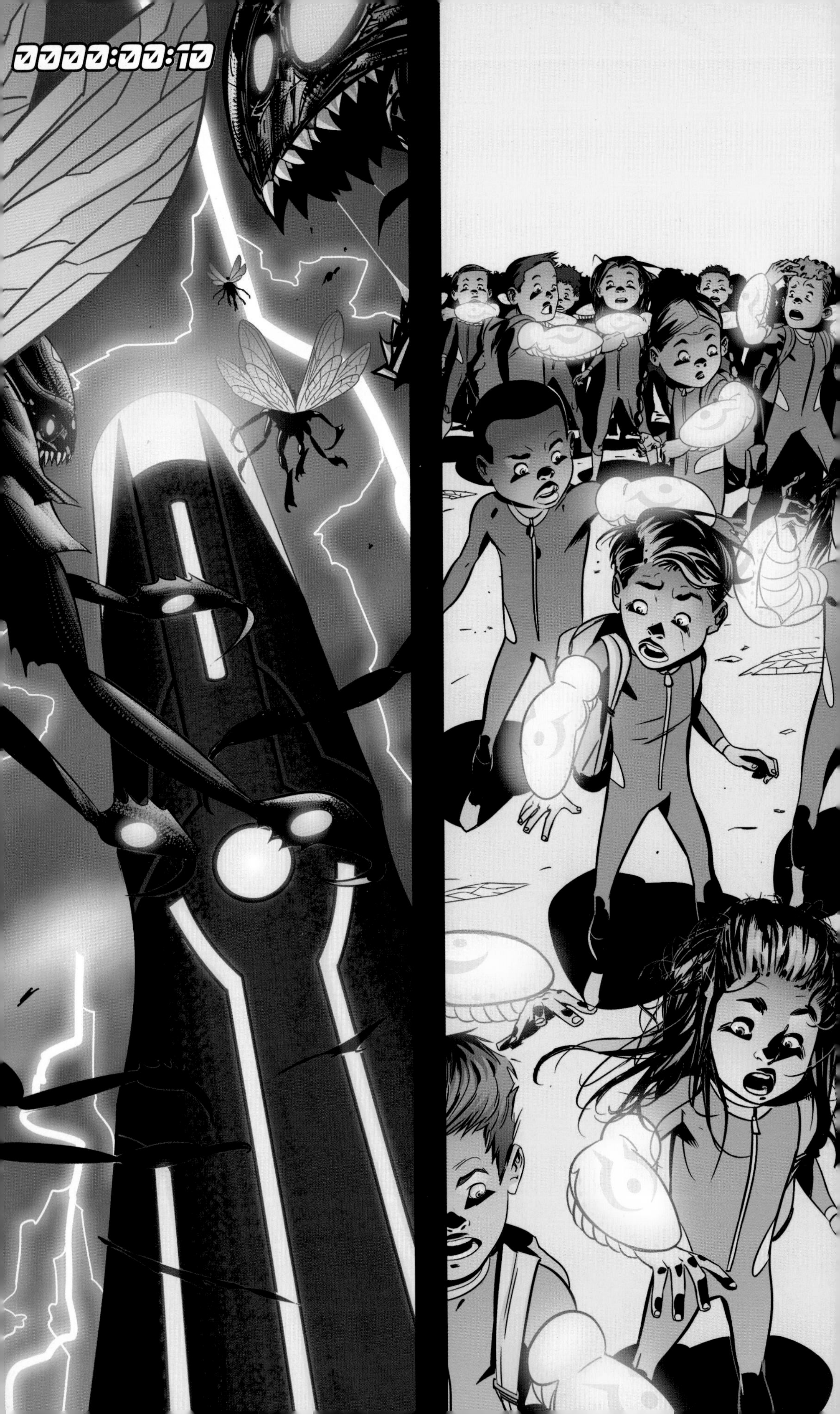
0000:00:10

0000000:00:00

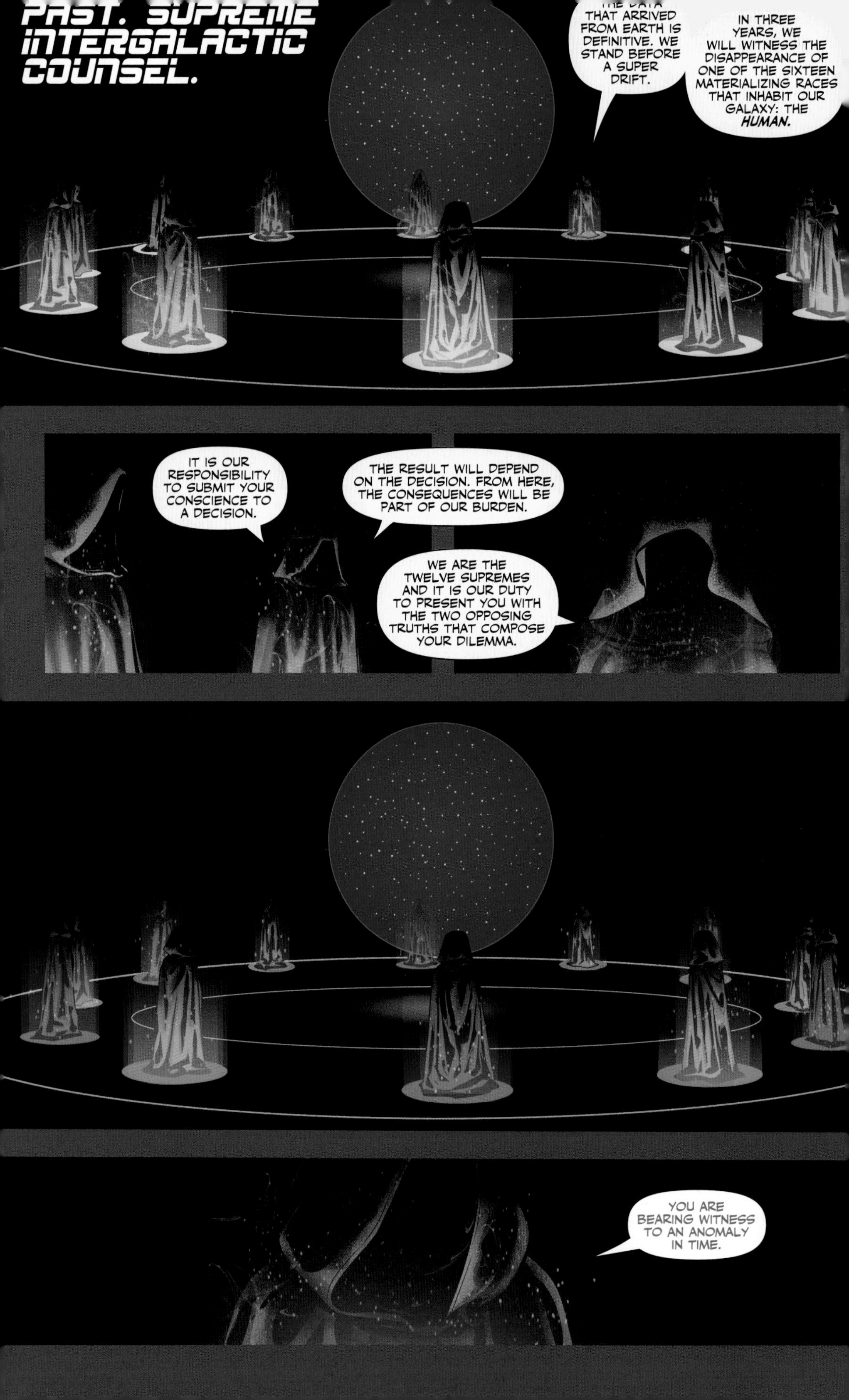
PAST. SUPREME INTERGALACTIC COUNSEL.
THAT ARRIVED FROM EARTH IS DEFINITIVE. WE STAND BEFORE A SUPER DRIFT.
IN THREE YEARS, WE WILL WITNESS THE DISAPPEARANCE OF ONE OF THE SIXTEEN MATERIALIZING RACES THAT INHABIT OUR GALAXY: THE *HUMAN.*
IT IS OUR RESPONSIBILITY TO SUBMIT YOUR CONSCIENCE TO A DECISION.
THE RESULT WILL DEPEND ON THE DECISION. FROM HERE, THE CONSEQUENCES WILL BE PART OF OUR BURDEN.
WE ARE THE TWELVE SUPREMES AND IT IS OUR DUTY TO PRESENT YOU WITH THE TWO OPPOSING TRUTHS THAT COMPOSE YOUR DILEMMA.
YOU ARE BEARING WITNESS TO AN ANOMALY IN TIME.

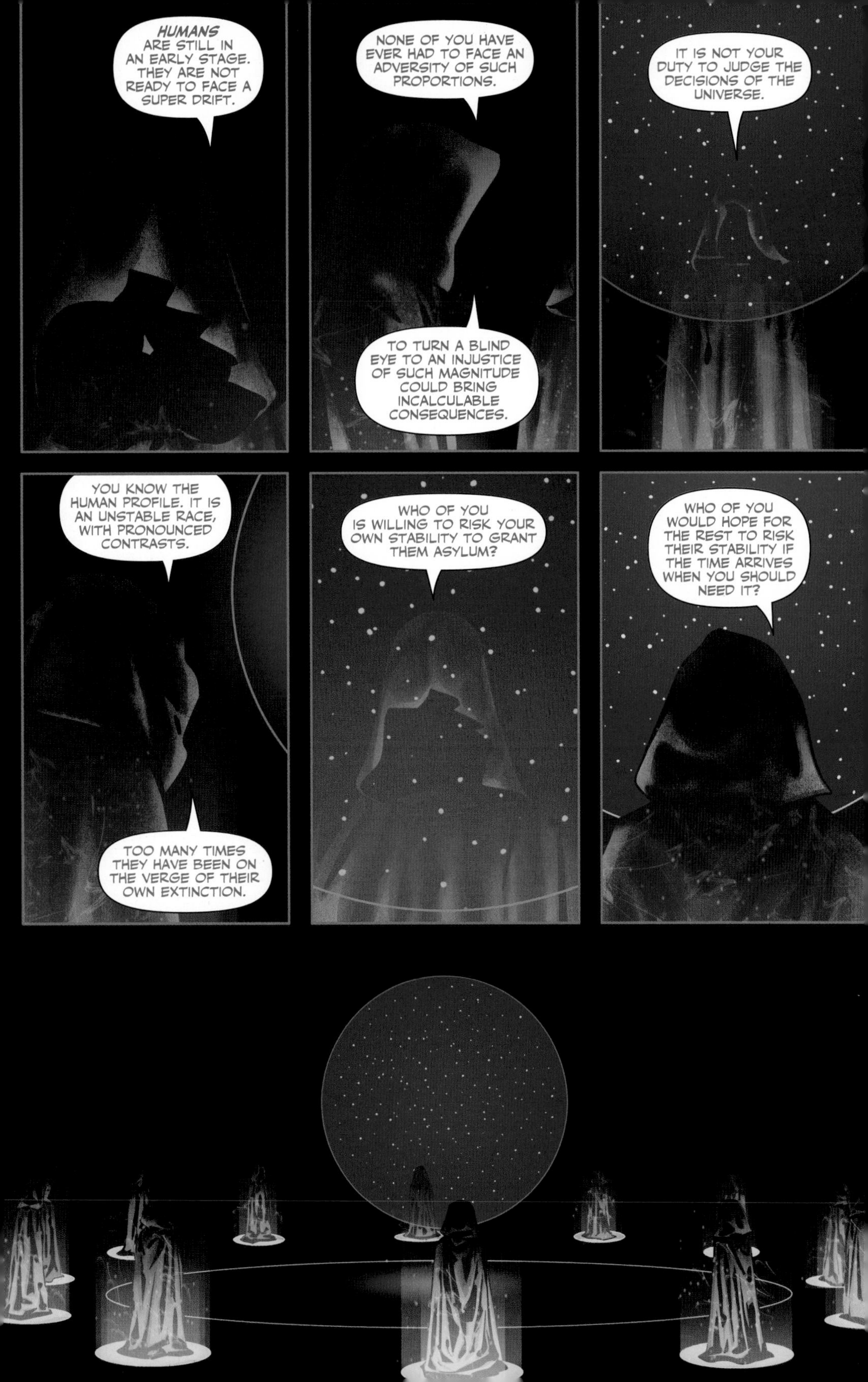

HUMANS ARE STILL IN AN EARLY STAGE. THEY ARE NOT READY TO FACE A SUPER DRIFT.
NONE OF YOU HAVE EVER HAD TO FACE AN ADVERSITY OF SUCH PROPORTIONS.
TO TURN A BLIND EYE TO AN INJUSTICE OF SUCH MAGNITUDE COULD BRING INCALCULABLE CONSEQUENCES.
IT IS NOT YOUR DUTY TO JUDGE THE DECISIONS OF THE UNIVERSE.
YOU KNOW THE HUMAN PROFILE. IT IS AN UNSTABLE RACE, WITH PRONOUNCED CONTRASTS.
TOO MANY TIMES THEY HAVE BEEN ON THE VERGE OF THEIR OWN EXTINCTION.
WHO OF YOU IS WILLING TO RISK YOUR OWN STABILITY TO GRANT THEM ASYLUM?
WHO OF YOU WOULD HOPE FOR THE REST TO RISK THEIR STABILITY IF THE TIME ARRIVES WHEN YOU SHOULD NEED IT?

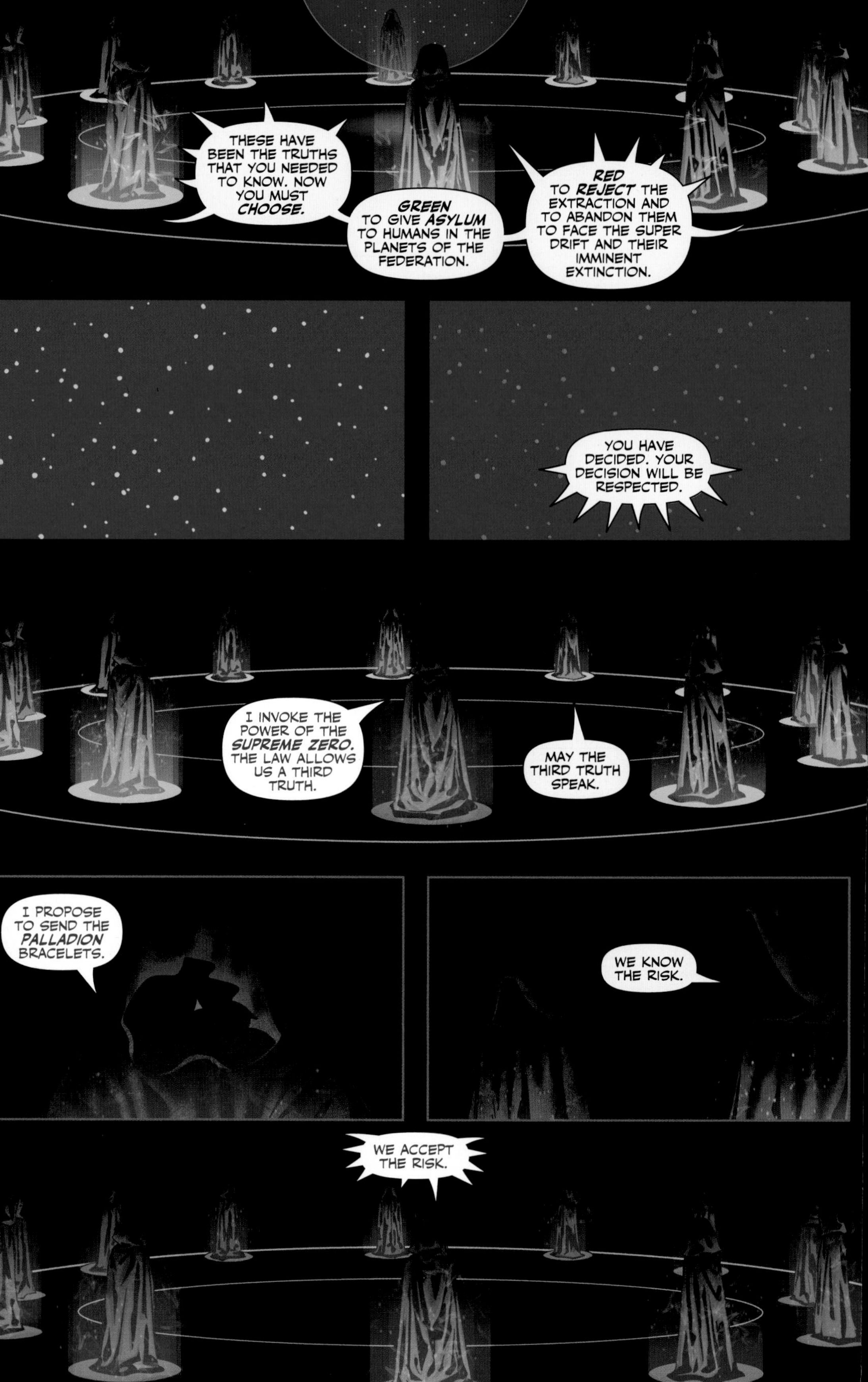
THESE HAVE BEEN THE TRUTHS THAT YOU NEEDED TO KNOW. NOW YOU MUST *CHOOSE.*
GREEN TO GIVE *ASYLUM* TO HUMANS IN THE PLANETS OF THE FEDERATION.
RED TO *REJECT* THE EXTRACTION AND TO ABANDON THEM TO FACE THE SUPER DRIFT AND THEIR IMMINENT EXTINCTION.
YOU HAVE DECIDED. YOUR DECISION WILL BE RESPECTED.
I INVOKE THE POWER OF THE *SUPREME ZERO.* THE LAW ALLOWS US A THIRD TRUTH.
MAY THE THIRD TRUTH SPEAK.
I PROPOSE TO SEND THE *PALLADION* BRACELETS.
WE KNOW THE RISK.
WE ACCEPT THE RISK.

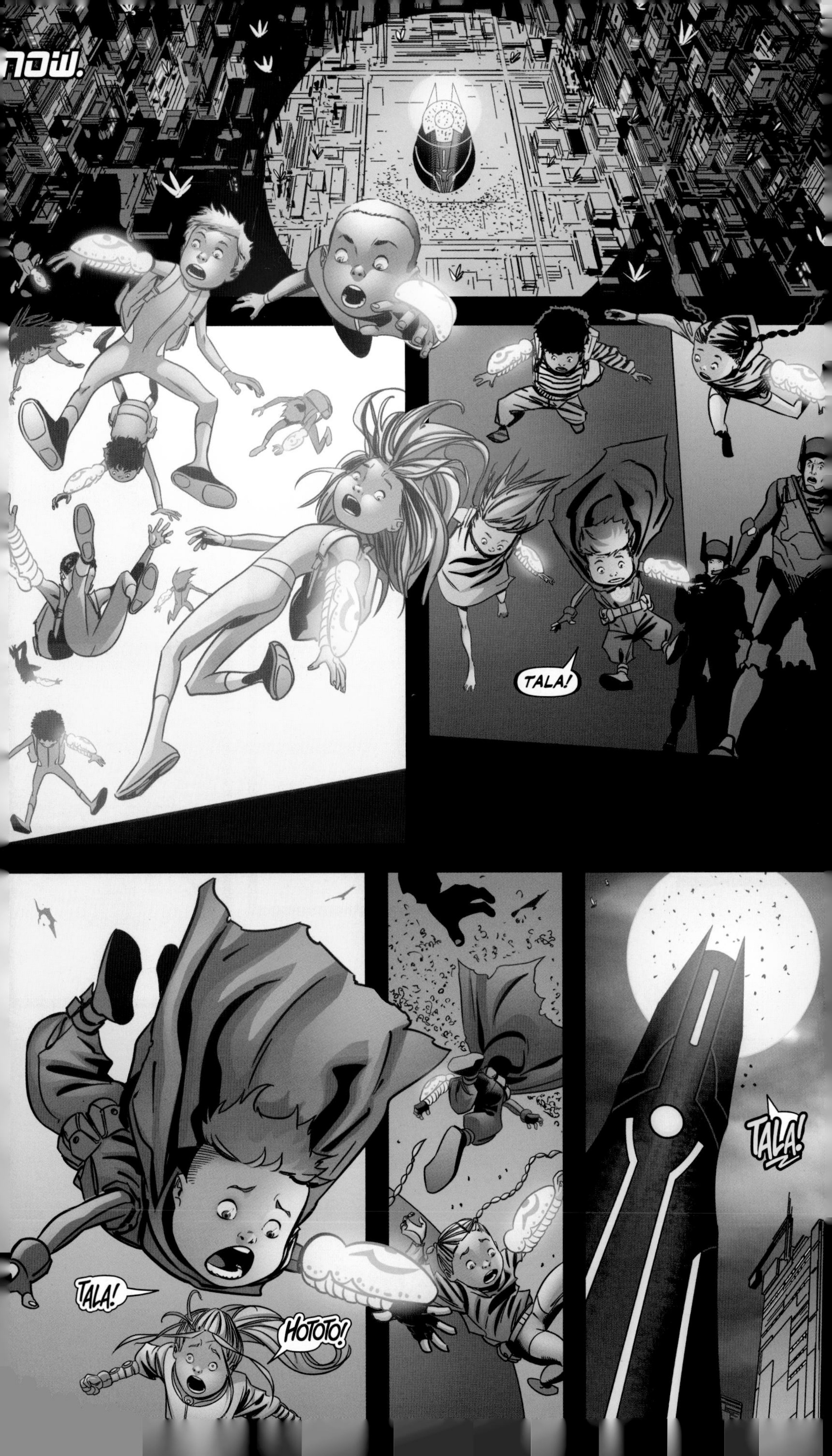
NOW.
TALA!
TALA!
HOTOTO!
TALA!

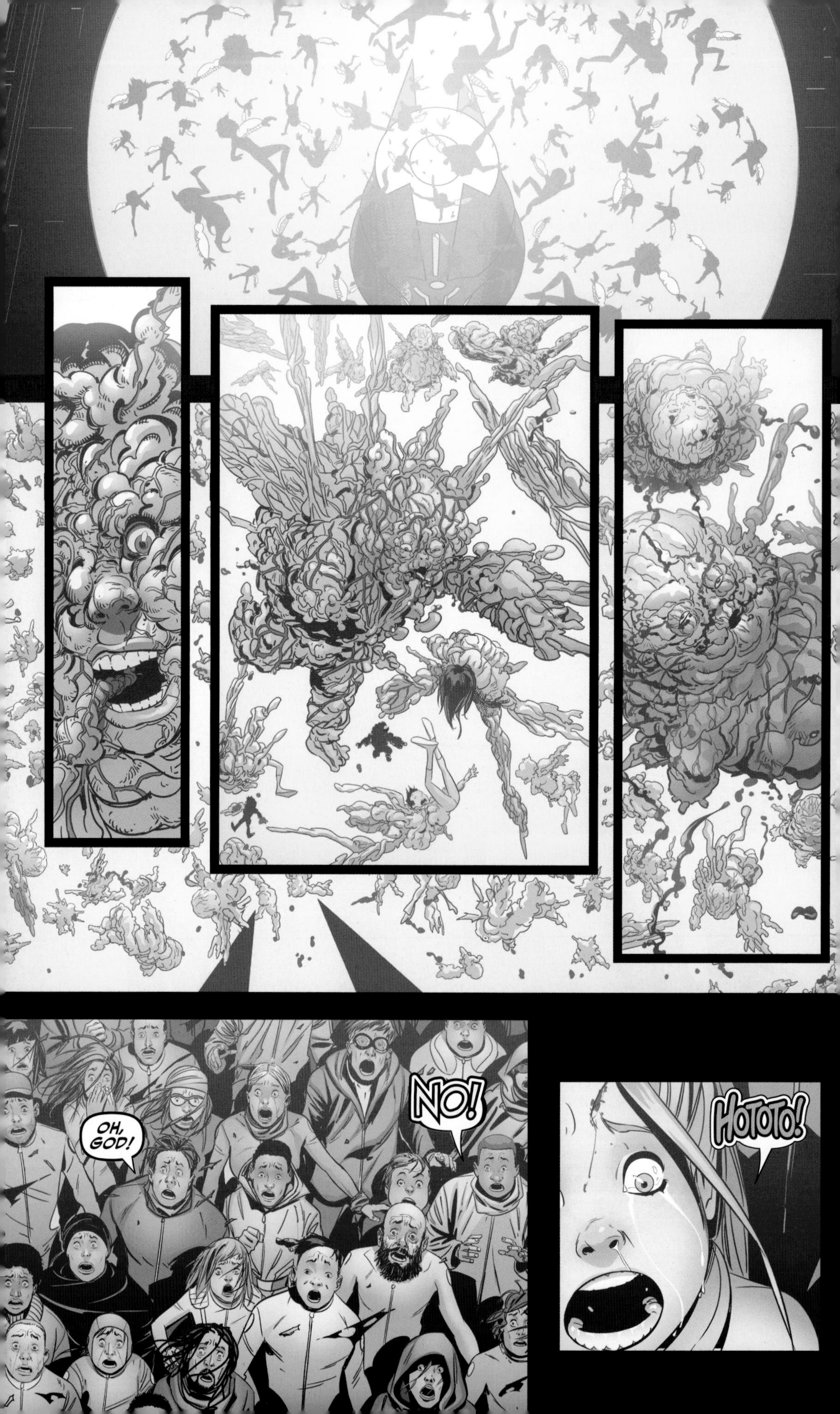
OH, GOD!
NO!
HOTOTO!

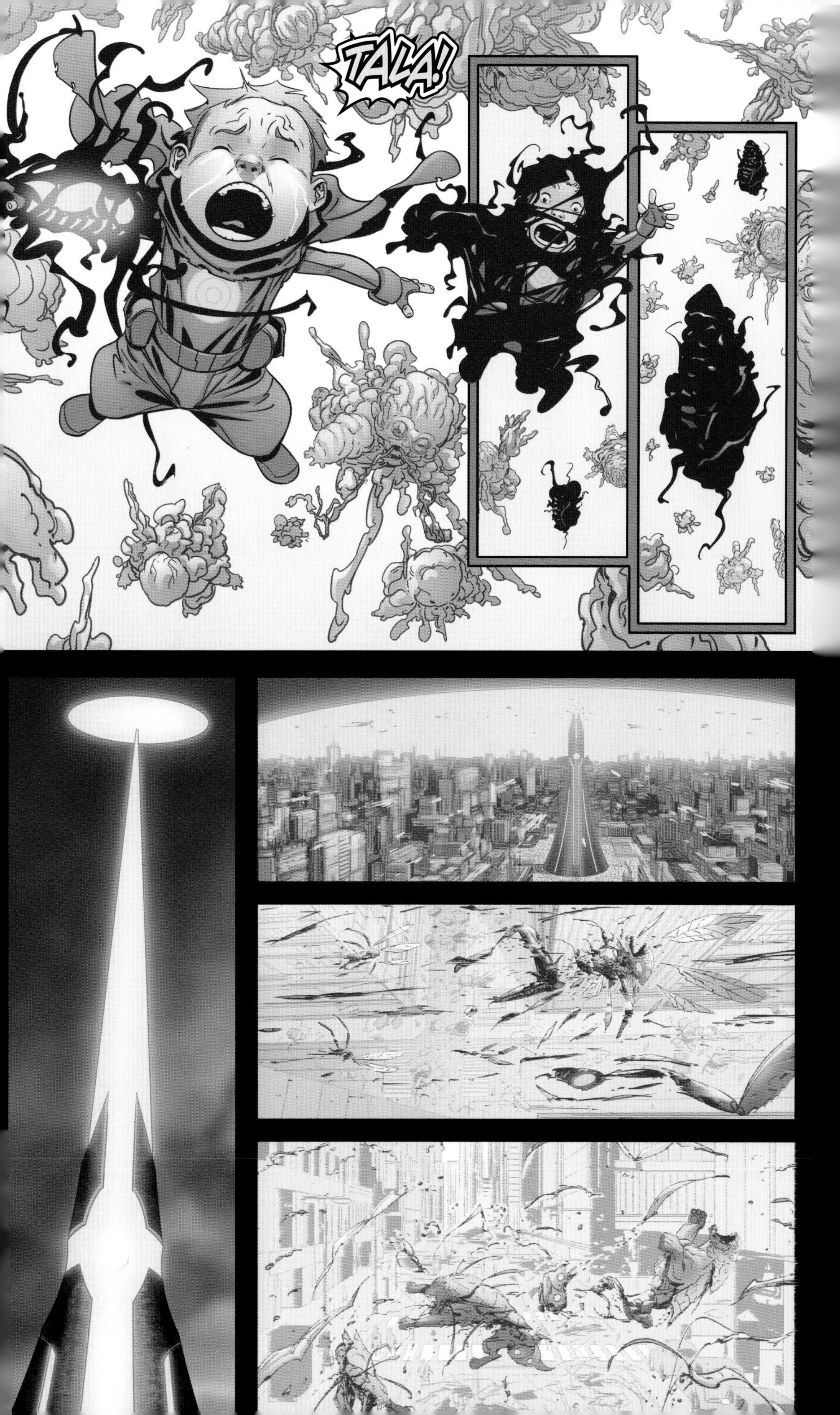
TALA!

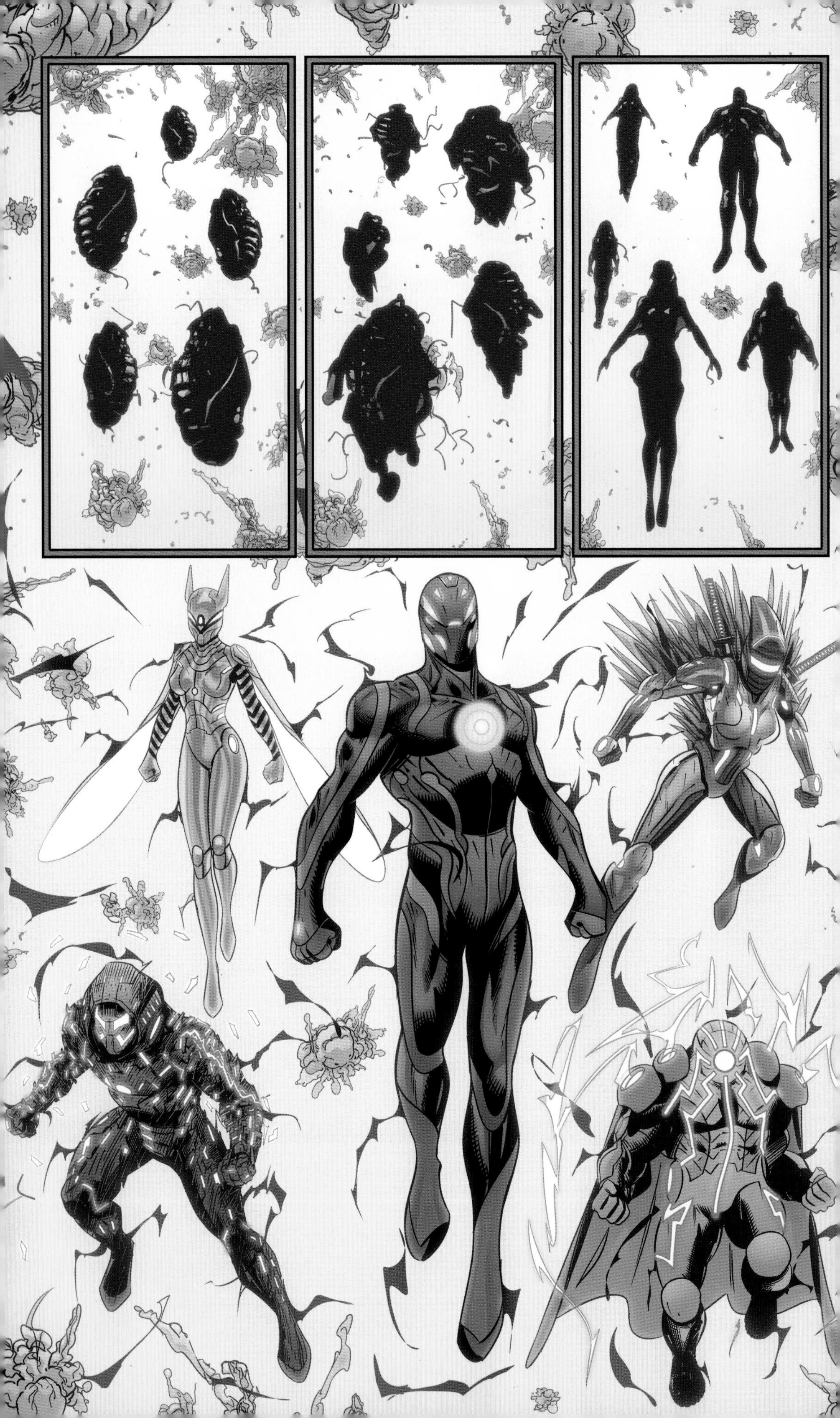

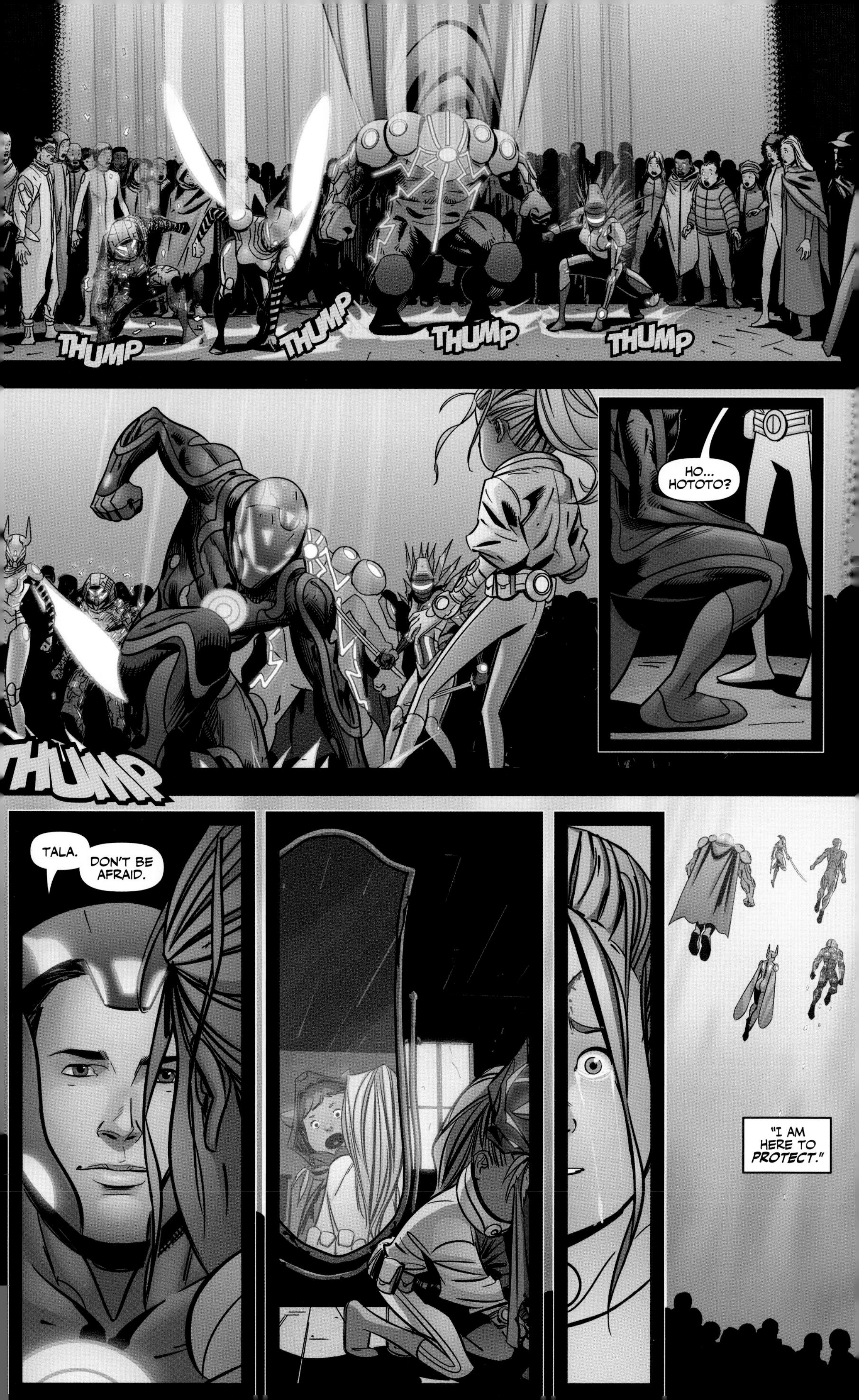
THUMP
THUMP
THUMP
THUMP
THUMP
HO... HOTOTO?
TALA.
DON'T BE AFRAID.
"I AM HERE TO *PROTECT.*"

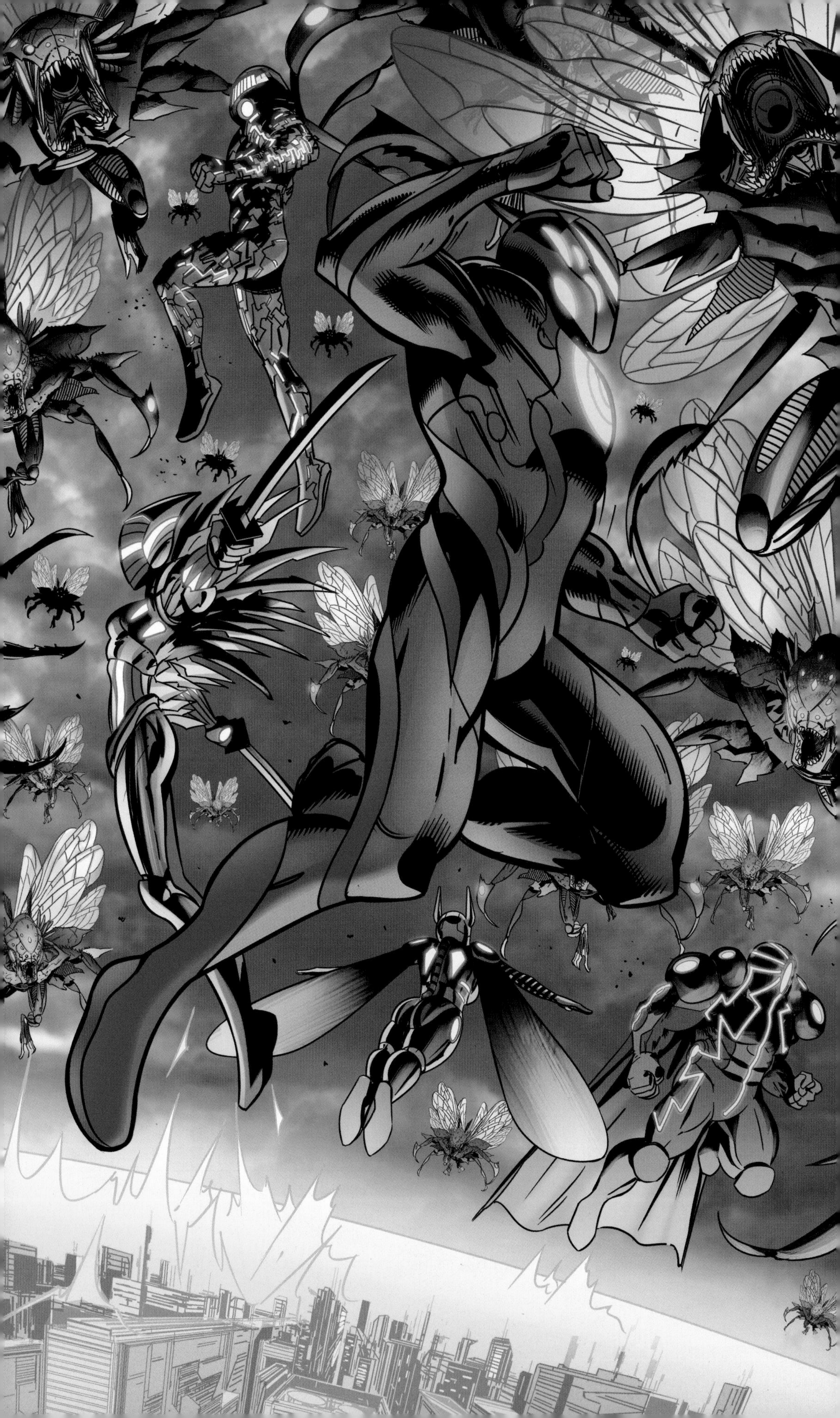

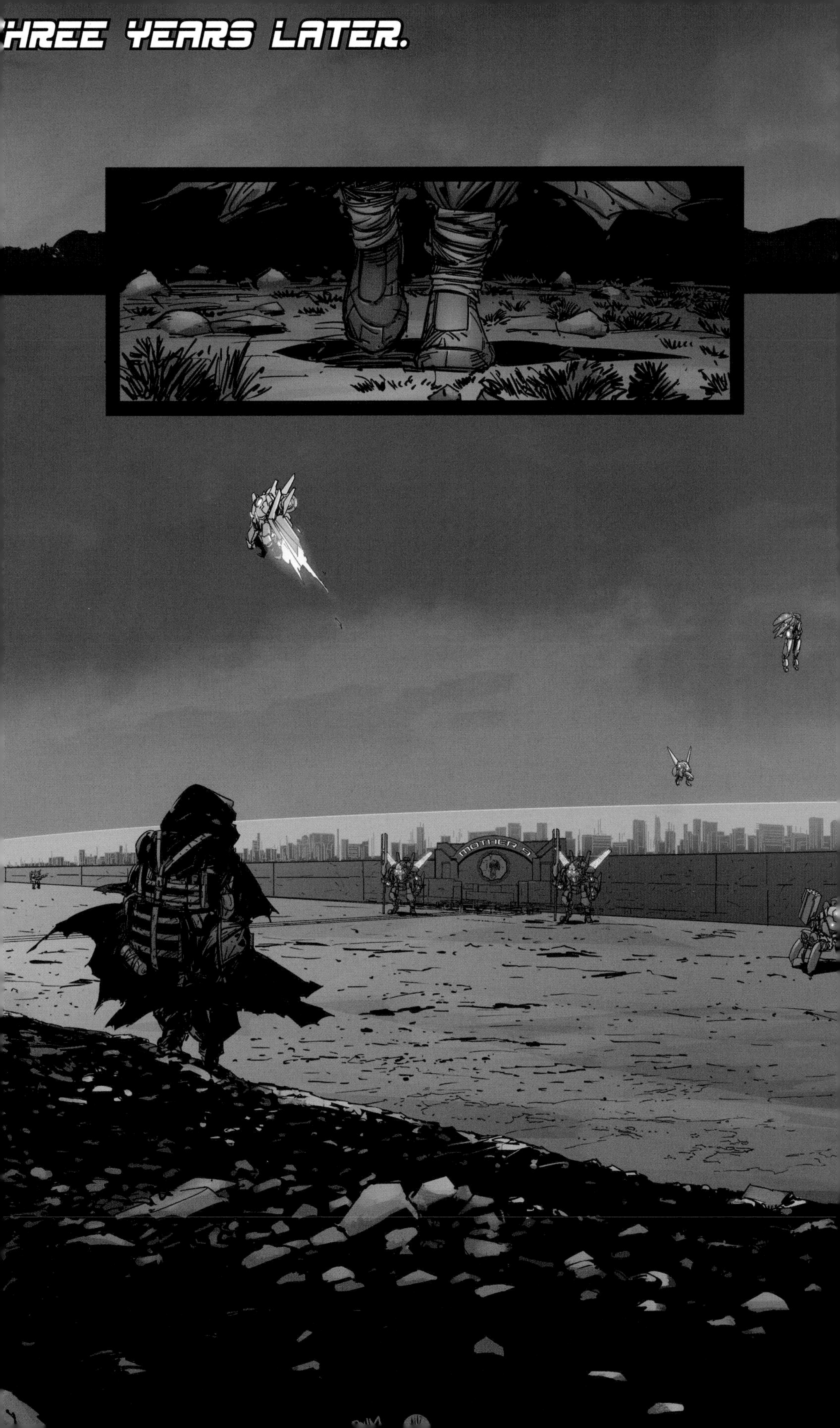
HREE YEARS LATER.
MOTHER 9

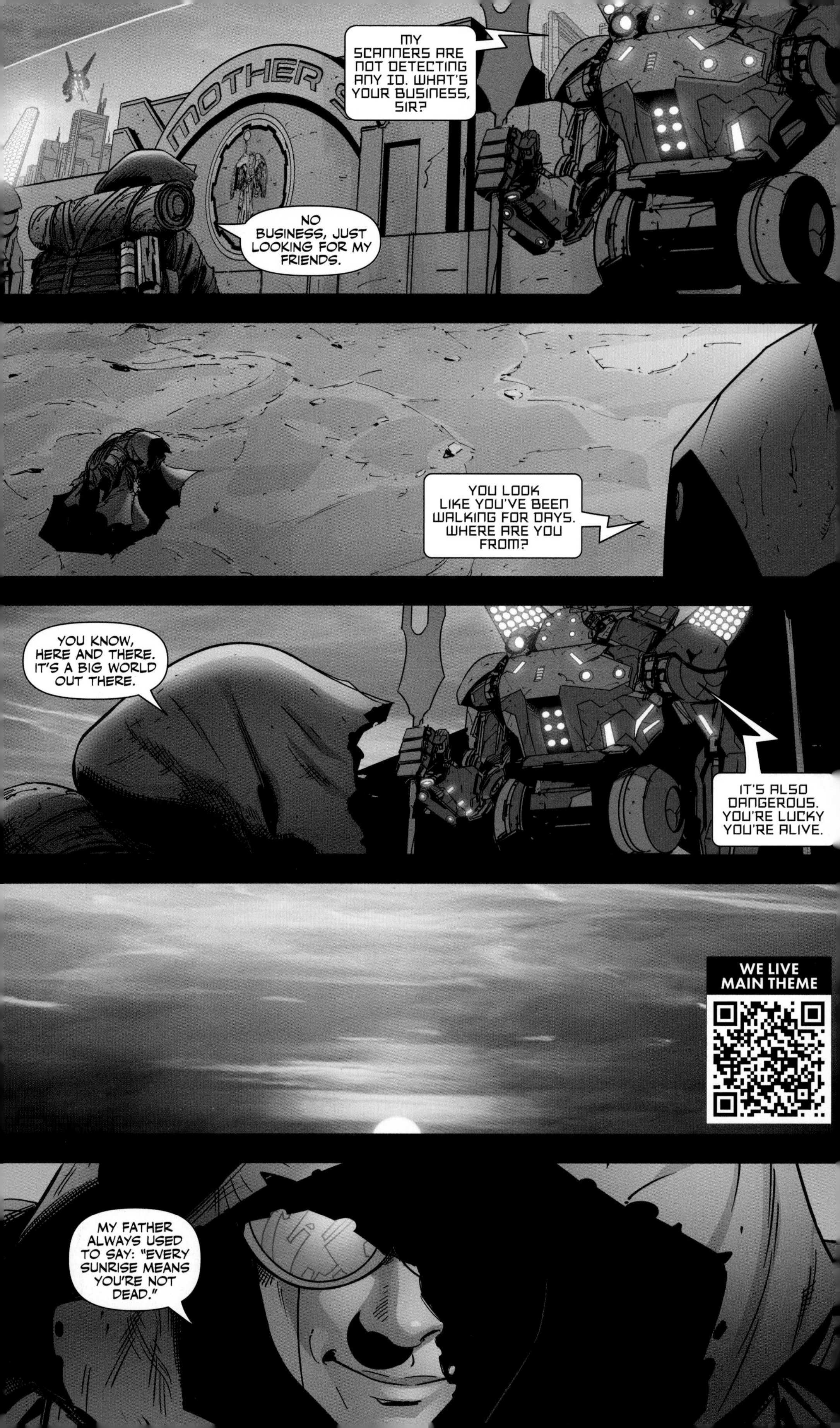
MOTHER S
MY SCANNERS ARE NOT DETECTING ANY ID. WHAT'S YOUR BUSINESS, SIR?
NO BUSINESS, JUST LOOKING FOR MY FRIENDS.
YOU LOOK LIKE YOU'VE BEEN WALKING FOR DAYS. WHERE ARE YOU FROM?
YOU KNOW, HERE AND THERE. IT'S A BIG WORLD OUT THERE.
IT'S ALSO DANGEROUS. YOU'RE LUCKY YOU'RE ALIVE.
WE LIVE MAIN THEME
MY FATHER ALWAYS USED TO SAY: "EVERY SUNRISE MEANS YOU'RE NOT DEAD."

WE LIVE™

COVER GALLERY

Main Cover

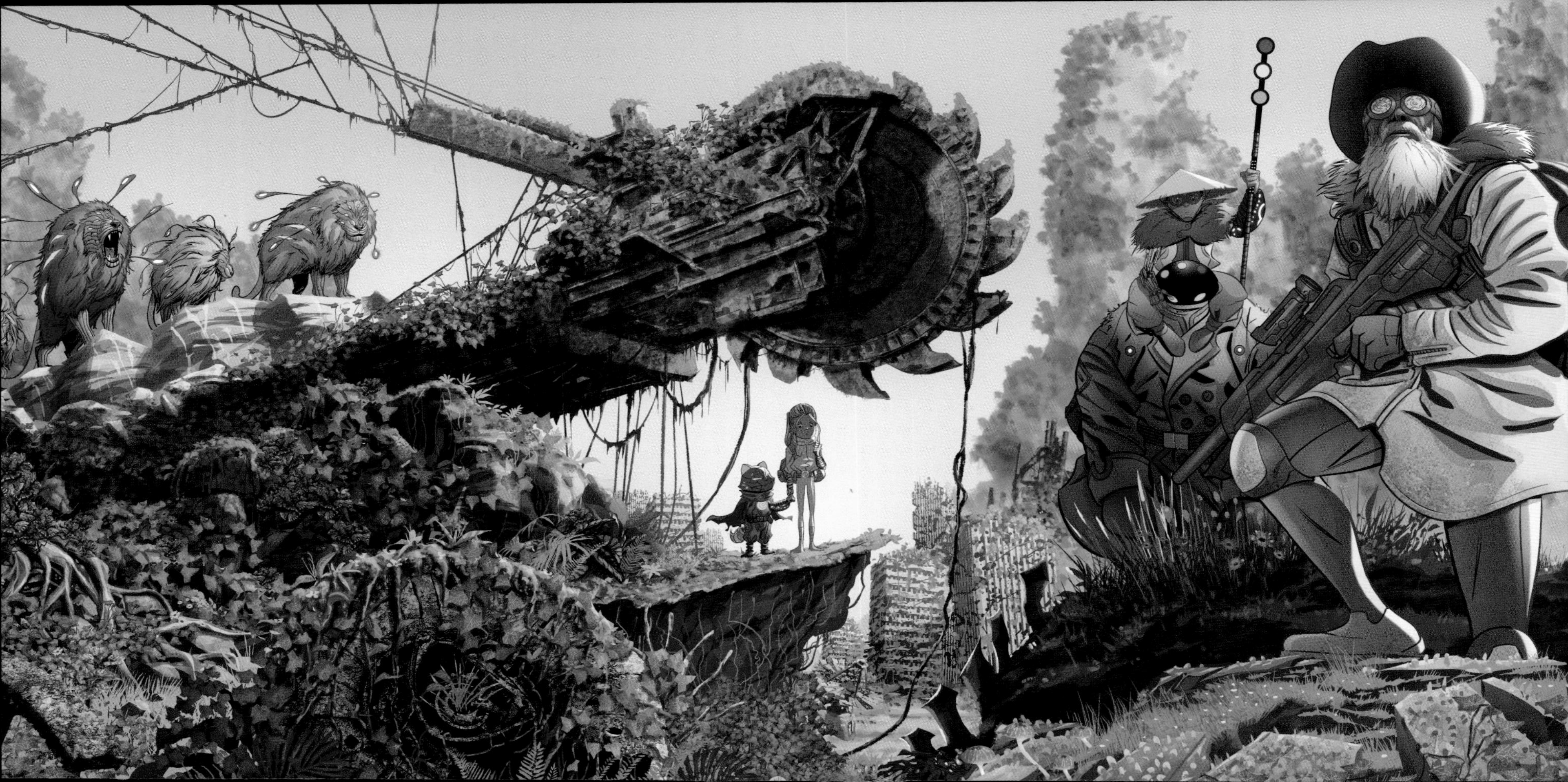

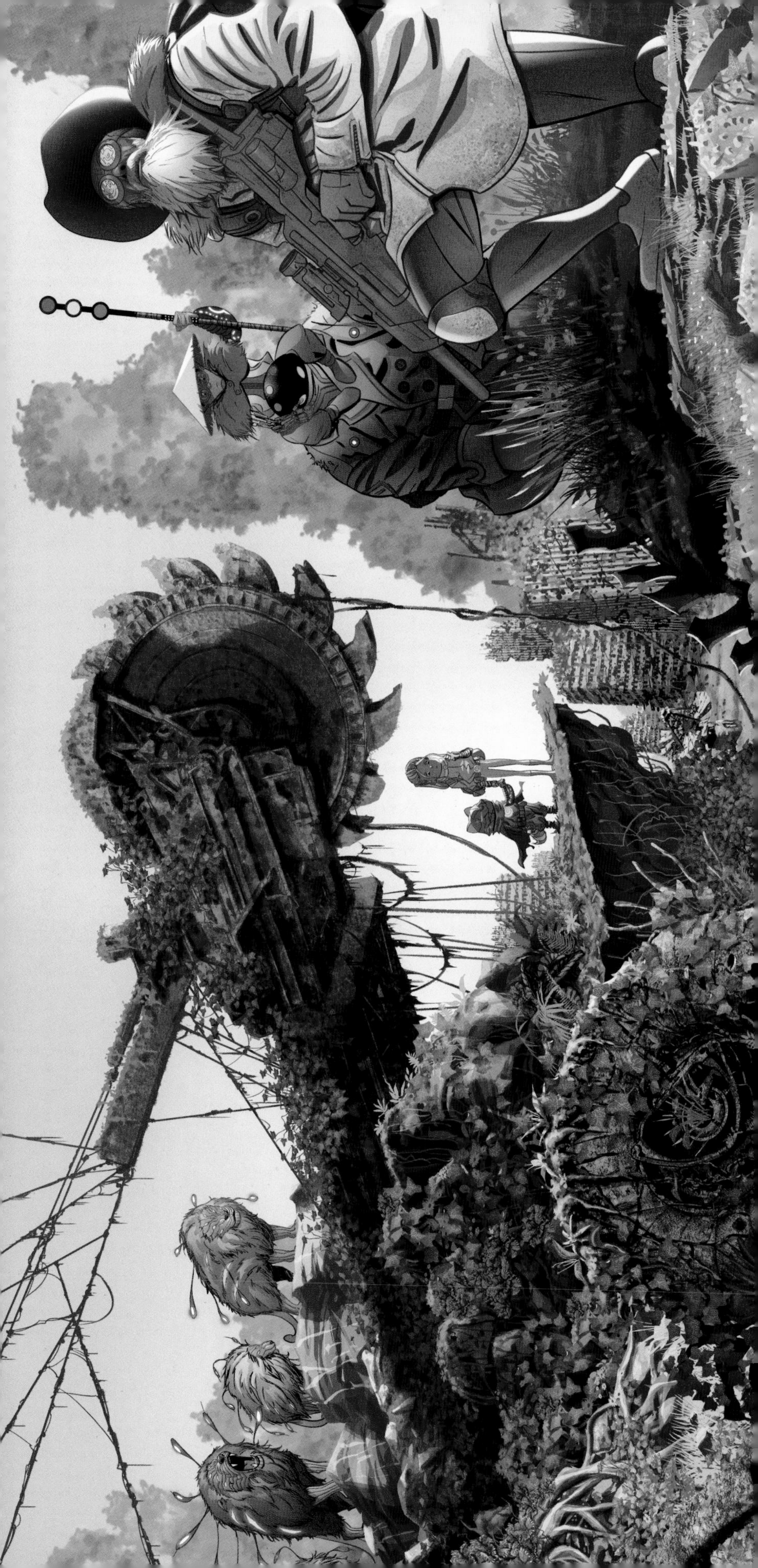

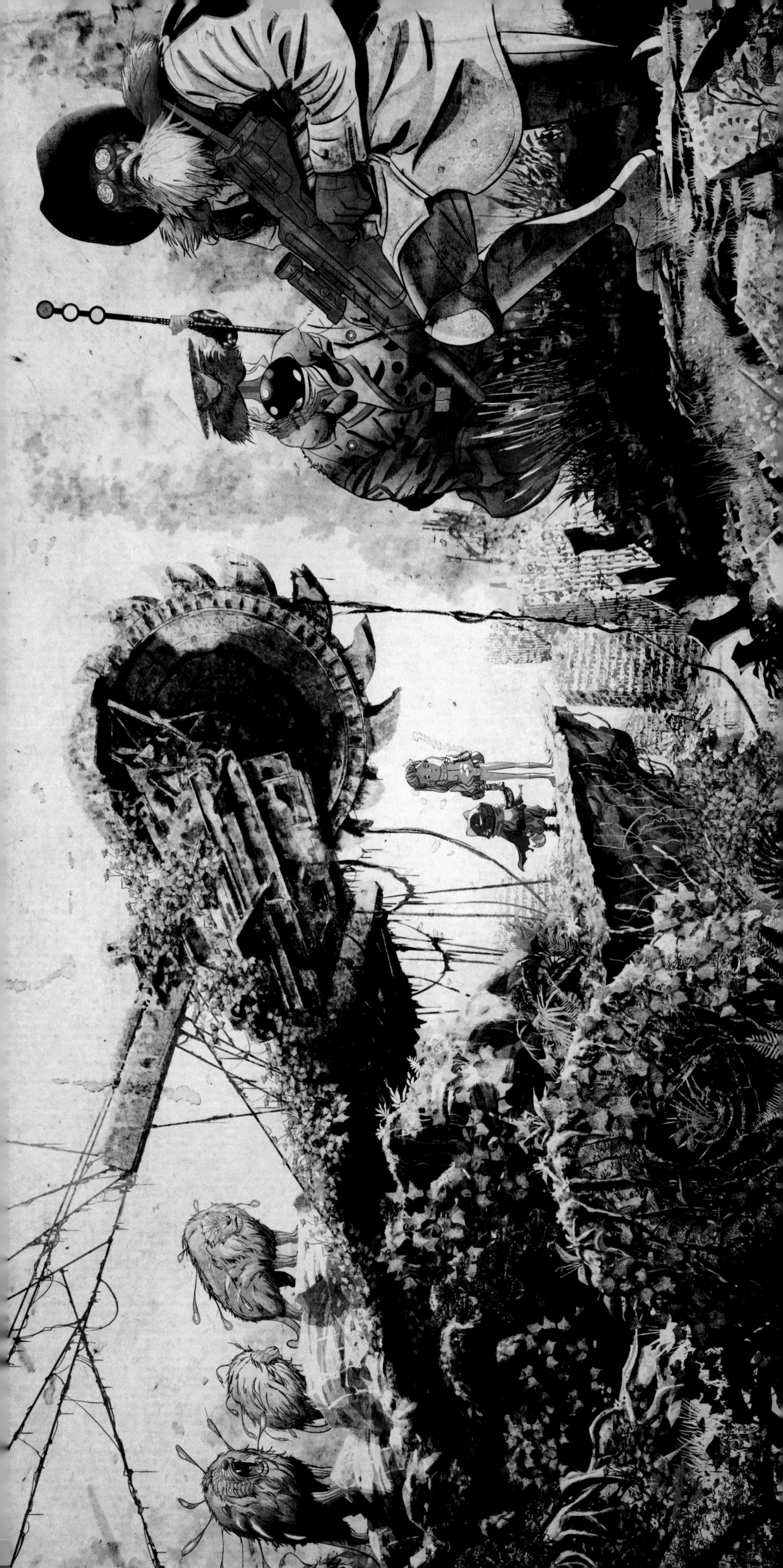

Issue 1
DUSTIN NGUYEN
Incentive Cover

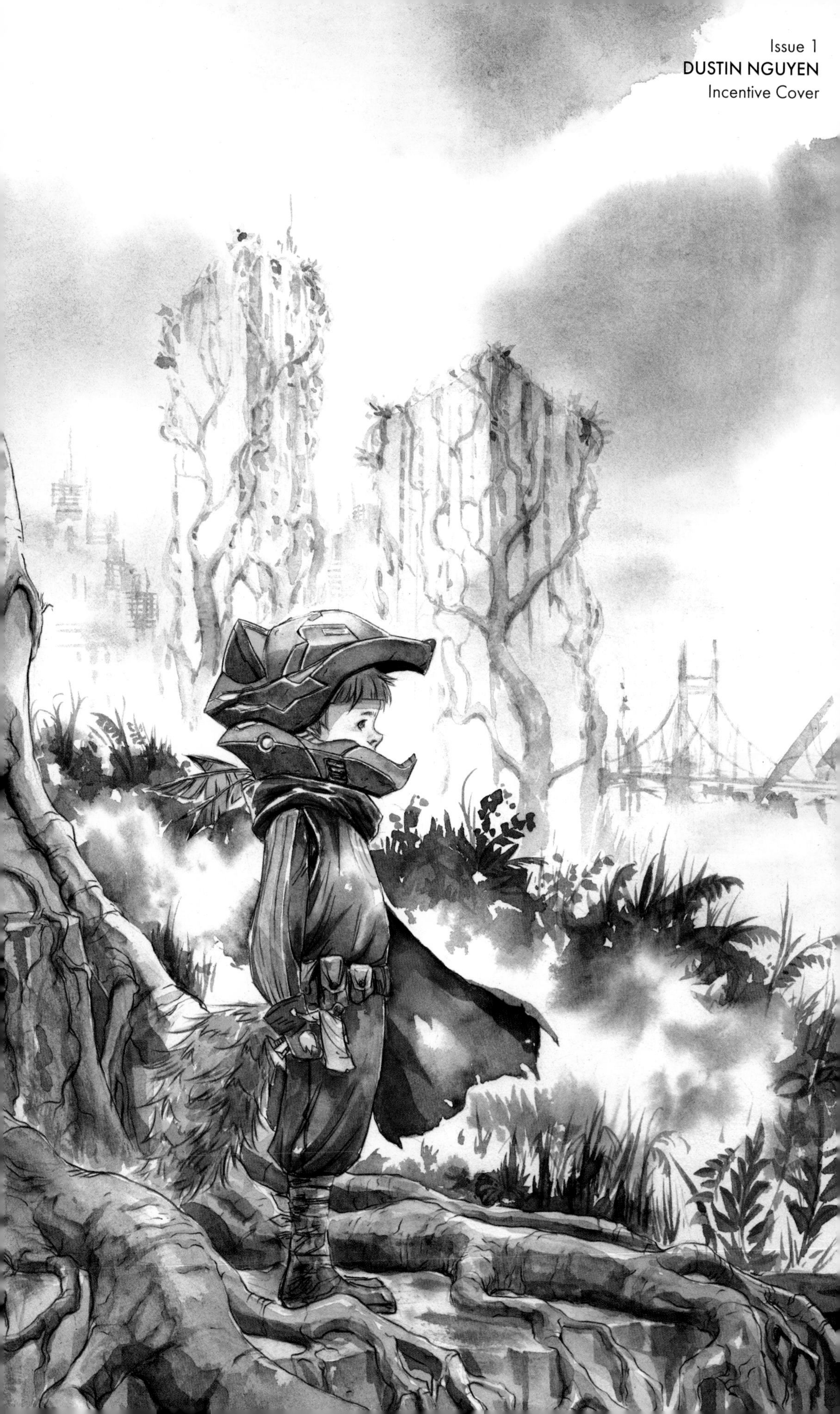

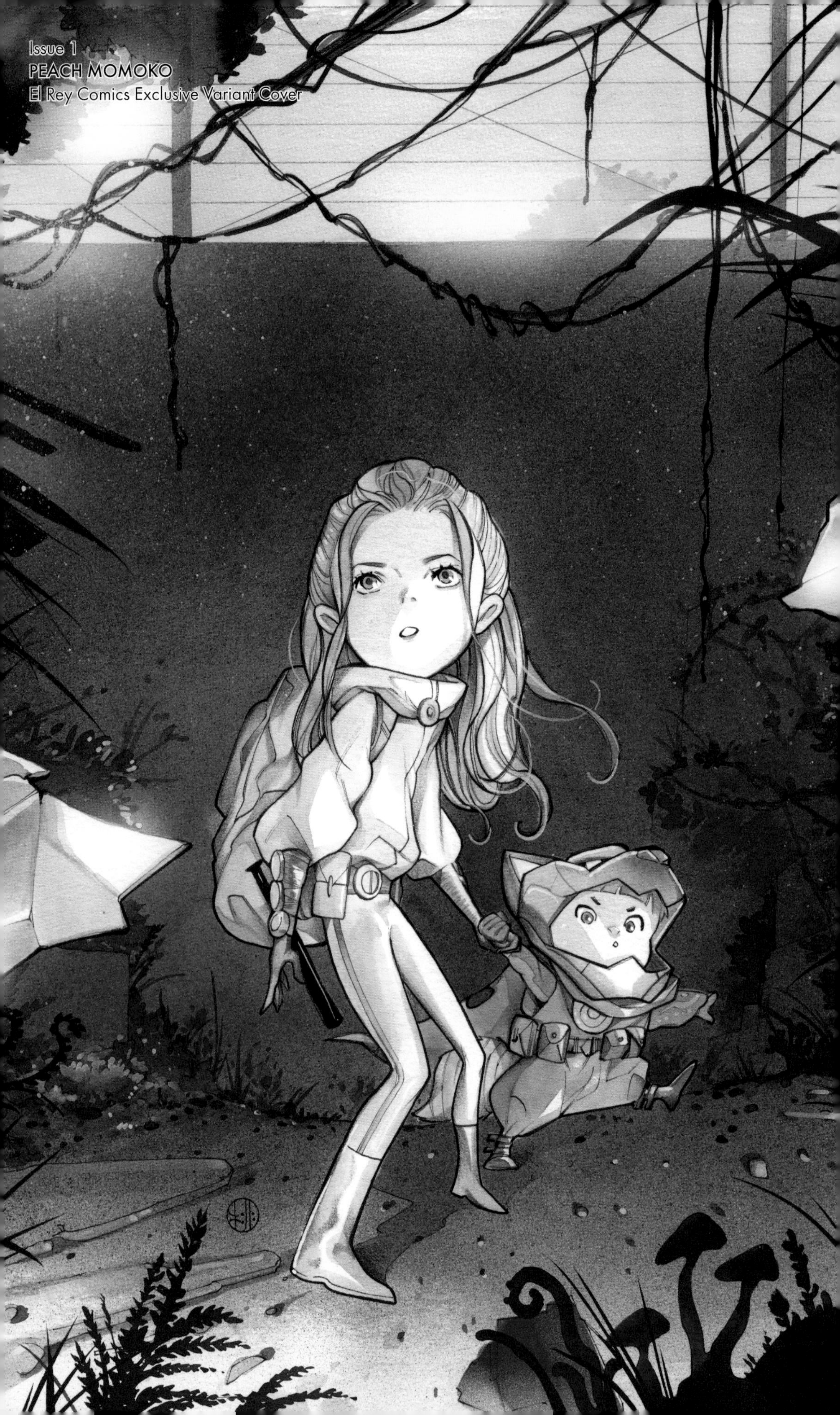

Issue 1
PEACH MOMOKO
El Rey Comics Exclusive Variant Cover

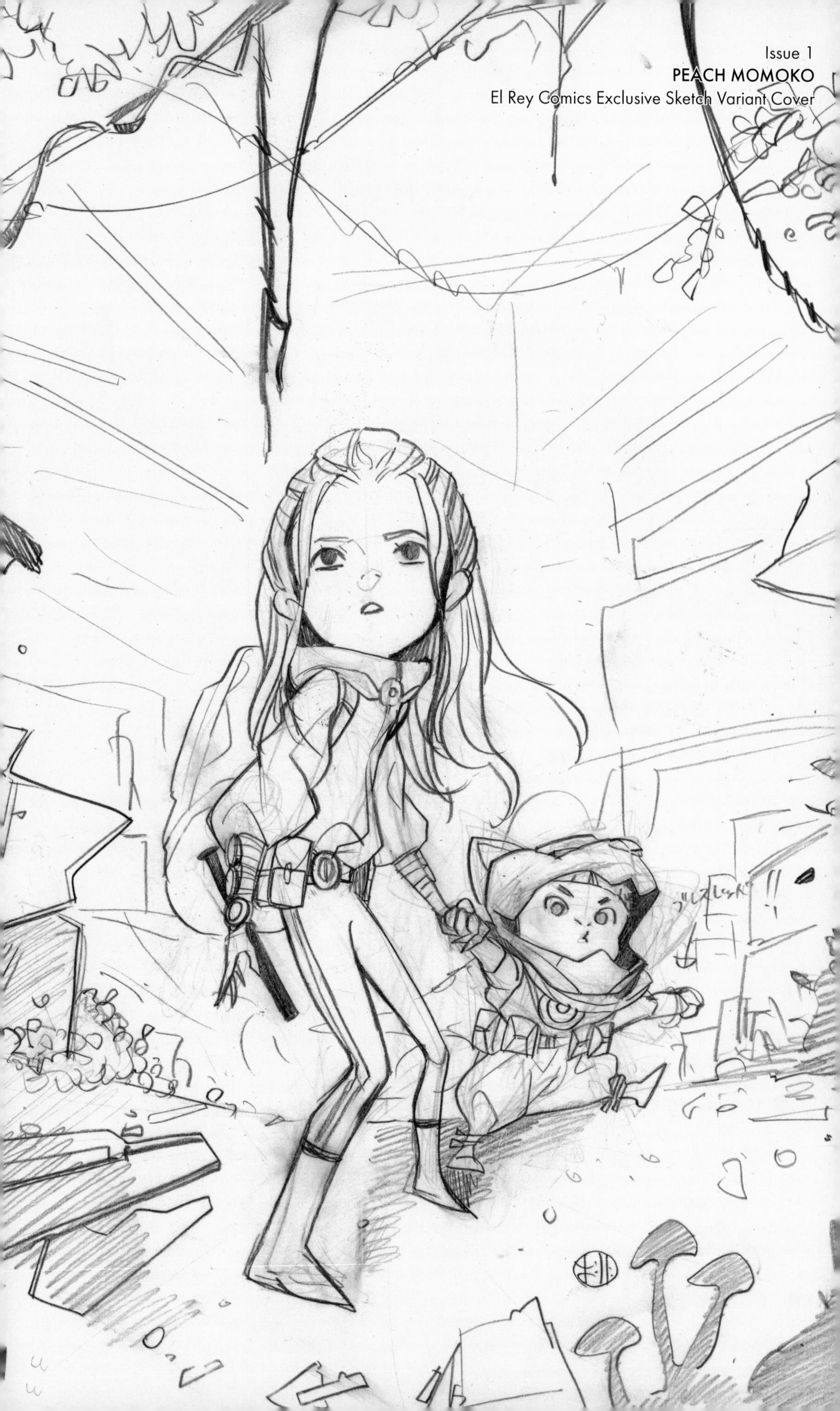

Issue 1
PEACH MOMOKO
El Rey Comics Exclusive Sketch Variant Cover

Issue 1
DAVID SANCHEZ
The Comic Mint Exclusive Variant Cover

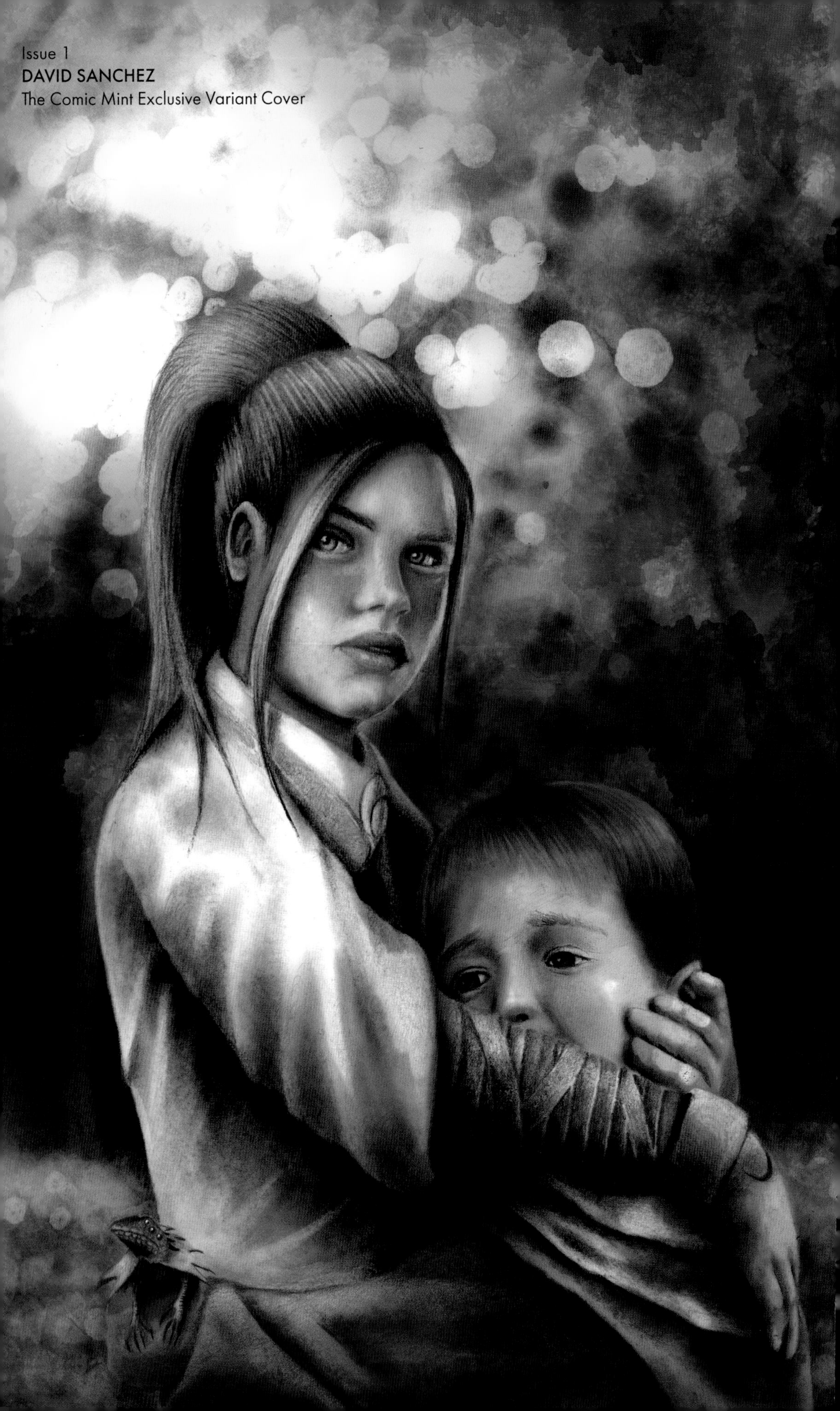

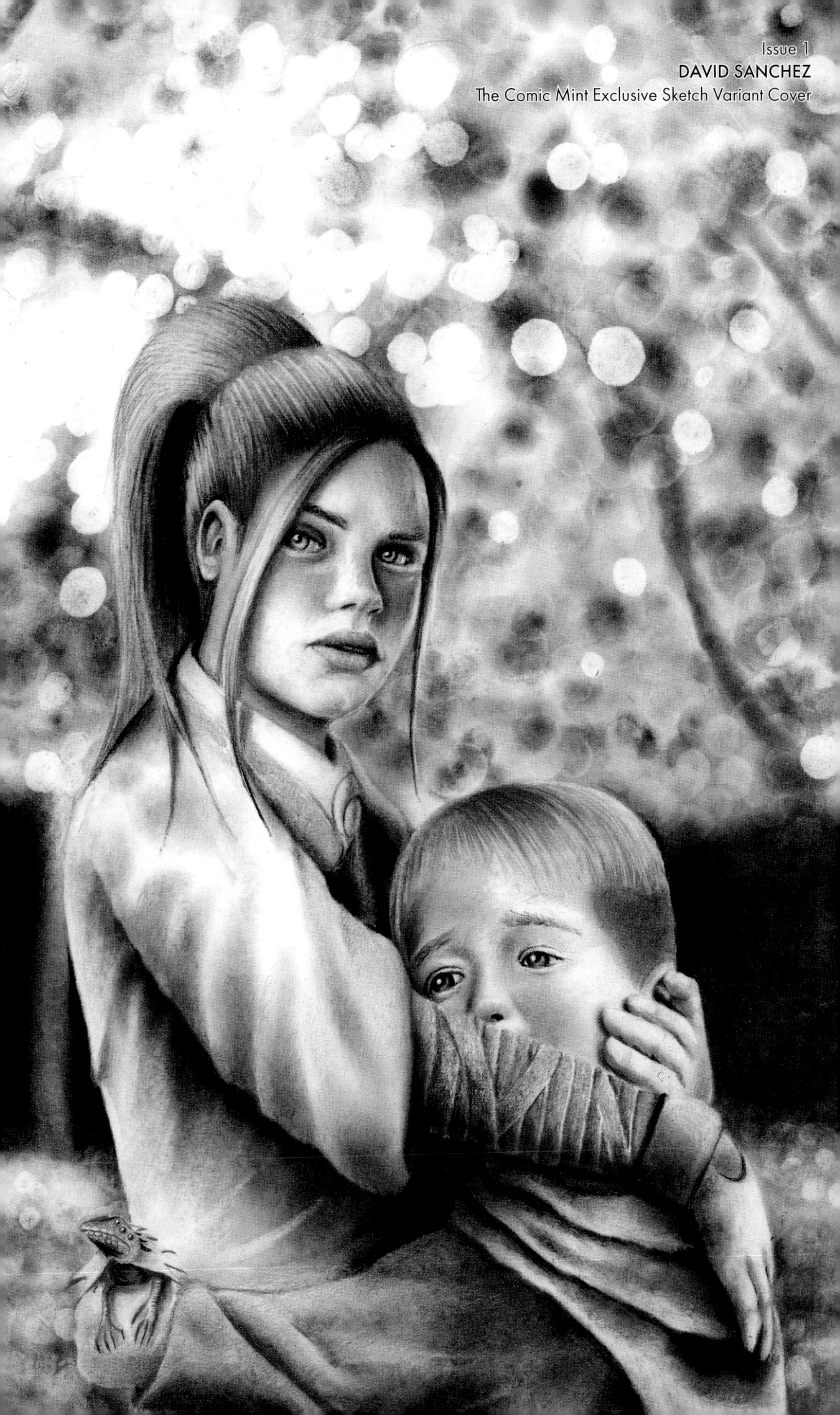

Issue 1
DAVID SANCHEZ
The Comic Mint Exclusive Sketch Variant Cover

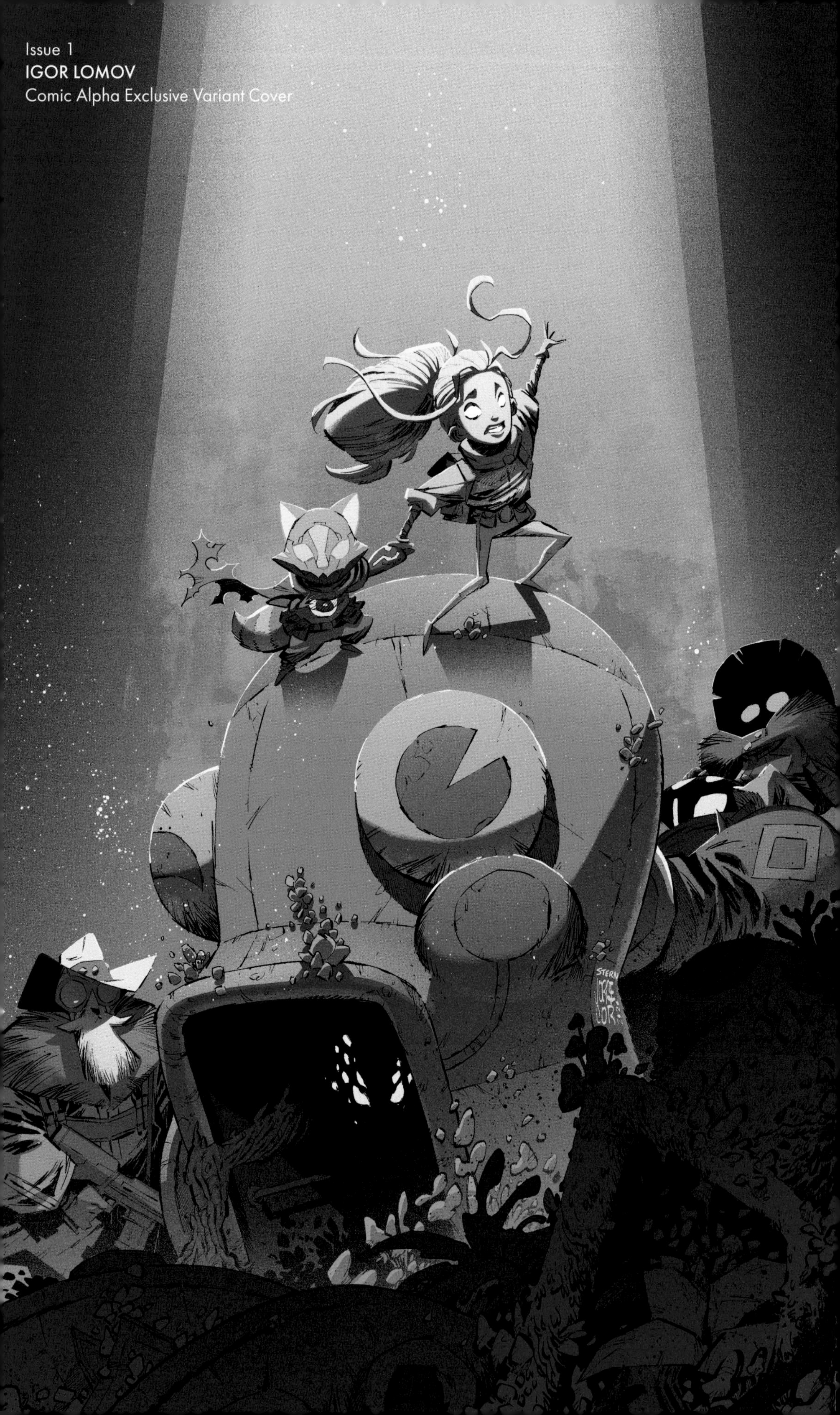

Issue 1
IGOR LOMOV
Comic Alpha Exclusive Variant Cover

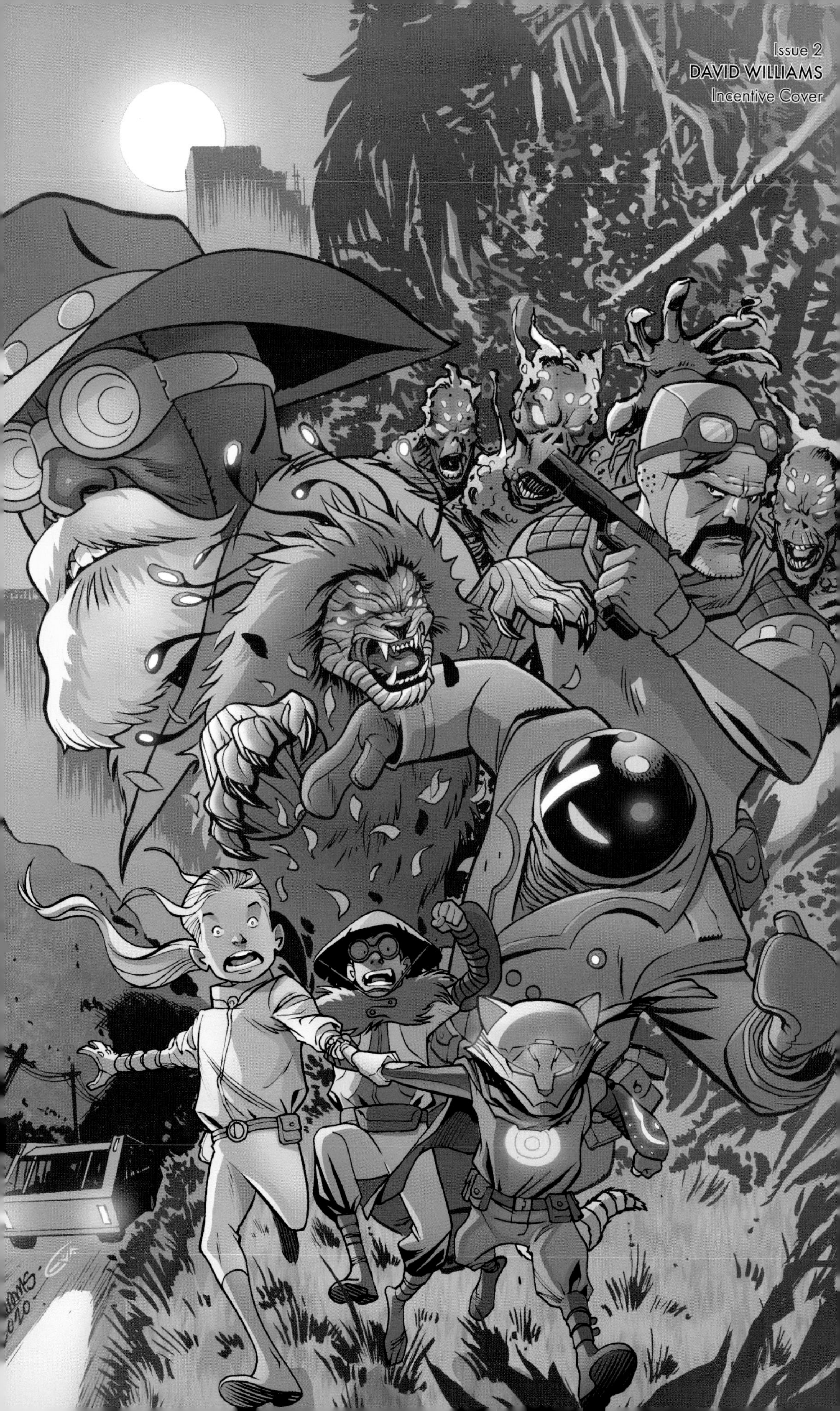

Issue 2
DAVID WILLIAMS
Incentive Cover

Issue 2

INAKI MIRANDA

The Comic Mint Exclusive Sketch Variant Cover

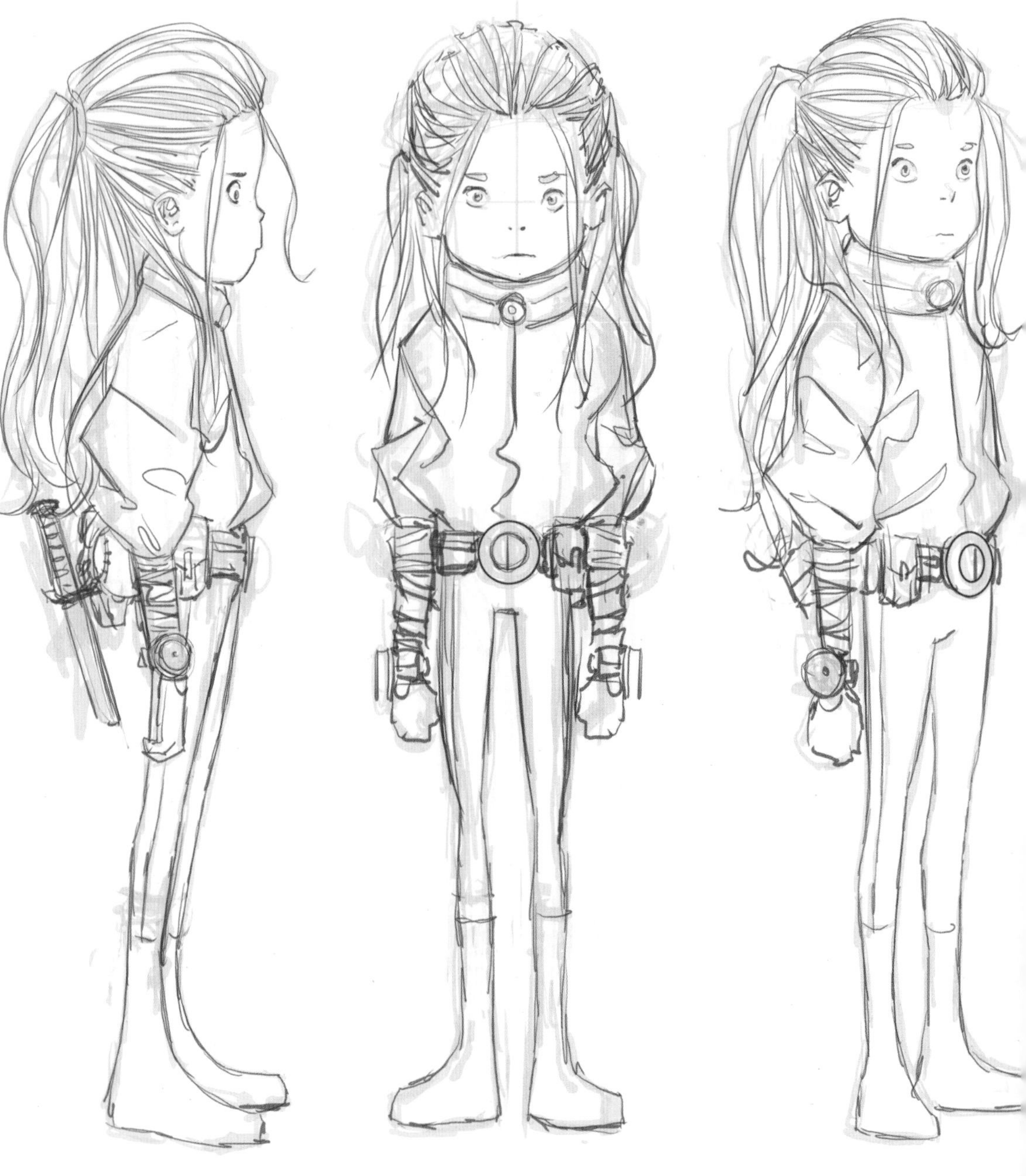

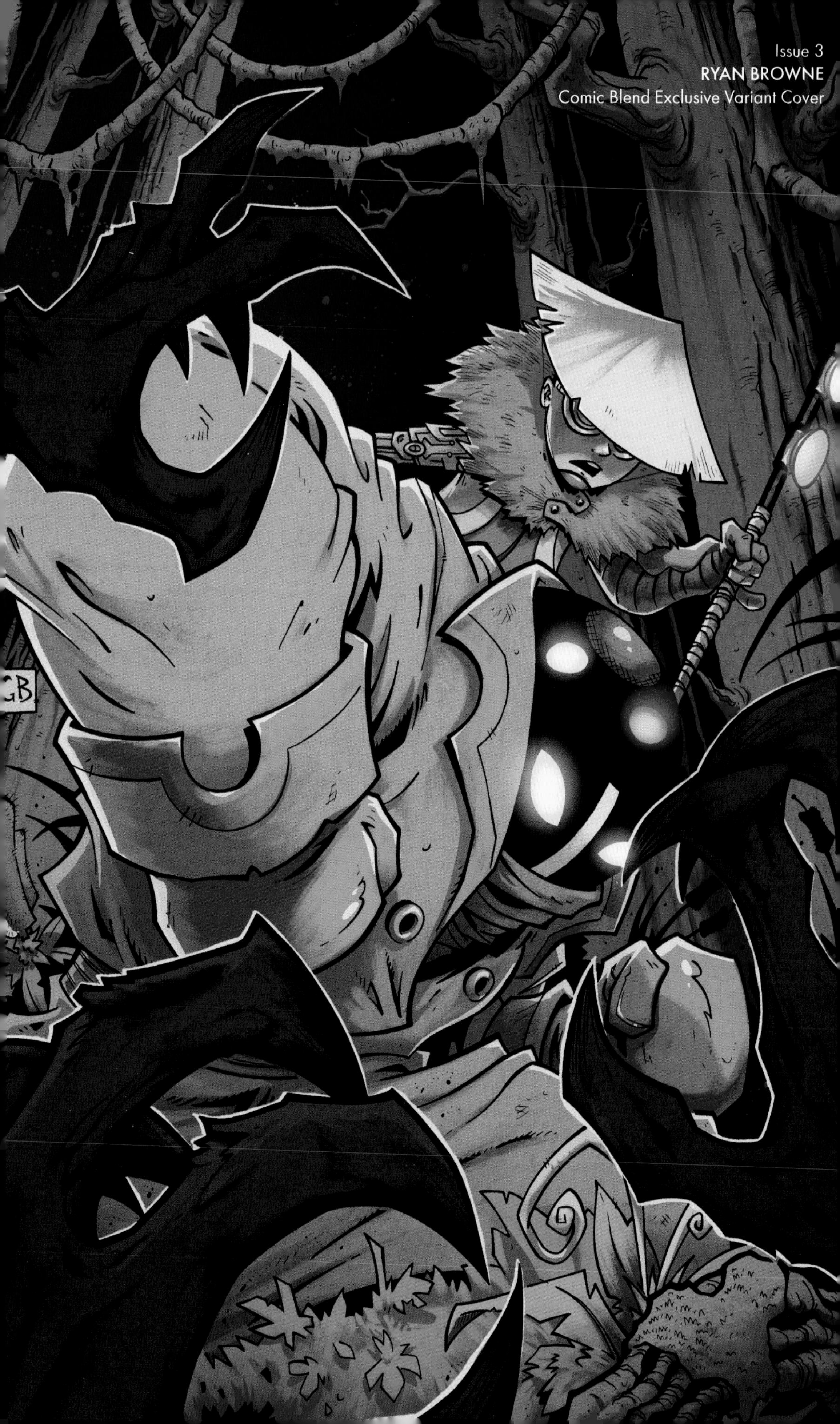
GB

Issue 3
RYAN BROWNE
Comic Blend Exclusive Variant Cover

Issue 3

INAKI MIRANDA

The Comic Mint Exclusive Sketch Variant Cover

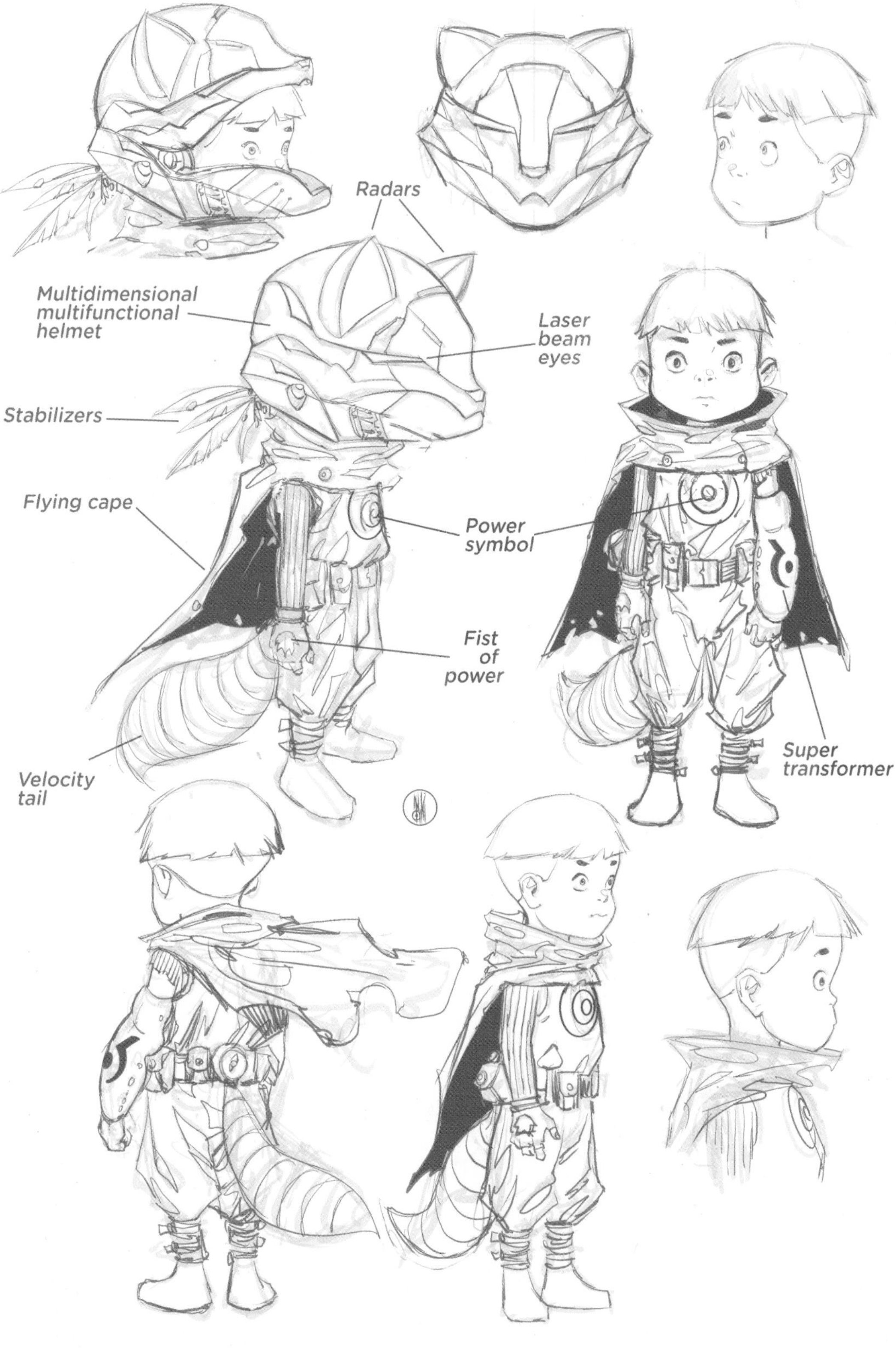
Radars
Multidimensional multifunctional helmet
Laser beam eyes
Stabilizers
Flying cape
Power symbol
Fist of power
Super transformer
Velocity tail

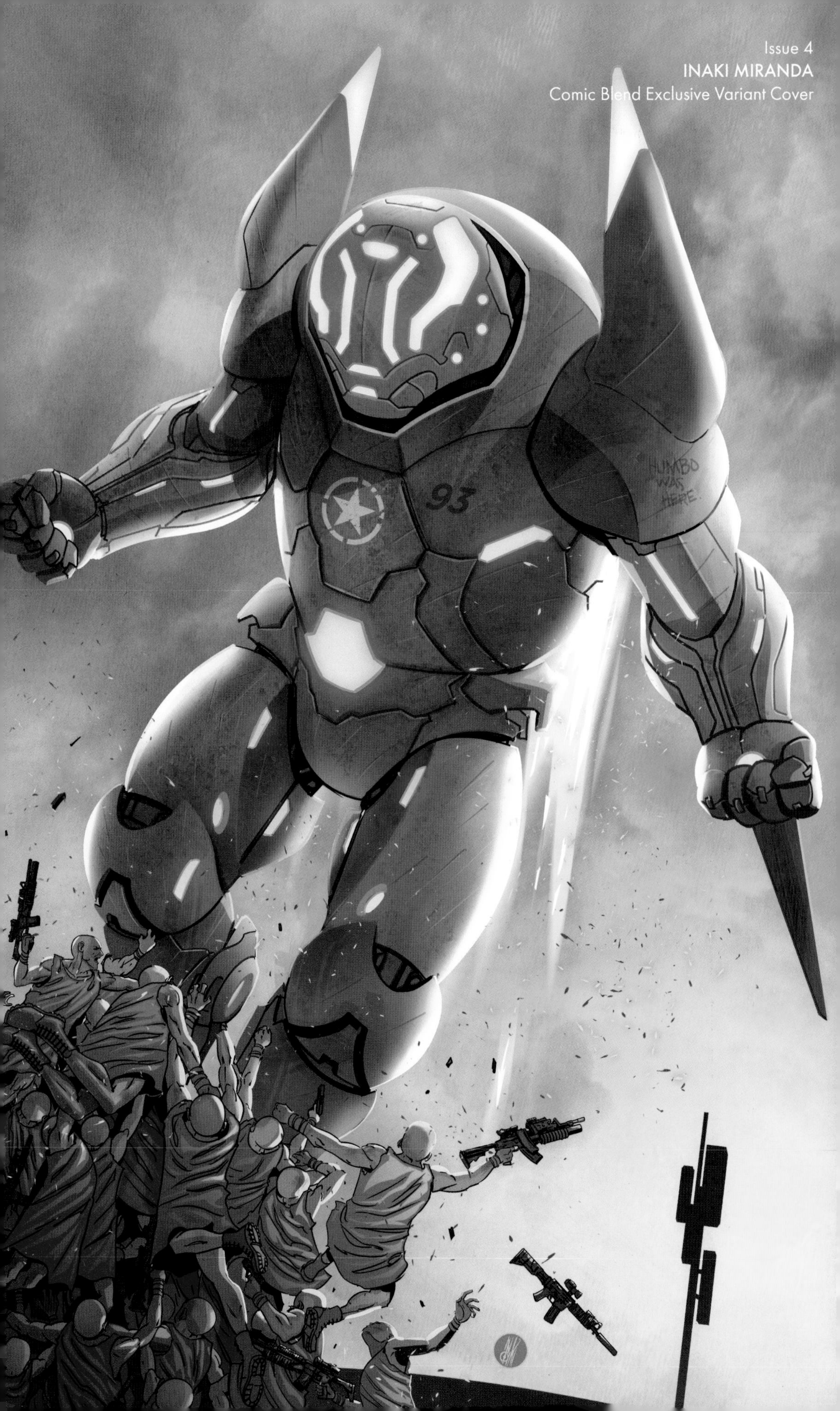
93
HUMBO WAS HERE

Issue 4
INAKI MIRANDA
Comic Blend Exclusive Variant Cover

Issue 5

INAKI MIRANDA

Trinity Comics Exclusive Sketch Variant Cover

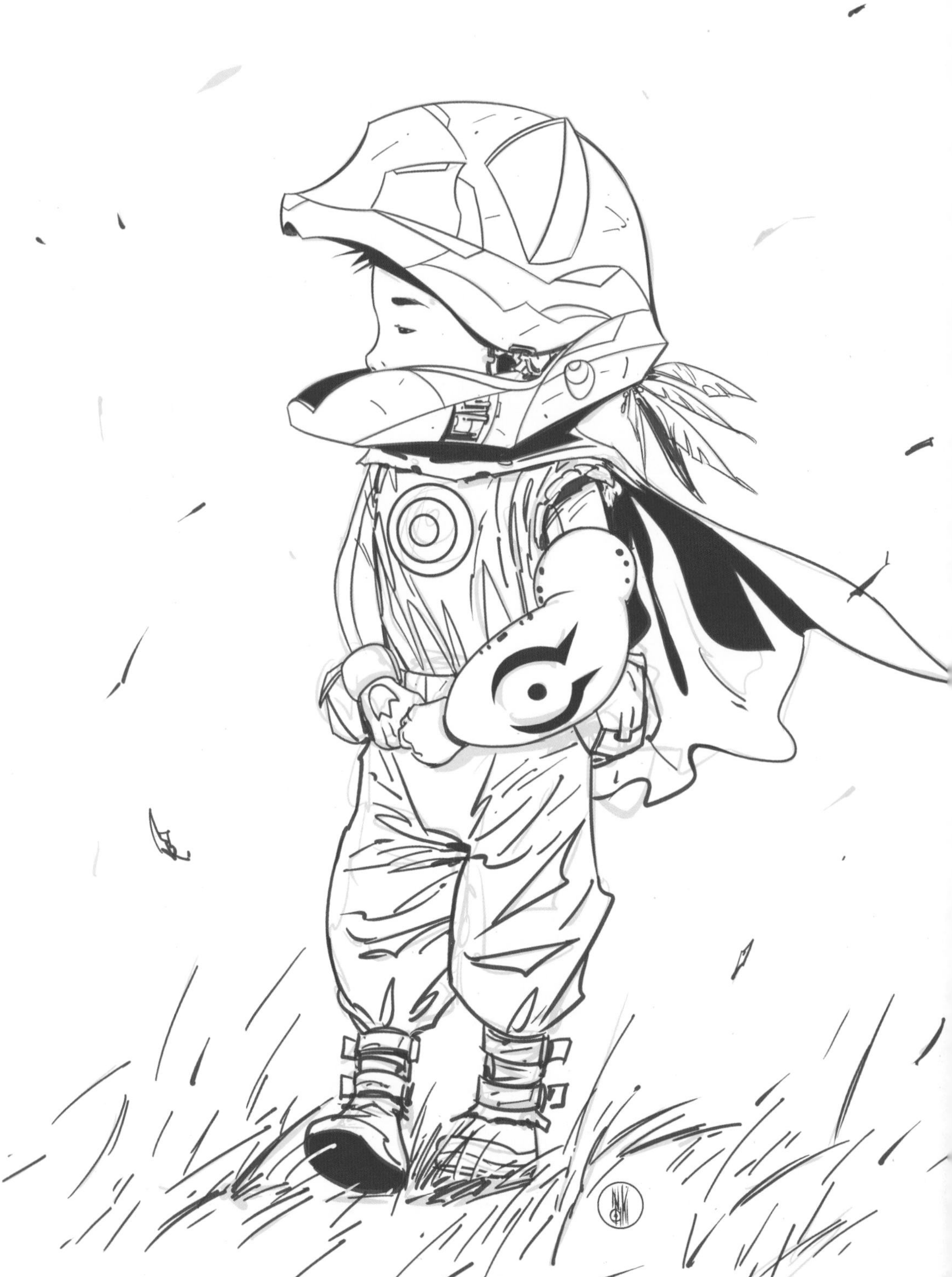

WE LIVE

EXTRAS

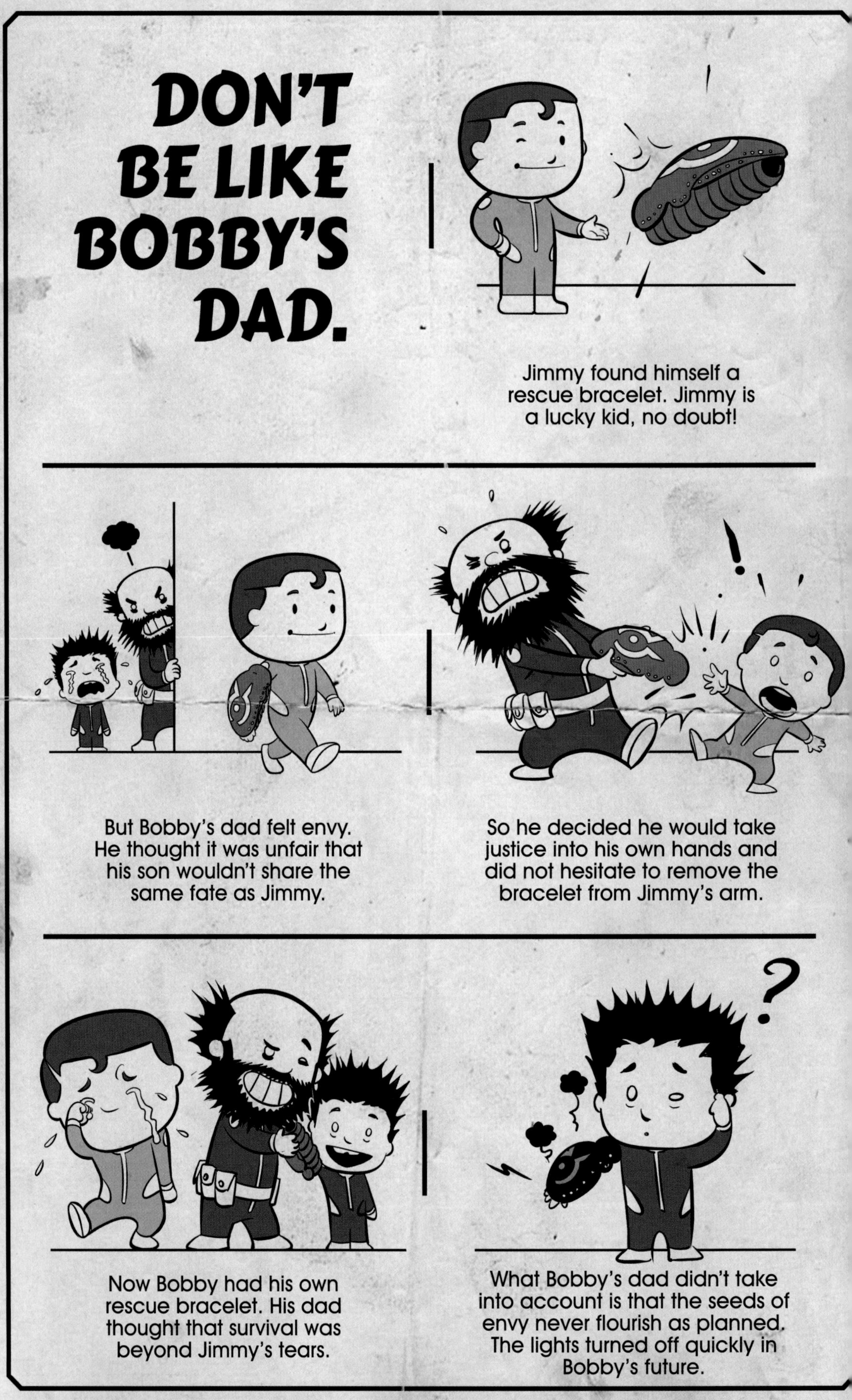
DON'T BE LIKE BOBBY'S DAD.
Jimmy found himself a rescue bracelet. Jimmy is a lucky kid, no doubt!
But Bobby's dad felt envy. He thought it was unfair that his son wouldn't share the same fate as Jimmy.
So he decided he would take justice into his own hands and did not hesitate to remove the bracelet from Jimmy's arm.
Now Bobby had his own rescue bracelet. His dad thought that survival was beyond Jimmy's tears.
What Bobby's dad didn't take into account is that the seeds of envy never flourish as planned. The lights turned off quickly in Bobby's future.

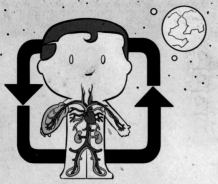

The bracelet hides a sophisticated symbiotic mechanism that connects to the blood system. Inside, an advanced hemodialysis process prepares the body for its adaptation to the new home planet.

Once the dialyzer attaches to a human, it can't be transferred. It will loose all functionaltiy and will turn off permenantly.

I'm sorry, Bobby, your dad was wrong.

Bobby's dad not only failed in his selfish attempt to save his son, but he also sentenced Jimmy when he removed the bracelet. Don't be like Bobby's dad.

Let Jimmy live.
Protect our chosen children.
They are our future.

THIS IS AN OFFICIAL CIVIL DEFENSE ANNOUNCEMENT

PRODUCED IN COLLABORATION
BY THE NINE MOTHER MEGALOPOLIS

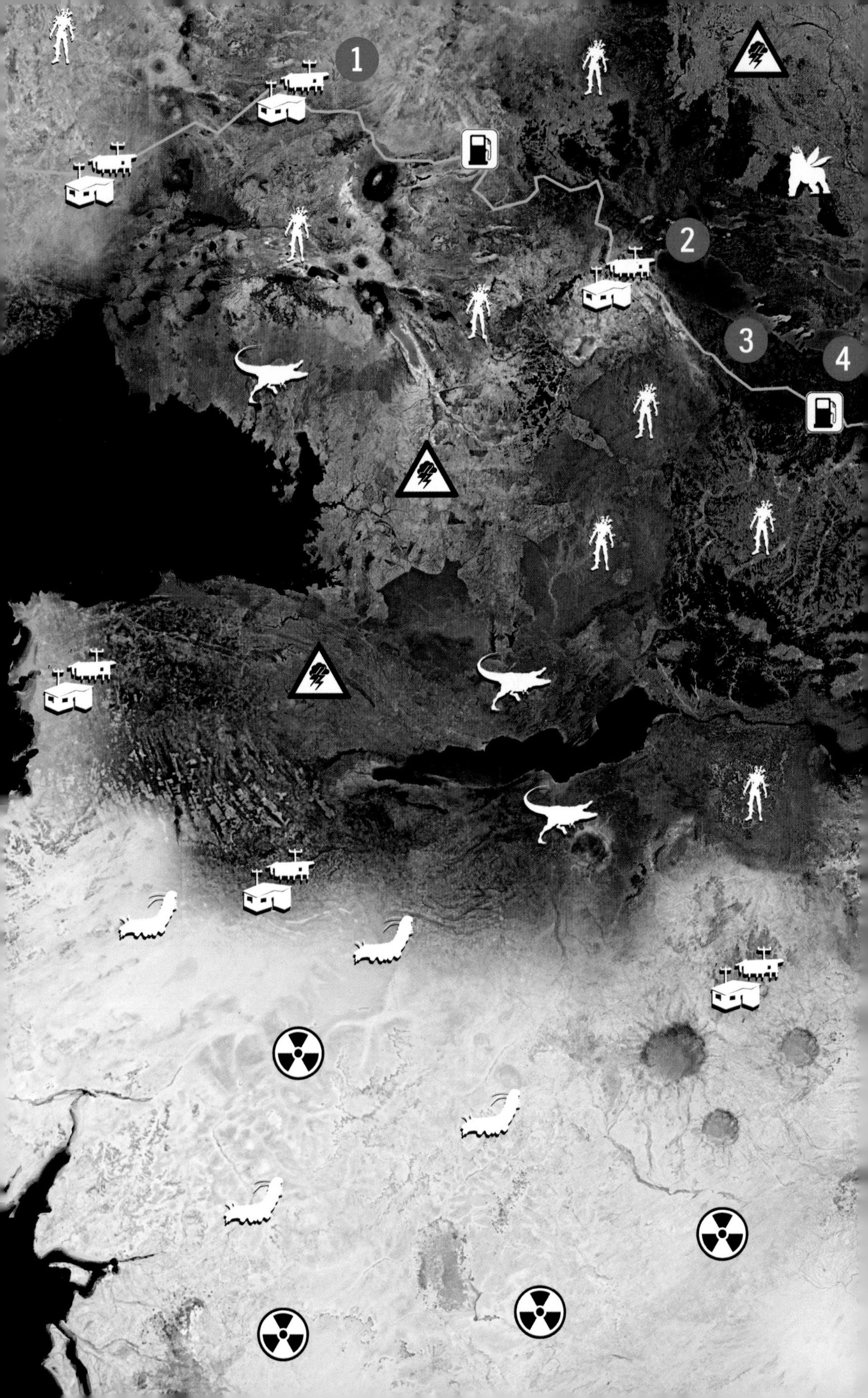
1
2
3
4

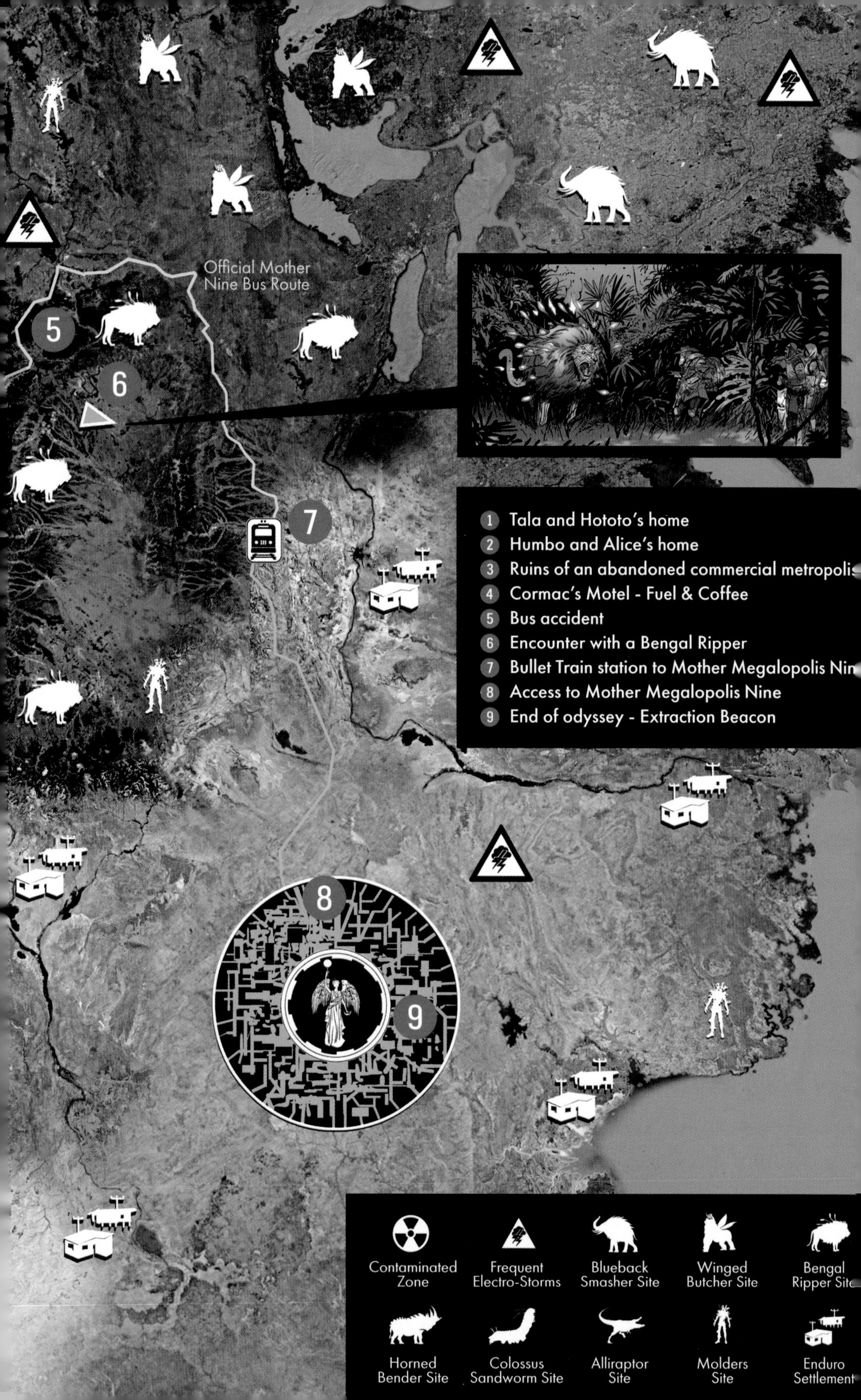

Official Mother
Nine Bus Route
5
6
7
8
9
1 Tala and Hototo's home
2 Humbo and Alice's home
3 Ruins of an abandoned commercial metropoli
4 Cormac's Motel - Fuel & Coffee
5 Bus accident
6 Encounter with a Bengal Ripper
7 Bullet Train station to Mother Megalopolis Nin
8 Access to Mother Megalopolis Nine
9 End of odyssey - Extraction Beacon
Contaminated Zone
Frequent Electro-Storms
Blueback Smasher Site
Winged Butcher Site
Bengal Ripper Sit
Horned Bender Site
Colossus Sandworm Site
Alliraptor Site
Molders Site
Enduro Settlement

Unlock original music composed by Elhombreviento and Mario "gonzo" Lorente exclusively for WE LIVE by scanning this QR Code—including "Summer Cornfields" (Bonus Track), found only in this collection.

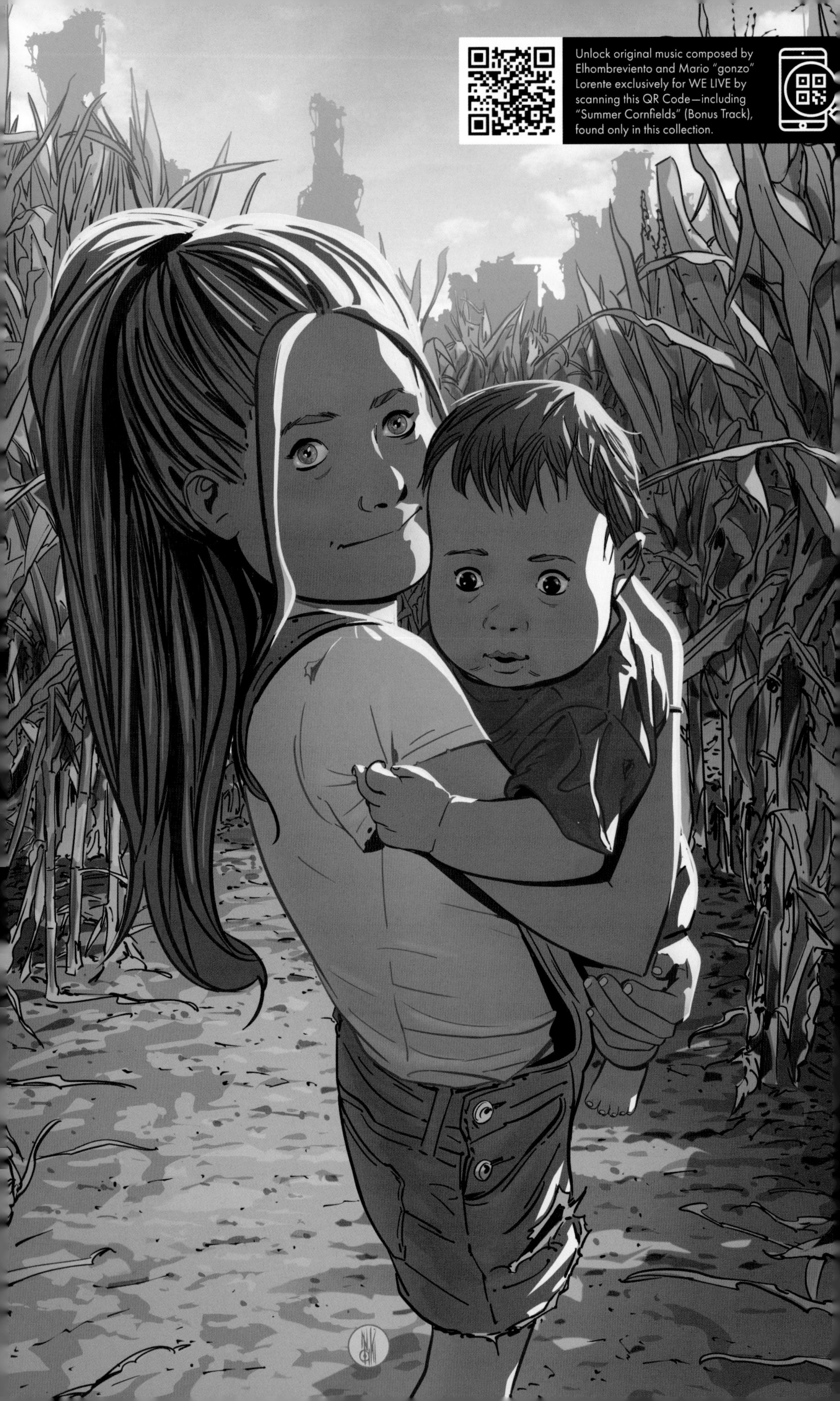

WE LIVE

INAKI MIRANDA
sketchbook

Here's a secret: Hototo, Tala and Humbo are the stylized echoes of three real life little persons.

I believe that the simplified lines of a drawing must always try to capture life; and in the case of WE LIVE, these three little souls already came with their own complex personalities developed, with their funny gestures, their own way of walking, talking and reacting to life, their sounds—their unique non-transferable colors.

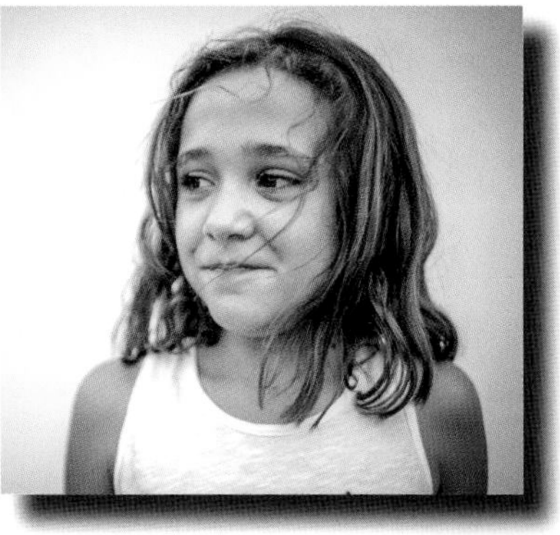

Noa, Roy's sweet daughter turned into the sweet brave TALA.

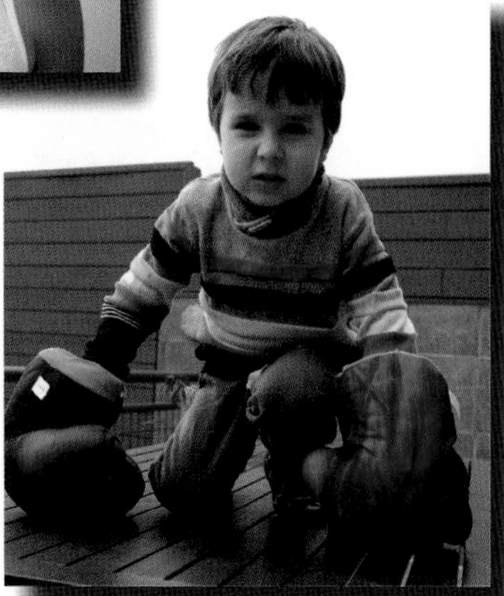

Mael, the little dreamer, the son of my sister Cynthia, gave life to our little superhero HOTOTO.

The intrepid smile of Jaime, the son of my brother Michaux, brought us the humour of the young gifted HUMBO.

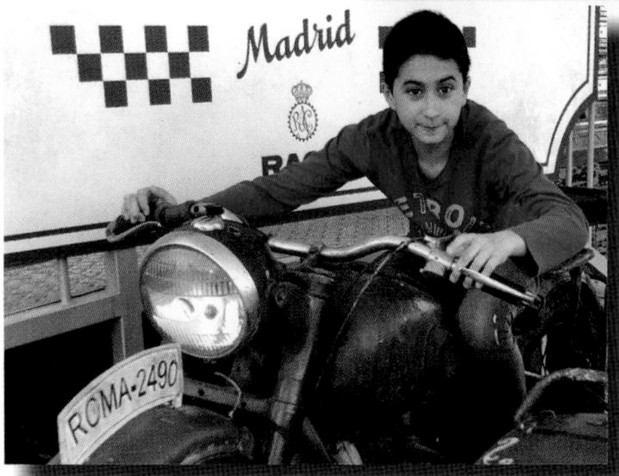
Madrid
ROMA-2490

These three young Mirandas slipped into this fantastic apocalyptic world and took over the story forever.

When Roy and I sat down to write this book, we just had to look behind our backs and connect the pieces of those vital cogs that we know and love so much.

Always together.

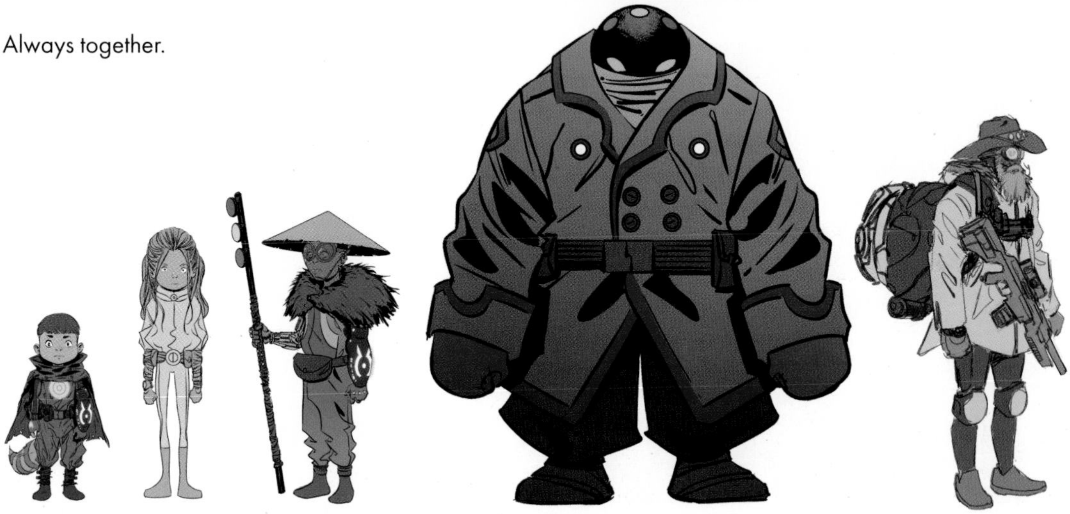

HOTOTO **TALA** **HUMBO** **ALICE** **SIMON**

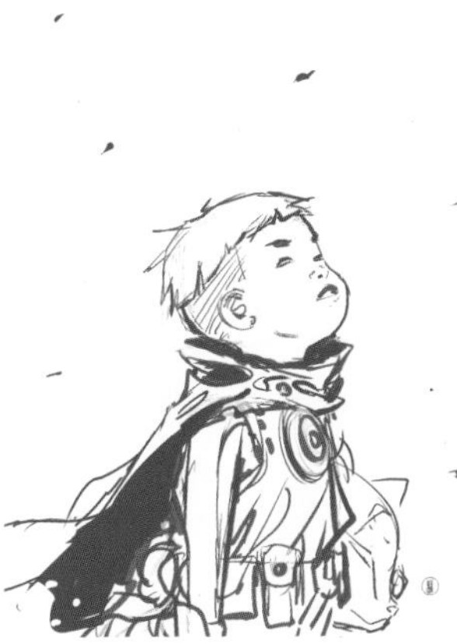

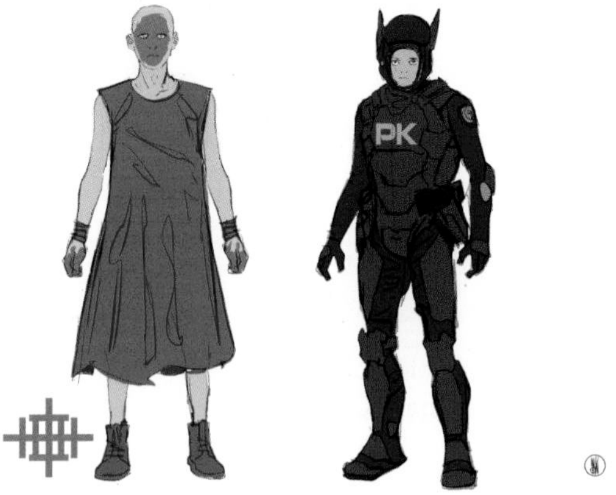
PK

ACCEPTIST

PEACEKEEPER (PK)

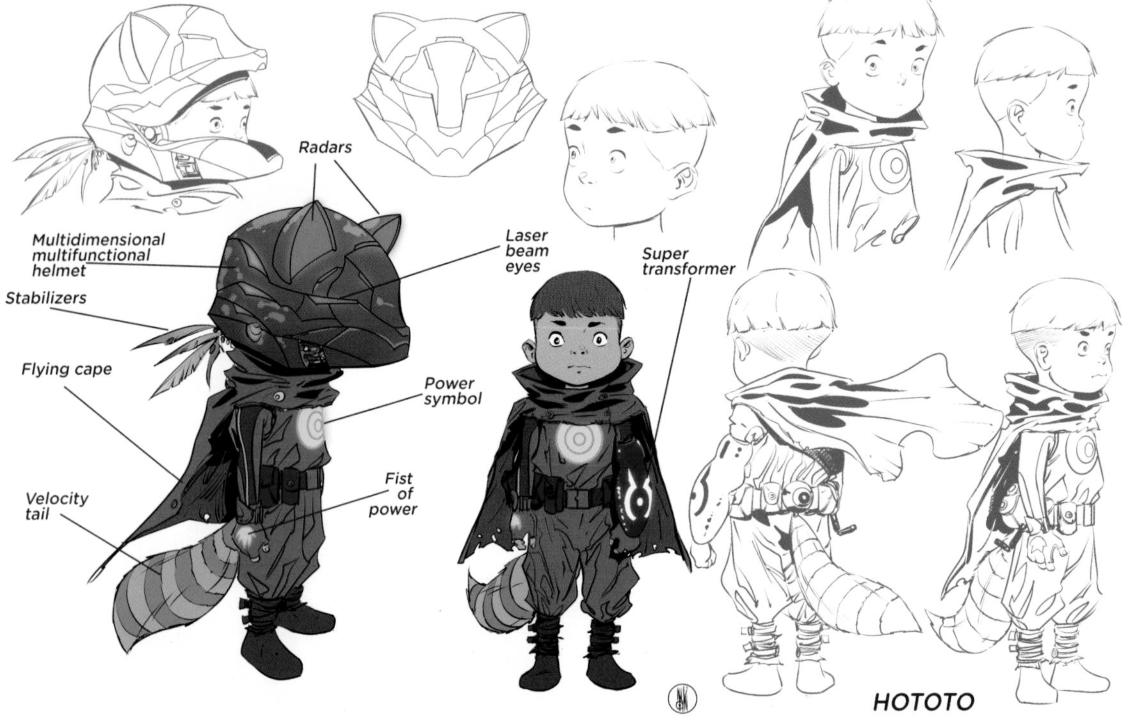
Radars
Multidimensional multifunctional helmet
Laser beam eyes
Super transformer
Stabilizers
Flying cape
Power symbol
Fist of power
Velocity tail

HOTOTO

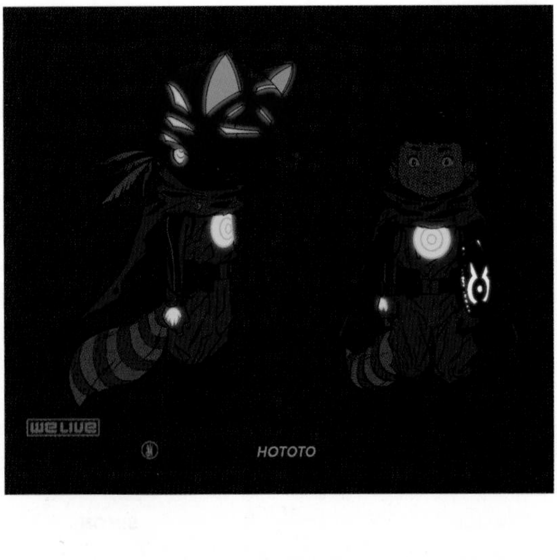
WE LIVE
HOTOTO

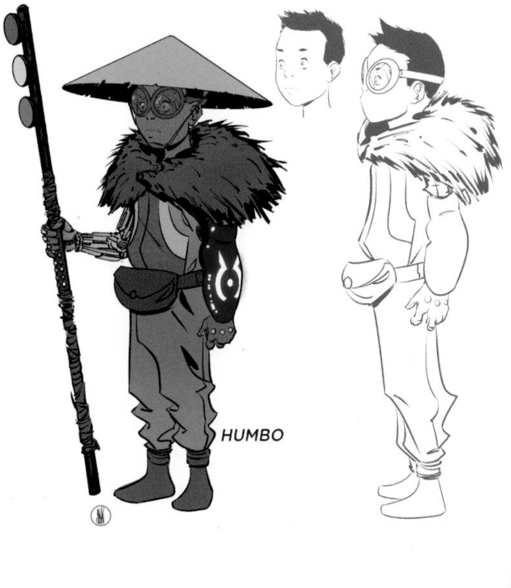
HUMBO

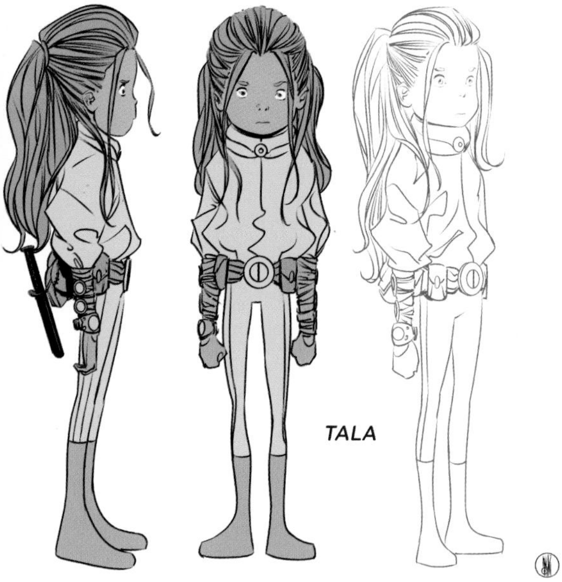
TALA

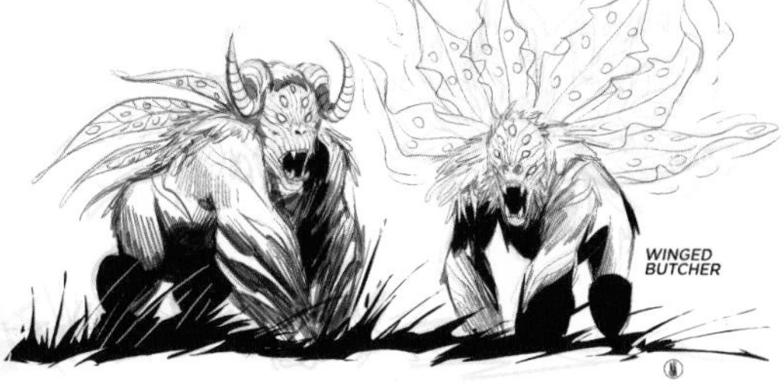
WINGED
BUTCHER

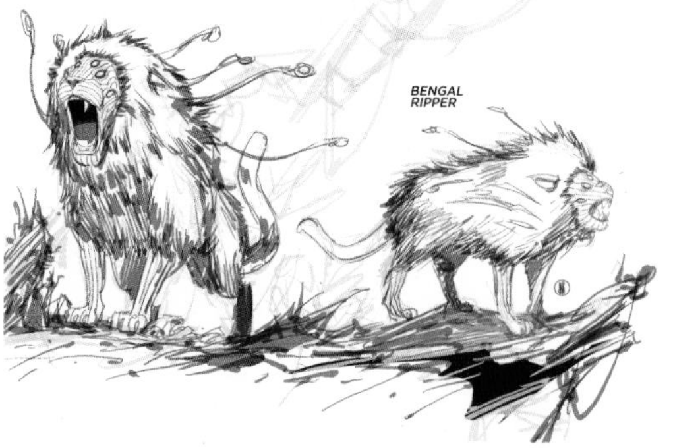
BENGAL
RIPPER

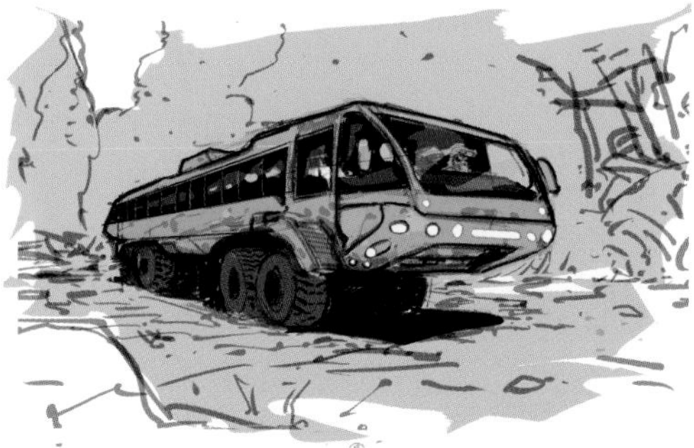

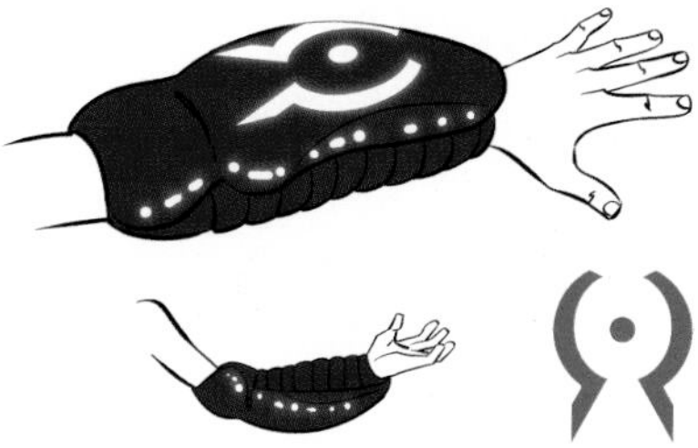

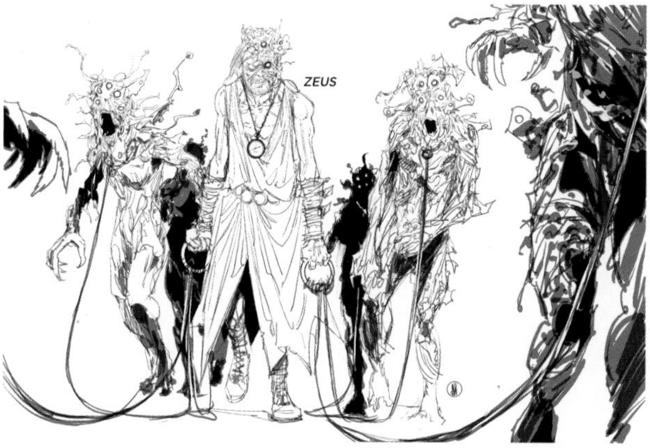
ZEUS

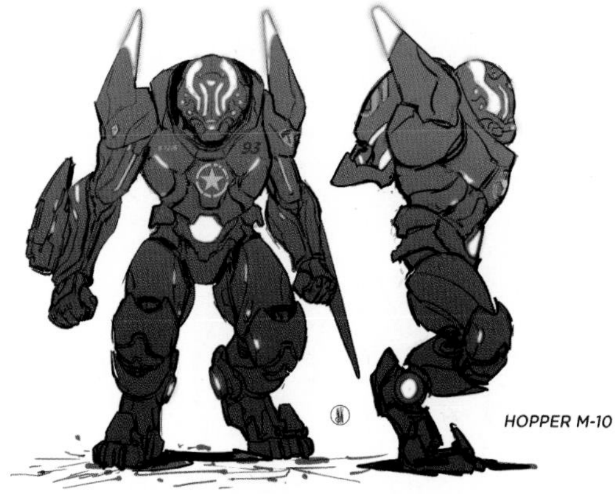
HOPPER M-10

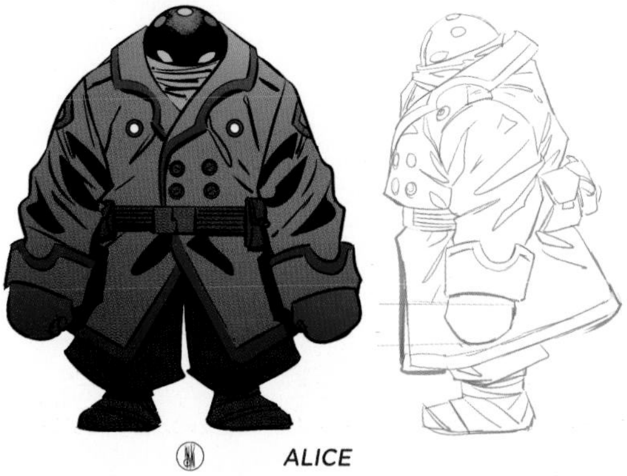
ALICE

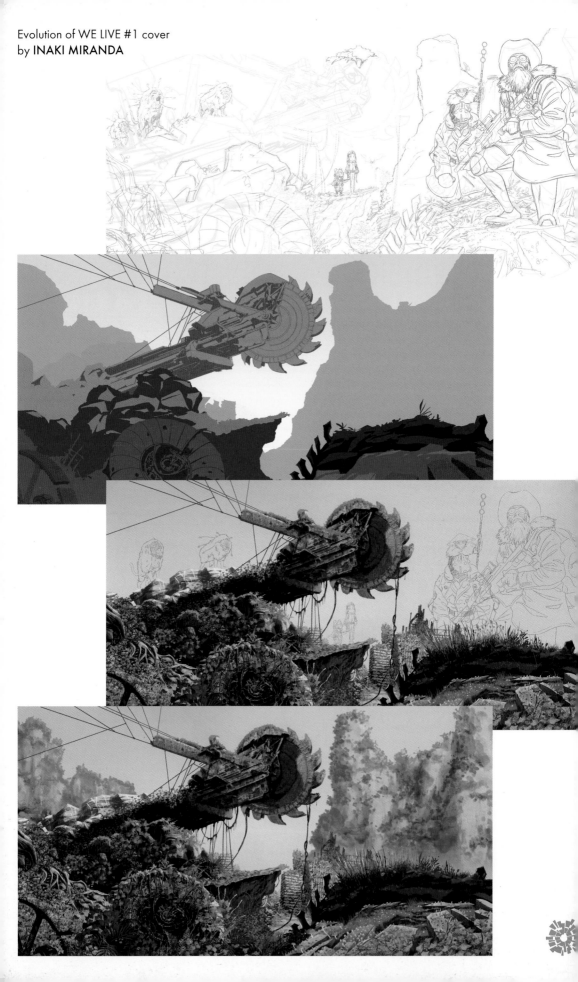

Evolution of WE LIVE #1 cover
by INAKI MIRANDA

THANK YOU

Now that you have followed us through these five chapters and have reached the end of thisfirst season of WE LIVE, it's time for you to know that what we are about to tell you, we can do because of you.

This first season was pitched to AfterShock as the prologue to a new universe of superheroes. It could have stayed forever as one self-contained story if the sales weren't on our side. But thanks to all of you who have been a heartfelt part of Tala and Hototo's journey, today we can say that this is just the beginning of something bigger. The story of these two siblings is much more extensive. The WE LIVE universe has many more corners yet to be discovered and explored.

But we first needed you to know (feel) the origin of Tala and Hototo without being aware that they would be the trigger point of a new heroic universe. Without their humanity, superpowers wouldn't mean a thing to us. Their bond is the essence of this story. A superhero symbol needs to have real heart and meaning.

We also wanted to fill this new universe with all the painful complexities that darken the path of human existence: death, fear, disappointment, lies, despair, helplessness, cruelty...the real villains to Hototo's symbol: love, hope, innocence, imagination.

So, we're here now, in this strange new place, and while it might seem that light has somehow prevailed, you must also know that our characters and the remains of the human race have a very tough road ahead; things are not going to be easy for them. Human life is still far from safe, and far from redemption--they (we) have done too much damage to Mother Earth. Let's not forget that nature has always found a way to open its own path and adapt to adversities.

We hope you are ready for what's coming, and that you follow us to the uncertain tomorrow we are heading towards.

If that's the case, we want to welcome you to The Era of The Palladions. See you in Season Two!

Thank you.
The Miranda Brothers.

WE LIVE

THE MIRANDA BROTHERS writers/artist

🐦 @InakiMiranda   🐦 @RoyleFlaco

They come from different professional worlds. Inaki earned a degree in Fine Arts and established a place for himself in the comics industry, collaborating with DC Comics for more than a decade on such titles as *Coffin Hill*, *Catwoman*, *Harley Quinn* and *Batman Beyond*. In 2020, he inaugurated his first JOII contemporary art show in Madrid, titled Superdragon Genesis. Roy hails from both the music industry and the stage. He supplements his long career as a Hip Hop singer—in bands such as LEFlaco, Roy Mercurio, Dremen, La Zurda—with his job as a Creative Director

Different life paths that met in the territory of ideas and narration. The Brothers watched the same films, played the same vide games, read the same comics and shared the same Star Wars and He-Man action figures. Their natural imaginative impulse led them to join forces and create stories together...as if they were returning to that messy bedroom they shared as children.

EVA DE LA CRUZ colorist

📷 evadlcruz.colorist

Eva de la Cruz graduated in Fine Art at Complutense University in Madrid. She made her professional comics debut in the pages of 2000AD coloring *Judge Dredd*. Since then, she has continued to enjoy various collaborations with publishers like 2000AD, DC Comics, Vertigo, IDW, Dark Horse and Scholastic. Eva was voted as one of ComiCon's Seven Best Colorists of 2018.

DAVE SHARPE letterer

🐦 @DaveLSharpe

Dave grew up a HUGE metalhead, living on Long Island, NY while spending summers in Tallahassee, FL. After reading Micronauts (and many other comics), Dave knew he had to have a career in the business. Upon graduating from the Joe Kubert School in 1990, he went on to work at Marvel Comics as an in-house letterer, eventually running their lettering department in the late 90s and early 00s. Over the years, Dave has lettered hundreds of comics, such as *Spider-Girl*, *Exiles*, *She-Hulk* and *The Defenders* for Marvel, and *Green Lantern*, *Harley Quinn*, *Sinestro* and *Batgirl* for DC Comics. Dave now works on both *X-O Manowar* and *Faith* for Valiant Comics in addition to his lettering duties on several AfterShock titles. Dave also plays bass and is way more approachable than he looks.